# OLITICAL FREUD

# Political Freud

## A HISTORY

Eli Zaretsky

Columbia University Press  New York

Columbia University Press
*Publishers Since 1893*
New York   Chichester, West Sussex
cup.columbia.edu
Copyright © 2015 Columbia University Press
Paperback edition, 2017

Library of Congress Cataloging-in-Publication Data
Zaretsky, Eli, author.
   Political Freud: a history / Eli Zaretsky.
      p. ; cm.
   Includes bibliographical references and index.
   ISBN 978-0-231-17244-8 (cloth: alk. paper)—ISBN 978-0-231-17245-5 (pbk. : alk.
paper)—ISBN 978-0-231-54014-8 (e-book)
I. Title.
[DNLM: 1. Freudian Theory—history. 2. History, 20th century. 3. Politics.
4. Psychoanalysis—history. 5. Psychoanalytic Theory. WM 460.5.F9]

616.89'17—dc23                                                    2015007307

*Cover design by Philip Pascuzzo*

*For Natasha Zaretsky*
*My Beloved Daughter*

In 1953 I turned to a deep study of Freud feeling the need to reappraise the nature and destiny of man. Inheriting from the Protestant tradition a conscience, which insisted that intellectual work should be directed toward the relief of man's estate, I, like many of my generation, lived through the superannuation of the political categories which informed liberal thought and action in the 1930s. Those of us who are temperamentally incapable of embracing the politics of sin, cynicism and despair have been compelled to re-examine the classic assumptions about the nature of politics and about the political character of human nature.

—NORMAN O. BROWN, *LIFE AGAINST DEATH*

# CONTENTS

# ACKNOWLEDGMENTS

As always, my greatest debt is to Nancy Fraser who shaped every idea in this book, and even many sentences. I received especially valuable readings at crucial times from John Judis, a dear friend who has helped me with many labors besides this one, and Philip Leventhal, a wonderful editor. Leonard Helfgott, Elliot Jurist, Jeremy Safran, Richard Bernstein, and Donald Pease read early versions of the book, or parts of it, and made extremely helpful comments. The chapters were written separately and later revised. Early versions of the chapters include "Psychoanalysis and the Spirit of Capitalism," *Constellations* 15, no. 3 (2008): 366–81; "Beyond the Blues: Richard Wright, Psychoanalysis and the Modern Idea of Culture," in Joy Damousi and Mariano Plotkin, *The Transnational Unconscious* (New York: Oxford University Press, 2007); "The Place of Psychoanalysis in the History of the Jews," *Psychoanalysis and History* 8, no. 2 (2006); "Psychoanalysis, Vulnerability and War," in Adrienne Harris, ed., *First Do No Harm* (New York: Routledge, 2010); and "Psychoanalysis, Authoritarianism and the 1960s," in Joy Damousi and Mariano Plotkin, *Psychoanalysis and Politics: Histories of Psychoanalysis Under Conditions of Restricted Political Freedom* (New York: Oxford University Press, 2012).

# POLITICAL FREUD

# Introduction—Political Freud

In 1968, at a convention of Students for a Democratic Society, I spied a pamphlet by Herbert Marcuse on the book table: *The Obsolescence of the Freudian Conception of Man.* That ideas such as the unconscious and repression could become obsolete shocked me. I remember this today because it encapsulates the two meanings of *Political Freud.* First, for a New Leftist like myself, Marcuse epitomized the ideas that it was impossible to understand politics without insight into the irrational forces that shaped history and that Freudian thought was incomparably the deepest path we had to such insight. Second, the pamphlet's title suggested that Freud's thought was itself historical, depending on the social and cultural conditions that gave rise to it and that could also render it obsolete. In the next few years I watched as Freudian thought *did* become "obsolete," at least in part, and for reasons having nothing to do with its intellectual merits. Its plausibility was undermined through the dynamics of consumer capitalism, the commercial ambition of pharmaceuticals and insurance companies, the openness of the public sphere to any sensational claim, no matter how ill-founded, the politics of gender and sexuality, and the changing meanings of private life.

Years later, having become a historian of psychoanalysis, I concluded that both senses of Political Freud—as a way of understanding history and as a product of history—were valid. On the one hand, Freudian thought was integral to many if not all of the great progressive currents of the twentieth century, including the cultural rebellions of the 1920s, African American radicalism, surrealism, Popular Front antifascism, the New Left, radical feminism, and queer theory. Its focus on the psychic bases of societal domination generated some of the landmark political-critical books of the last century, such as Wilhelm Reich's study of the psychofamilial roots of Nazism (*Mass Psychology of Fascism*, 1933), Frantz Fanon's excavation of racialized colonial violence (*Black Skin, White Masks*, 1952), and Juliet Mitchell's rereading of psychoanalysis as a theory of patriarchy or male domination (*Psychoanalysis and Feminism*, 1974). As these examples suggest, political Freud had an affinity with the left and, at times, with heterodox Marxism. On the other hand, every aspect of psychoanalysis, from the recruitment and training of the profession to the most private recesses of the analytic hour, had been shaped, and often warped, by such powerful political forces as anti-Semitism, racism, sexism, homophobia, and economic self-interest. Even within the privileged space of the consulting room, there was always a tension between free associations, whose center of gravity was depth, and the surface traffic of everyday life.

I was repeatedly struck, too, by the costs of the obsolescence of political Freud. The shallowness and manipulativeness of the late-twentieth-century political sphere; the power of collective emotions like hope, fear, and denial; the weakness of social bonds when based on identification alone; the ease with which group paranoia was mobilized; the role of projection in justifying aggression; the futile longing for leadership; the powerfully unfolding and deeply positive racial, sexual, and familial revolutions, and so much more, seemed to me to cry out for psychoanalytic insight. Absent that insight, and the radical temperament that accompanied it in the past, I watched at least one great nation lose its way. At the same time, I was struck by the ignorance that surrounded the figure of Freud, the ease with which words like *sexism* or *homophobia* were applied to some of the deepest and most complex concepts he originated, the shockingly false claims of refutation advanced by ahistorical and unphilosophical gatekeepers like Frederick Crews, and the effortlessness with which the news media was manipulated, especially when the subject was what counted as science.[1] What surprised me, above all, was the lack of resolution on the part of American psychoanalysts, their almost pathetic inability to defend either themselves or their project.

What made the situation particularly distressing was my understanding, as a historian, that psychoanalysis had had a critical or political side from the first. In Europe, where it was born around 1900, amidst a crumbling feudal past, incipient dictators, and omnipresent threat of violence, that meant it trained its critical side on the "father complex." In the 1920s and 1930s, many drew upon Freud's insights into the wish to submit, to idealize "father-figures," as well as into the ubiquity of aggression and sadism, to illuminate the fascist preoccupation with a leader or *Fuehrer.* Later, after Freudianism spread to the United States, others drew on Freud's insights into the loss of the ego in groups, the credulity of an unreflective "individualism," and the power of narcissism, to illuminate the "mass" or consumer society that triumphed after World War II. In both Europe and America, psychoanalysis clarified the weakness or loss of individual autonomy that ran through the new mass societies. Whereas under fascism the threat to autonomy came in the form of submission to masters and father figures, in consumer society it came in the form of the merging of one's identity with a "crowd," "mass," or market, or through a one-sided retreat into private life and a fashionable contempt for politics. A shared subterranean current of critical thought seemed therefore to unite the European and American strands of Freudianism.

Yet at some point in the 1970s the critical tradition of political Freudianism was largely obliterated, especially outside the university, and a shrunken and distorted image of Freud installed in its place. Conceiving this book as a response, I set myself two interrelated tasks: first, to reaffirm the critical element in Freudianism and, second, to explain the reasons why political Freud had become "obsolete." My guiding intuition was that the two tasks were interconnected. On the one hand, political Freudianism had arisen to meet a felt need to understand the irrational or unconscious dimension of historical experience. Thus it arose among African Americans because the psychic costs of slavery went so far beyond political and economic deprivation or social exclusion. It arose among Jews because the Nazi project so far exceeded any instrumental Great Power ambition. It arose among women because misogyny was inexplicable simply as a means of gaining control over women's labor or even over women's bodies. In each case something "extra" needed to be explained. The chapters that follow identify this "extra"—unconscious mental life—and chart the efforts of political Freudians to probe its depths.

At the same time, I knew that there was something deeply irrational in the rejection of psychoanalysis. To be sure, I knew there was much truth in the criticisms. As the product of an immigrant Jewish background, I had never encountered a truly sexist professional milieu until I observed upwardly mobile, nouveau riche American psychoanalysts, especially in their homes. While I knew that Freud had been quite progressive for his time on the question of homosexuality, I also knew that many later analysts held views that were repulsive to me. I understood very well why women did not feel comfortable with a concept like "penis envy." I knew that the psychoanalytic profession was overwhelmingly white and middle class. And although I was aware that American culture was inhospitable to any form of thought that did not yield immediate short-term benefits, I was not convinced that this was always a bad thing. But none of this changed my fundamental sense that the one-sided rejection of Freudianism was part of a huge step backward politically and culturally, that the baby was being thrown out with the bathwater, and that it was necessary to look at both the critical side of Freudianism as well as the affirmative, even oppressive side, and to work through their entanglement. This book is the result.

The first chapter, "Psychoanalysis and the Spirit of Capitalism," can be read as an attempt to create a context for political Freudianism, especially its American wing. It situates the sweep of psychoanalytic history, from its charismatic origins to its "obsolescence," amid the shift from nineteenth-century competitive capitalism, with its strong work ethic and its demand for saving, to twentieth-century corporate capitalism, with its encouragement of a hedonistic and expansive consumerism. This shift precipitated a new understanding of personal life. In the older, tradition-bound competitive capitalist era, family, community and work largely determined individual identity. The new horizons of corporate capitalism enabled a new sense of interiority, not reducible to societal relations but powerfully shaped by early familial experiences. Psychoanalysis gave voice to this sense of a unique, idiosyncratic intrapsychic life. What propelled it to its leading place was its conviction that existing controls over sexuality and the instincts were irrational and unjust, a conviction that had an affinity with the new possibilities of large-scale capitalism.

The chapter explains this affinity by arguing that analysis helped provide "a new spirit of capitalism"—in Max Weber's sense of the term—for the era of mass consumption. As analyzed by Weber, capitalism's original spirit—the Protestant ethic—was ascetic, compulsive, and "pharisaic" or hypocritical, justifying profit and even exploitation so long as it brought in money. In contrast, the newer spirit was tolerant of sexuality, attuned to the emotional currents of personal life, frank, direct, and straightforward. The original spirit had been part of a traditional culture that relied on obedience, hard work, and frugality and in which the family was generally the unit of production. The newer one reflected a world in which the family was a unit of consumption and there was an ongoing drive to expand spending. The transition to a consumer-centered ethic included a long-term revolution in sexual and familial norms to which Freudianism was central, one that reached its high point in the 1960s and 1970s. In the end, however, this revolution diverged from Freudianism in elevating instinctual release or gratification over and against Freud's goal of instinctual renunciation or sublimation.

Throughout this chapter, both meanings of political Freud are in play. On the one hand, I use psychoanalysis to extend Weber's account by showing that capitalist society affected not only the preconscious structure of economic motivation and behavior but also released primary processes and unconscious fantasies at the level of mass culture, while undermining paternal authority by revealing its unconscious sources. On the other hand, I historicize psychoanalysis. By situating it vis-à-vis the transition from societies oriented to restraint, control, and guilt to those oriented to release, spontaneity, and empowerment, the chapter helps explain how Freudianism itself spawned conditions that gave rise to its own obsolescence. Yet understanding those conditions raises the possibility that psychoanalysis can remain relevant in analyzing the new repressive or desublimizing aspects of "release."

Chapter 1 discloses the interplay between Freudianism and the "American century," meaning the spread of an American-style mass consumerist ethic throughout the world. It thereby suggests that the ideal of individual freedom, based on access to technology and consumer goods, is only the outer face of American capitalism. At a deeper level, the United States is still grounded in an unmastered—unconscious—past. Slaveholding, the plantation system, and Jim Crow are basic to this past, along with violence, dispossession, and war. Understanding America more deeply therefore raises the issue of *memory*, a popular and collective process that can be distinguished from history and is the subject of chapter 2. In "Beyond the Blues" I examine the radical African American and Afro-Caribbean intellectuals who drew on the Freudian critique of the father complex, in the form of the master-slave relationship, in order to build a collective memory in the Black community. Here, too, the problem of obsolescence looms, since from reading most contemporary history or cultural studies one might conclude that Black America had been immune to the pervasive Freudianism of the twentieth century.

In fact, psychoanalytic thought was central to three great episodes of African American and Afro-Caribbean radicalism that preceded the civil rights movement: the Harlem Renaissance of the 1920s, the Popular Front of the 1930s, and the existentialist-inflected anticolonial and postcolonial paradigm that emerged after World War II. In each case, political Freudianism aimed less at a theory of racism (though attempts at this were made) than at uncovering the memory of the slave experience and its aftermath. W. E. B. Du Bois deciding he had "not been Freudian enough" when he observed the body parts of a lynched Negro displayed in a local store. Richard Wright helping found a psychoanalytic clinic in Harlem that could speak to the experience of Southern migrants. Frantz Fanon fearing that he could never shake off the memory of a child's street cry, "'Dirty nigger!' or 'Look a Negro.'"[2] In each case an African American or Afro-Caribbean intellectual was drawing on Freud not just to probe the damage to the inner world left behind by slavery and colonialism but to turn that reconstructed memory toward politics. To be sure, political Freudianism was a supplement to other vehicles of collective Black self-examination and self-expression, including, most importantly, music. The blues especially demonstrated the African American capacity and will both to remember and transcend the legacy of slavery. Yet political Freudianism added something to the blues. In the hands of figures like DuBois, Wright, and Fanon, it turned self-deprecating humor, wisdom literature, and odes to ambivalence into direct statements of anger and pain, encouraging political action in place of endurance.

Effectively then, chapters 1 and 2 disclose the way in which political Freudianism can appear as a critical intervention into the historical process and then disappear, become "obsolete." The third chapter, on Freud's *Moses and Monotheism* (1938), focuses directly on that process by interrogating an idea crucial to the Freudian approach to history, the idea of *regression*. Freud's first substantial use of this idea was in *The Interpretation of Dreams* (1900) where he wrote, "If we call the direction which the psychic process follows from the unconscious into the waking state progressive, we may then speak of the dream as having a regressive character."[3] The concept had broad implications by suggesting that the history of the human species, like that of the individual human mind, does not exist on a single "progressive" surface, but rather has active layers or strata, formed in the past, to which we can *return* or regress. This broad sense is in play when we say that fascism involved regression. But it was also in play when Theodor Adorno claimed that consumer society fostered "narcissistic regression" in the form of Warhol-style infinite celebrity. Used this way, the concept of regression offered a new way to think about history. Against the standard approach, which contrasts progress with decline or decadence, political Freudians posited that history unfolds at different levels and at different timescales, that there are points in the past to which we regress, predispositions, stages, or conflicts to which we "return." In this Freudians refused to accord exclusive authority to the straightforwardly empirical approach to historical study and instead linked historical thinking with philosophical and political critique as well as with a theory of memory.

Written on the eve of World War II, and in the shadow of the Nazi terror, *Moses and Monotheism* used the idea that there are unconscious processes in history to analyze the founding of monotheism in ancient Egypt, the accompanying creation of the Jewish people, and the subsequent rise of anti-Semitism. The history of the Jewish people, Freud argued, had been marked by *repetitions*, events that *returned*, in such forms as internally felt commands, categorical imperatives, or religious injunctions, but only after being worked over by unconscious processes. Such processes, Freud argued, could not be explained through behavioral accounts that focus on education or training; rather, they "escaped the constraints of logical thought." Unlike many recent interpretations of the book, such as those of Yosef Yerushalmi and Jacques Derrida, which confine themselves to the question of Jewish identity, then, my reading reveals a *Moses and Monotheism* centered on the problem of how genuine spiritual advances, such as monotheism, philosophy, and—Freud's special concern—psychoanalysis, can be preserved in the face of an ever present pull toward regression.[4] It was the question of progress or, more starkly, *survival* that animated Freud's interest in Jewish identity.

In my reading, *Moses and Monotheism* is at bottom a reflection on the history of psychoanalysis, a *summa*, centered on Freud's preconscious identification of psychoanalysis with Judaism. Just as Freud believed that regression from monotheism to sensual experience was the main threat faced by the Hebrews in biblical times, so he held that knowledge of the repressed unconscious was in danger of being destroyed by the regressive forces of his time. Importantly, the threat to psychoanalysis came from *two* sources—on the one side, the Nazis, and, on the other, the integration of psychoanalysis into a debased, American-dominated mass culture. The rise of the Nazis—a horrific regression in what many considered the most advanced country in Europe—precipitated the writing of the book. But, by broadening the theme of regression to include the fate of psychoanalysis in the United States, Freud's interrogation of progress had implications that went beyond the looming war. In addition to the light it sheds on Judaism and anti-Semitism, the book raises the question of whether the obsolescence of psychoanalysis also included an element of regression.

The Jewish people survived World War II, but could the same be said for psychoanalysis? To be sure, the psychoanalytic profession survived, above all in the United States and England, from whence it was reexported after the war as part of the remaking of the postwar world. Nevertheless, something important had been lost. Not only were the most important societies and centers in Vienna, Budapest, Berlin, and Frankfurt destroyed, not only were many analysts and followers killed, but the internal spirit of the analytic world was compromised by the attempts of central figures, including Freud, to keep an analytic presence going in Germany even after the Nazis had expelled the Jews from the profession. Once again the political side of psychoanalysis became irrepressible, this time in an immediate and practical sense. In 1933 Freud exclaimed, "Free me from [Wilhelm] Reich," because Reich wanted to organize sex clinics against the Nazis and Freud feared this endangered the psychoanalytic institutes. I regard Reich as exemplary of the political Freudian tradition for seeing the need to organize against the Nazis and I see a tragic flaw in Freud for his deluded hope that psychoanalysis could survive in Nazi Germany even after the expulsion of the Jewish analysts.

After World War II, the question of the survival of the critical element in Freudianism became increasingly pressing. This problem is probed in chapter 4, "The Ego at War: From the Death Instinct to *Precarious Life*," which examines political Freudian thinking concerning war during World War I, World War II, and the U.S. invasion of Iraq, which followed 9/11. In 1932, prodded by the League of Nations, Freud wrote to Albert Einstein, asking, "How long shall we have to wait before the rest of mankind become pacifists too?" Freud's view that human beings are instinctually aggressive was well known, so what could he have meant by calling himself a pacifist? The answer lies amid the outbreak of shellshock (today termed post-traumatic stress disorder) during World War I. The cause of the syndrome, according to Freud, was not aggression but rather passive waiting, which became pathological because of the soldier's defensive denial of vulnerability, or what Freud called his "preference for the active role." In contrast to other antiwar strands of his time, such as those associated with Marxism and some strands of maternalism, Freud believed that aggression was a normal and healthy part of civilization, but only insofar as its roots in vulnerability, dependence, and in the continued presence of infantile states in the adult mind were recognized. Freud's formulation became central to a political Freudian tradition that grappled with war, and through tracing that tradition we can discern a significant shift in the conception of the human being during the twentieth century.

The century's earliest approach to war rested on the older, father complex–inflected warrior ethic associated with such ideals as glory, honor, and self-sacrifice. The shell shock incident of World War I led Freud to formulate his theory of the ego, which, insofar as it retains its connections to infancy and the unconscious, challenged those ideals. In doing so, Freudians seemed to affirm the spirit of jazz age modernism and to make common cause with the antiwar movements

and pacifist feminisms of the time. As psychoanalysis matured, however, its interest shifted from the father complex to the preoedipal
mother. During the Second World War, the British analysts around
Melanie Klein used the theory of the earliest relation to the mother
to explain the country's appeasement of Hitler, which they interpreted
as male soldiers and citizens' abandonment of their mothers, sisters,
and daughters. They thereby replaced Freud's theory of the ego with
a theory of object relations. Decades later, after the 2001 attacks on
the World Trade Center, the philosopher Judith Butler again drew on
political Freudian traditions to argue that the wound to American narcissism brought about by the attacks precipitated the self-destructive,
defensive reaction of the invasion of Iraq. By Butler's time, however,
the theory of the ego, now coded "male" or "Cartesian," had become
suspect. Thus she conceived her project as disrupting the bounded
and protective sense of self that the jihadist attacks had breached.
Hence the political Freudian tradition reflects a shift from the classical
Cartesian or Kantian view of the rational, independent, "bounded"
ego to the view that the ego is formed through recognition, object
relations, and language. While this shift deepened the Freudian interrogation of vulnerability, it also threatened to lose the focus on ego
autonomy that gave psychoanalysis its critical force. This loss, integral
to the problem of obsolescence, is further explored in chapter 5, "From
the Maturity Ethic to the Psychology of Power."

Chapter 5 concerns the Freud of the New Left and of radical
feminism, arguably the last incarnation of political Freud. The chapter
begins in cold war America, when Freudian thought was being integrated into an anticommunist "maturity ethic," a new Puritanism or
Calvinism. This cold war version of Weber's spirit of capitalism echoed
its predecessor by condemning narcissism or self-love and so became
a target of radical movements in the 1960s. If Herbert Marcuse's *Eros
and Civilization* became the psychoanalytic "Bible" of the New Left, it
was largely because the book extolled the primary, antinomian narcissism of the infant-mother relationship, which—so Marcuse wrote—
pointed the way "from sexuality constrained under genital supremacy"

to eroticization of the entire body, more or less as an infant's body may be said to be eroticized everywhere, not merely in the genital region. In the seventies, however, the terrain shifted again. The boundlessness, "polymorphous perversity," and oceanic feeling of the antinomian moment gave way to secondary narcissism in the form of "good works," meritocracy, and self-assertion, especially in the feminist movement, which argued that power, not sexuality, was the central, driving force in the private sphere. Thus, 1970s feminists, drawing on the New Left precedent, substituted a sociological and political account of domination for the "individual explanations" characteristic of psychoanalysis. The eventual result was a new ethic of personal life that converged with the neoliberal critique of traditional, familial, and kinship-based authority and unwittingly facilitated the emergence of full-scale consumer capitalism. Bringing us full circle to the story begun in chapter 1, then, the cultural revolutions of the sixties and seventies completed the critique of the Protestant ethic that classical Freudianism had begun. Narcissism replaced asceticism, flexibility (the network society) replaced compulsivity, and the "pharisaic" or hypocritical spirit of the older capitalism gave way to a full-throated valorization of "empowerment." As the restraints and inhibitions that once animated it seemed to crumble, Freudianism became "obsolete."

In general, then, the book charts the rise and fall of political Freudianism. Each chapter highlights two seemingly antithetical moments: a critical moment when political thinkers and social movements looked to psychoanalysis to clarify the irrational sources of domination and an affirmative moment when Freudianism became submerged in a larger history and appeared to become obsolete. Read together, the chapters disclose a subterranean struggle to guard a critical perspective against forces conspiring to repress, suppress, or abandon it. These struggles are taken up directly in the afterword, "Freud in the Twenty-first Century."

Written on the occasion of the 150th anniversary of Freud's birth, the afterword asks whether psychoanalytic thought is relevant in today's world or is merely of historical interest. In its heyday, it argues, Freudianism was a synthesis, combining a theory of the mind, a new paradigm for interpreting culture, and an ethical commitment to self-reflection. During the 1970s, with the waning of the traditional, family-centered culture of restraint, the three currents came apart. The theory of the mind gave way to neuroscience. The approach to culture found a home in the university, especially in cultural studies, women's studies, queer theory, postcolonial theory, and film studies. But the fate of the ethical commitment to self-reflection, like the fate of political Freudianism as such, remains in doubt. What is at stake in the resolution of this doubt?

To answer this question requires that we, like Freud before us, situate ourselves in the long durée of evolution and history. What made Moses a transcendent figure, and drew Freud to him, was the realization that a great idea, such as monotheism, meant nothing if it remained restricted to a small, intellectual elite. It needed rather to be internalized by a whole people. However, there is a crucial difference between movements centered on reforming the spiritual life of a people, such as monotheism or Calvinism, and psychoanalysis. Earlier movements sought to align an individual's internal state to an objective moral or "axial" order by promoting a focus on morality, sin, or conduct. Psychoanalysis, in contrast, posited a new and essentially postaxial conception of the individual. According to that conception, stimuli that come to the individual from the society or culture are not directly registered but are first dissolved and internally reconstituted in such a way as to give them personal, even idiosyncratic, meanings. As a result, there is no direct or necessary connection between an individual's subjectivity and the social order. The goal of analysis, then, is not the internalization of any particular value but that of the analytic attitude itself: the capacity to examine one's thoughts, wishes, and conflicts without judging them, at least at first.

The spread of the analytic attitude represented a great advance in moral thought, because it extended critical self-reflection from acts to thoughts and wishes. This book argues that a similar extension or inward turn had begun to take place in radical politics as well. Whereas mainstream and cold war liberals opposed fascism or "totalitarianism," radicals were critical of capitalism as well. Thus liberals saw progress as blocked by *external* antiliberal forces, while democratic leftists saw progress as blocked by forces that were *internal* to their own societies, such as class exploitation and ideological mystification. In the same way, Freud saw the resistances to rationality and progress as *internal* to consciousness and the ego and not as external obstacles such as lack of education or ignorance. What distinguished political Freudianism, then, was the effort to identify the obstacles to progress from *within* the movement toward progress itself. African American Freudians showed that slavery and ethnocidal violence were *internal* to liberalism and even to the Black freedom movement itself, not marginal or contingent; feminist Freudians showed that misogyny was *internal* to the family and to women themselves; antiwar Freudians showed that violence was *internal* to mass democracies and the modern nation-state. An important substream of the twentieth-century radical tradition, then, involved collective processes of self-reflection, beyond what either communists or mainstream liberals sought to accomplish. If political Freudianism is incomplete, how can we preserve this achievement in the present and for the future?

Today few people need to be convinced that we need higher levels of cooperation and foresight than earlier liberal societies promoted if we are to address such problems as the increase in social inequality during the decades of neoliberal ascendance or the dangers of climate change. What cries out for explanation are the *internal* obstacles that prevent us from achieving those levels. As in the past, the obstacles are rooted not only in the sometimes narrow self-interest of the elites but also in the superficiality of progressive movements themselves. If a new stage in the radical tradition is to emerge, it has to be able to look at its own history and identity. In so doing, it will see that contemporary radicalism's sense of itself as self-created a mere generation ago is worse than an illusion—it is a repression. The result of this repression has been the failure to appreciate not only the political Freudians of the past but also the general crisis of the twentieth century to which we are heirs. This failure makes it more likely that we will reenact the blind spots of the past while failing to identify the regressive forces of our own time, which, as always, present themselves as the most progressive.

# I

# Psychoanalysis and the Spirit of Capitalism

Although *The Interpretation of Dreams* was published over a century ago, the integration of psychoanalysis into the broad matrix of modern social and cultural history has barely begun. During his lifetime, Freud's charisma was so powerful that the historical landscape surrounding him remained in shadows. Only decades after his death did light begin to dawn. The earliest significant attempt to historicize psychoanalysis appeared in 1980. Situating Freud in the context of the decline of classical liberalism and the rise of mass politics and mass culture, Carl Schorske's *Fin-de-Siècle Vienna* was an inspired beginning.[1]

Schorske was right to situate psychoanalysis in a broad historical frame. The brilliant debut of psychoanalysis in 1899, its spectacular entry into American-style mass culture, the widespread fascination it inspired among youth, flappers, artists, and intellectuals, as well as among advertising writers and industrial psychologists, its critical contribution to the post–World War II welfare states, the revival of its utopian dimensions during the 1960s, the central place it occupied in the history of second-wave feminism, gay liberation, and Latin American Marxism—all this attests to the depth and pervasiveness of the connections between psychoanalysis and twentieth-century culture. In psychoanalysis, it is possible to say, one encounters the *spirit* of twentieth-century culture, at least until the mid 1970s.

If so, then the problem of situating psychoanalysis historically may have an affinity with the problem Max Weber faced when he made the phrase "the spirit of capitalism" famous in 1905. Whereas Adam Smith and the British school of political economy tended to take the psychology and culture of capitalism for granted, Weber and his contemporaries, faced with the late development of the German economy, viewed psychology and culture as problems requiring explanation.[2] Distinguishing the "form" of capitalism, especially exchange relations, from its spirit (*Geist*), and describing the modern economic order as a "tremendous cosmos" of meanings, Weber's *The Protestant Ethic and the Spirit of Capitalism* isolated one crucial moment in the evolution of the spirit of capitalism, namely the origins of such bourgeois virtues as thrift, discipline, and self-denial in the Protestant reformation of the sixteenth and seventeenth centuries.[3] According to Weber, the Calvinist idea of a rationalized, methodical life plan devoted to worldly affairs—a "calling" (*Beruf*)—was crucial in precipitating the spirit of capitalism. Originating in aspirations for salvation, Weber reasoned, rational, goal-directed, methodical self-organization remained integral to the emerging commercial and industrial order even after it had left its religious connotations behind.[4]

When he wrote *The Protestant Ethic,* Weber believed that capitalism no longer needed a transcendental justification, i.e., a *Geist* or spirit. "This-worldly asceticism" or Calvinism, he remarked, having successfully remodeled the world, had flown from the iron cage. In its place stood "victorious capitalism" resting on "mechanical foundations," meaning that economic necessity and cause-and-effect relations drove the capitalism that had left the reformation behind. The truth

is, however, that capitalism always requires a "spirit"; it never justi-
fies itself purely instrumentally but the spirit changes. In this chapter,
accordingly, I will show that psychoanalysis played a crucial role in
bringing about the changes in the spirit of capitalism that we associate
with the *second* industrial revolution—the rise of mass production and
mass consumption—a process that was just beginning when Weber
wrote his famous book.

To make this argument, I will draw on another of Weber's ideas,
one that barely appears in *The Protestant Ethic*, the idea of charisma.[5]
According to Weber, even social transformations as vast as the rise of
capitalism cannot be explained by objective factors alone. They also
involve reorientations to meaning sparked by charismatic individuals,
individuals who motivate their followers by giving personal expression
to new or innovative goals or ideas.[6] Such reorientations to meaning
neither reflect nor cause objective social change; having rather an "elective affinity" with such change, they serve as *catalysts* for them.[7] Whether
encountered still warm in individuals and sects or routinized in institutions, charisma guarantees that the aspirations and legitimations that
accompany social change will be rooted at an inward and personal level,
rather than remaining at the level of material interests or coercion. For
Weber, then, early Calvinist or Puritan charisma helped spark the crucial inward transformations without which capitalism would not have
taken off, or at least would have taken a very different form.[8]

Charisma played an important role in the rise of capitalism especially because of its effects on the family. Normally, Weber believed,
charisma was directed against everyday, mundane economic life and
therefore *against* the family. Thus Jesus and Buddha—early charismatic figures—urged their followers to *leave* their families to create
an authentic spiritual community. By contrast, the Puritan "Saints" of
the seventeenth century redefined the family as a locus of charismatic
meanings, sanctifying its everyday labor and giving it a religio-ethical
character. During the early centuries of capitalism, when the family was
the engine of economic development, this redefinition fostered such
family-based virtues as thrift, industry, and discipline. Several centuries

later, Methodist revivals and awakenings served related ends. Embraced by the English and American industrial working classes, Methodism served not only as an "opiate" but also as a vehicle of personal transformation encouraging the sobriety and familial responsibility that enabled the first industrial revolution. In both cases, then, the infusion of everyday familial and economic life with charismatic or sacred meaning was crucial in precipitating a socioeconomic transformation.

The second industrial revolution—the rise of the vertically integrated, bureaucratically organized corporation with its orientation toward mass consumption—also involved a charismatic reorientation toward work and the family, one comparable to, if not as intense as, the Reformation.[9] Just as men and women did not embark on the transition from agrarian society to industrial capitalism for merely instrumental or economic reasons, so in the twentieth century they did not become consumers in order to supply markets. Rather, they separated from traditional familial and communal morality, gave up their orientation to self-denial and thrift, and entered into the sexualized "dreamworlds" of mass consumption on behalf of a new orientation to what I will call personal life. Psychoanalysis—I will argue—was the "Calvinism" of this shift. But whereas Calvinism sanctified mundane labor in the family, Freud urged his followers to leave behind their "families"— the archaic images of early childhood—not to preach but to develop more genuine, that is, more personal, relations.[10]

I will make this argument in four parts, each of which focuses on a phase in the history of psychoanalysis. In the first phase, which runs from the 1890s until World War I, and which encompasses the early years of mass production, psychoanalysis was effectively a sect expressing, in an intensely charismatic form, then new aspirations for "personal life." In a second phase, which encompasses the interwar period (1919–1939), psychoanalysis became a mass cultural phenomenon, integral to and diffused by the new mass media, such as film and radio. It thereby helped generate the utopian ideology of individuality that accompanied mass consumption. In a third phase, which runs from World War II to the mid-1960s, psychoanalysis was integrated into the

Keynesian welfare states, becoming, in Weber's phrase, a "this-worldly program of ethical rationalization," and supplying what I will call the maturity ethic for post–World War II domesticity. Finally, in a fourth phase, running roughly from 1965–1974, the New Left and women's movement attacked the maturity ethic and the welfare state, ushering in the post-Fordist network or communication-based spirit of capitalism that characterizes the present. In half a century, then, psychoanalysis ran through the familiar Weberian cycle of charisma, routinization, and diffusion, although even in its long period of decline it continued to spark new if transitory upheavals.

I.

Let me begin by quoting Luc Boltanski and Éve Chiapello's description of the nineteenth–century bourgeoisie: "owning land, factories and women, rooted in possessions, obsessed with preserving their goods, endlessly concerned about reproducing, exploiting and increasing them . . . thereby condemned to meticulous forethought . . . and a quasi-obsessive pursuit of production for production's sake."[11] The essence of the description is the attempt to deepen authority by extending control and enforcing restraint. Since most property was either rooted in land or small-scale, and since the family was the center of small-scale property, the family was at the center of this system of authority. It organized not just daily life but lineage, inheritance, and marriage. Its patriarchal or paternal relations were reproduced in shops and trades as well as being at the center of communal life. The depressing devotion to duty that resulted was what Weber—who grew up among burghers—referred to when he wrote that the Puritans wore their economic responsibilities "like a light cloak, which can be thrown aside at any moment," while for his generation the cloak "had become an iron cage"

When he wrote *The Protestant Ethic*, Weber believed that duty, restraint, and savings had lost the association with charismatic meaning they originally had. Writing the book during his own psychic crisis, he never abandoned hope that a new asceticism, a new turn inward, might emerge and challenge or modify capitalist rationalization. In fact, his sense of the exhaustion of the Protestant ethic and his desire to escape from the iron cage were widely shared. The coming of the market, the railroad, the steamship, new forms of communication such as mass newspapers and popular lectures, and especially wage labor, allowed "the young to emancipate themselves from local communities, from being enslaved to the land and rooted in the family, [and thus] to escape the village, the ghetto, and traditional forms of personal dependence."[12] It was within the consciousness that resulted, which we often call modernism or modernity, that psychoanalysis—the new asceticism for which Weber longed—attained its special place. The charisma of analysis arose, I believe, because it gave voice to the aspiration to be free from the spirit of nineteenth-century capitalism. In *Secrets of the Soul* I called this aspiration "personal life."[13]

By personal life I mean the experience of having an identity distinct from one's place in the family, in society, and in the social division of labor. In one sense, the possibility of having a personal life is a universal aspect of human life, but that is not the sense I have in mind. Rather, I mean a historically specific experience of singularity and interiority sociologically grounded in industrialization and urbanization. The separation (both physical and emotional) of paid work from the household, which is to say the rise of industrial capitalism, gave rise to new forms of privacy, domesticity, and intimacy. At first—in the Victorian era—these were experienced as the gendered familial counterparts to the impersonal world of the market. Later, they became associated with the possibility and goal of a personal life distinct from and even outside of the family. Expressions of this possibility include the "new" (or independent) woman, the emergence of public homosexual identities, and the turning of young people away from a preoccupation with business and toward sexual experimentation, bohemia, and artistic modernism. Personal identity became a problem and a project for individuals as opposed to something given to them by their place in the family or the community. Psychoanalysis was a theory and practice of this new aspiration for a personal life. Its original historical telos was *defamilialization*, the freeing of individuals from unconscious images of authority originally rooted in the family.

That psychoanalysis was a theory and practice of personal life can be seen in the signature concepts of its formative years—the unconscious and sexuality. Neither concept was new, of course, but Freud gave them both radically innovative meanings. In the case of the unconscious, he articulated the new experience—also evoked by such figures as Baudelaire, for example, in the figures of the poet or the *flaneur*—of no longer being defined by one's social relations, such as parentage, religion, nationality, or even gender. Thus, the subject of *The Interpretation of Dreams*, published in 1899, is a sleeping individual, someone who is completely separated from the real social world. With the external world at a distance, all stimuli arise from within. No thought that comes to the individual—whether it originated in childhood or comes from the "day residues," everyday impressions—is directly registered; rather it is first dissolved and internally reconstituted in such a way as to give it a unique and contingent meaning. The result was a new conception of the relations between the individual and the surrounding community. Traditional healers were effective because they mobilized symbols that were *both* internal *and* communal. In psychoanalysis, by contrast, there is no direct relation—no isomorphism or complementarity—between the community and the intrapsychic world. Whereas the communal world is composed of collective symbols, such as God or *la République*, in the intrapsychic world, symptoms replace symbols: a nervous cough, a tic, the washing of hands. In learning to interpret their private worlds, modern men and women distanced themselves from collectivities. Psychoanalysis taught individuals to withdraw from the painful tensions involved in their relation to society while encouraging them to relate "more affirmatively to their depths."[14]

The same reorientation toward a uniquely personal, intrapsychic world characterized the psychoanalytic approach toward sexuality. Whereas, in the nineteenth-century world described by Boltanski and Chiapello, sexuality was largely organized through familial relations, psychoanalysis emerged in a world in which many circles were repudiating the family-centered morality of the bourgeoisie.[15] These included the *Männerbunden* (male sects centered on a charismatic leader, such as Klimt or Marinetti); artistic bohemias, in which free love was common, and Marxist currents such as the one centered around Trotsky, who covertly supported Russian psychoanalysis until his exile. Most important, male homosexuals, such as the London gay society exemplified by Edward Carpenter, pioneered the idea of sexual life outside the family and not defined by reproduction, while "new women" promulgated Elizabeth Cady Stanton's wish to move beyond the "incidental relations of life, such as mother, wife, sister, daughter" to focus instead on what she called the "individuality of each human soul."[16]

In that context Freud, who began with an inherited schema that stressed gender difference aimed at reproduction, soon dropped it. Instead, he argued that the distinction necessary to understand psychic life was not between male and female but between libido and repression. Distinguishing the sexual object or target from the sexual aim, meaning the libidinal impulse the sexual act aimed at satisfying, Freud restricted the question of gender to the question of object choice. In contrast to the gender-based Victorian theories of psychology and sexology, he claimed that psychoanalysis recognized that every person had a "special individuality in the exercise of his capacity to love—that is, in the conditions which he sets up for loving, in the impulses he gratifies by it, and in the aims he sets out to achieve in it."[17] In spite of the masculine pronoun, psychoanalysis had implications for both sexes. Whereas earlier debates over women's roles had pivoted on whether men and women were fundamentally the same or fundamentally different, psychoanalysis gave voice to a new sensibility whose governing norm was neither sameness nor difference, but individuality.

In its early years, then, Freudian analysis seemed to codify a set of post-Victorian intuitions that until then had been the preserve of artists, sexual and ethnic minorities, and philosophers. The result was a far-flung charisma stretching before World War I from Los Angeles to Russia (which published the largest number of Freud translations of any country) and that by the twenties extended to India, Mexico,

China, and Japan. Psychoanalysis appealed to women as well as men and to homosexuals as well as heterosexuals; indeed, arguably women comprised the largest number of readers.[18] Above all, its charisma was deeply felt and experienced. The emotional tone with which Freud was read and discussed in the pre–World War I period is nicely captured in Lincoln Steffens's autobiography. In 1911 Walter Lippmann, Steffens wrote, "first introduced us to the idea that the minds of men were distorted by unconscious suppressions. . . .There were no warmer, quieter, more intensely thoughtful conversations at Mabel Dodge's [a Greenwich Village salon] than those on Freud and his implications." In this first phase of its history, then, psychoanalysis seemed to offer a way out of the iron cage by putting sexuality at the center of psychology. As Max Weber wrote, evoking the dead "skeletal grasp" of corporate-led rationalization, sexuality was the "gate into the most irrational and thereby real kernel of life . . . eternally inaccessible to any rational endeavour."

In sum, then, even as capitalism was becoming more comprehensively organized, more systematic, and more integrated, it was simultaneously loosening the economic vise, making possible greater ease in the relations between the sexes and enhancing the sense of individual subjectivity, if at first primarily for certain strata. As a charismatic sect, psychoanalysis expressed the new sense of subjectivity in its most immediate, because most personal, form. As Freud admitted, its key ideas, such as instincts and the unconscious, were not original to it. What distinguished psychoanalysis, he wrote, was not the content of its ideas but its insistence that they "touch every individual personally and force him [or her] to take up some attitude" toward them.[19] Precisely because psychoanalysis reoriented individuals away from the compulsions and demands of the family-based community and toward those that arose from the self, it was to play a central role in the emergence of the new spirit of capitalism.

2.

Let me turn now to the second epoch in the history of analysis, 1919–1945. In this period, sometimes called Fordism for its most famous exemplar, one encounters a very different spirit of capitalism. The key figure is no longer the property-owning bourgeois, but rather the manager. Heading up a large, hierarchical, bureaucratized firm, corporation, or cartel, the manager was often an engineer or at least worked closely with engineers and was generally more interested in scientific planning and efficiency aimed at cheap, mass consumption goods than at immediate short-term profits. The rise of the large, managerially organized corporation entailed changes comparable to those that characterized the rise of capitalism. Whereas earlier, the expansion of production depended on increasing the labor time spent in production, now it resulted from technology, new forms of workplace organization, and the scientific mind. While the common school was indispensable to the first industrial revolution, the research university was the key to the second. Even on the assembly line, after the initial wave of scientific management, workers began to gain flexibility and control.[20] Above all, the age of the large corporation was the age of mass consumption. Until the twentieth century, consumer goods were produced mostly in quantities sufficient to reproduce the labor force; the goal now became to expand, not restrict, consumption.[21]

These changes were accompanied by a psychological revolution that had psychoanalysis at its heart. Turned into a global phenomenon by the World War I shellshock incident, struck by the difficulty in gaining cures, and developing in the shadow of the Bolshevik Revolution and the rise of Nazism—the so-called general crisis of the twentieth century—psychoanalysis shed much of its early utopianism.[22] It became a theory of aggression, the death instinct, and resistance, all of which complemented and complicated its earlier emphasis on sexuality. At the same time, like Calvinism in its relation to early family- and market-based societies, it had an elective affinity to the age of the large corporation. The basis for this affinity laid in the fact that psychoanalysis constituted an *immanent* critique of Calvinism in a period during which the Protestant ethic—the older spirit of capitalism—had become not only obsolete but also dysfunctional.

Recall that in Weber's account Calvinism had made three contributions to the spirit of capitalism. First, it contributed to the latter's *ascetic* spirit. What is "natural," Weber reasoned, is to work in order to satisfy needs. Capitalism *reversed* this relationship: it called for the postponement of need satisfaction in order to increase capital. The Calvinist idea of the calling helped justify this reversal. The religious roots of the calling also explains Weber's second attribute of the spirit of capitalism, namely its *compulsive* character. If men and women were to persist at unsatisfying and onerous occupations, they had to believe that they were called to do so by some transcendental and unfathomable authority. This was God, who the Calvinists also made present and immediate in a new way. Finally, Weber argued that Calvinism was crucial to releasing what Weber called the acquisitive instinct. "What the great religious epoch of the seventeenth century bequeathed to its utilitarian successor," Weber wrote, "was . . . an amazingly good . . . even a pharisaically good, conscience in the acquisition of money, so long as it took place legally."

As an immanent critique of Calvinism, psychoanalysis modified or transformed each of these characteristics in a way that helped to crystallize the new spirit of capitalism. Thus it qualified and complicated asceticism by making the ubiquity of the instinctual life—orality, anality, exhibitionism, narcissism, phallic pride, sexual pleasure in looking, sadism, masochism—manifest and natural. Second, in contrast to the spirit that Weber described as compulsive and inexorable, it called attention to a new question: how much repression is necessary and how much is not? Third, and perhaps most important, psychoanalysis helped liberate not merely the acquisitive but the aggressive instinct, often struggling to redeem it from the superego, especially from guilt, from moral masochism and moral hypocrisy. Thus, whereas Calvinism inspired a vicious circle, whereby each moral exertion produced a deeper sense of inadequacy, thereby generating guilt, which in turn generated aggression and further moral exertion and further guilt, psychoanalysis was, at root, an attempt to break out of that circle.

Freudianism's challenge to self-denial, compulsivity, and hypocrisy help explain its mass appeal during the epoch in which the large
corporation became the dominant economic form. During the 1920s,
psychoanalysis helped shape the powerful new media of the second
industrial revolution such as radio, photojournalism, and film. Even
from prison, Antonio Gramsci noted that psychoanalysis had provided
"a new myth of the [noble] 'savage' on a sexual basis."[23] The novelist
Nathaniel West called Freud the "modern Bulfinch," meaning that he
had collected and published the imaginative fables used by radio nar-
rators, film writers, and other storytellers. W. H. Hearst published the
first public account of an analysis, a key moment in the evolution of a
culture of personal revelation. In 1925 Sam Goldwyn sailed for Europe,
announcing that he would offer Freud $100,000 to assist in devising
"a really great love story" or, failing that, would get Freud to "come to
America and help in a 'drive' on the hearts of this nation." Who better
than Freud? queried Goldwyn, Freud with his insight into "emotional
motivations and suppressed desires."[24]

The mass diffusion of psychoanalysis simultaneously democra-
tized and banalized a newly psychological way of thinking. Increasingly the term by which psychological thinking in general was desig-
nated, Freudianism not only reflected but also helped construct a new
object: personal experience. It introduced into English, or profoundly
redefined, such words as *oral, anal, phallic, genital, unconscious, psyche,
drives, conflict, neurosis, hysterical, father complex, ego-ideal, narcissist,
inhibition, ego, id,* and *superego.* Similar lists can be developed for other
modern languages. In the age of the large corporation, then, an age
obsessed with standardization and mass reproducibility, it encouraged people to regard much of what they experienced as arising within
themselves, thereby contributing to the process of inward development
that is the only secure basis for progress.

Psychoanalysis influenced the new spirit of twentieth-century
capitalism deeply because of its intimate, even subterranean, connections to the Protestant ethic, and broadly because it rested on a new
mass basis, namely personal life. Thus situated, psychoanalysis helped

change the promise of modernity that had arisen with the Enlightenment and the democratic revolutions. To begin with, it helped provide
a new conception of autonomy. If one considers earlier conceptions of
autonomy, one can see that they were not personal in the twentieth-
century sense. For Kant, autonomy meant the freedom to exercise one's
reason in order to discover universally valid moral rules. For Freud, in
contrast, autonomy meant the freedom to discover what one wants to
do with one's life. This shift resonated deeply with the second industrial revolution. In the age of the large corporation, everyone feared
conformity, a fear marked in such iconic works as Charlie Chaplin's
*Modern Times* (1936), which opened with a herd of sheep entering a
subway, or Aldous Huxley's *Brave New World* (1932), a dystopic society
manipulated by a leader variously called "Our Ford" or "our Freud."
The pervasiveness of this discourse demonstrated the esteem in which
the new ideal of personal rather than moral autonomy was held. Huxley's quip notwithstanding, psychoanalysis spoke for this ideal.

In addition, psychoanalysis helped reorient individuals to a more
personalized ideal of family life, one that incorporated a heightened
level of intimacy, including sexual intimacy, between men and women.
Some have called this the new heterosexuality.[25] This change too was
associated with the second industrial revolution. As the family fully
lost its earlier identity as a productive unit based on the ownership
of property, psychoanalysis infused it with new meaning as the arena
of personal life. When individuals lost their sense of being part of an
integrated system of property and hierarchy, psychoanalysis offered
them a new sense, according to which individuality was rooted in one's
childhood and expressed in marriage and parenthood. In this period,
accordingly, psychoanalysis itself underwent a shift. Originally an
agent of defamilialization, it began to acquire a refamilializing role.

Finally, psychoanalysis helped pave the way for a new sense of identity, ultimately rooted in the experience of personal life, one that helped
render problematic the older emphasis on social class. This is not to say
that psychoanalysis did not influence the psychology of work, directly
in such areas as "human relations" and indirectly through its expansive

notion of the mind. Nevertheless, its most intense impact was felt in
life outside production. Premised on the view of the individual as infi-
nitely desiring rather than capable of satisfaction, psychoanalysis was
indispensable to an epoch that sought to expand consumption. It revo-
lutionized advertising, which shifted from addressing perceived needs
to addressing unconscious wishes and it had a profound influence on
the visual media including photography, which saw itself, like psychoanalysis, as a way of revealing what people were like when they were
least aware of themselves. Overall, psychoanalysis helped change the
way in which capitalism was understood, from a mode of production
to a mode of distribution and consumption.

Throughout all of these changes, the most important were those
that occurred in the realm of personal experience or introspection.
Weber singled out Calvinism from all the other sects and churches of
the Reformation because it alone encouraged what Weber called "deep
spiritual isolation." Referring to predestination, Weber wrote: "In what
was for the man of the age of the Reformation the most important
thing in life, his eternal salvation, he was forced to follow his path alone
to meet a destiny which had been decreed for him from eternity. No
one could help him." Psychoanalysis, at its core, reproduced this spiritual isolation. No less than Calvinism, only one thing mattered for
interwar psychoanalysis: not worldly success, not sensory satisfaction,
not "self-esteem," but the state of one's soul. This gave it a privileged
place among the critical currents of the day.

As an immanent critique of Calvinism, in conclusion, psychoanalysis subverted traditional, religiously based assumptions concerning family life, sexuality, and the work ethic. Just as seventeenth-century
capitalism rested on the sacralization of family life, and just as
nineteenth-century industrialization rested on a new work discipline,
so the rise of mass consumption society rested on analogous vehicles for
the transformation of subjectivity. Psychoanalysis was one of the most
effective of these vehicles, triggering internal, charismatically originated
motivations, helping to transform the family from a tradition-bound
and production-oriented unit into a carrier of expressive individuality.

3.

So far I have been writing about the impact of psychoanalysis on the spirit of capitalism; now I want to switch gears and describe the impact of capitalism on psychoanalysis. From its inception, psychoanalysis was divided between two impulses: one pushed toward absorption into mainstream institutions integral to twentieth-century capitalism, especially the research university, the "social control" professions such as social work, therapy, and testing, and the new mass culture; the other pulled toward sectarianism, that is, the wish to guard a Freud-centered, proto-Calvinist, ultimately Hebraic or Mosaic core. Both impulses had dangers. Absorption would destroy the unique character of psychoanalysis; sectarianism would preserve its identity, but at the cost of keeping it marginal and schismatic. Until the 1930s, psychoanalysis maintained a precarious balance. Beginning in the thirties, however, when psychoanalysis was destroyed in continental Europe and its refugees fled to England and the United States, the balance tipped. Psychoanalysis became, in Weber's term, a "this-worldly program of ethical rationalization," one with strong links to such normalizing agencies as the social service professions, medicine, and the welfare state.

This third phase had its roots in the New Deal and the Popular Front. During World War II, especially in England, the relation to the mother came to dominate analytic theory. *Ego, sexuality,* and *individual* gave way to *object, mother,* and *group.* Analysts developed a new "relational" view of the ego as ethically responsible. Ethical responsibility was less a matter of observing universal moral norms than of meeting concrete obligations to particular others. Not incidentally, Bloomsbury, with its ethic of transfamilial sociality, played an important role in the evolution of object-relational thinking. Under the impress of the terrible war, the older metapsychology—id, ego, superego—was replaced by clinical and theoretical concerns with attachment, loss, and mourning.

In the United States, postwar psychoanalysis spoke with a somewhat different accent. The New Deal and the war experience encouraged a revolution in American society, from forms of status and traditional authority to new ideas of internalized self-control. Freudian ego psychology, with its stress on the power that the ego has to guide and control unconscious processes, was institutionalized in the epoch of the postwar welfare state. During the war, the United States Surgeon General's Office had ordered that every doctor in the military be taught the basic principles of psychoanalysis.[26] When doctors could not meet the demand for treatment, the newly founded professions of clinical psychology and psychiatric social work stepped into the breach. After the war, psychiatry shed its custodial image by turning to analysis. As department heads in hospitals, analysts helped transform counseling, testing, welfare, education, personnel, and law, especially new branches such as juvenile and domestic relations and criminology.[27] Religion became a center for psychological, not just spiritual, counseling; the schools were transformed by their concern for psychology.[28] Medicine itself turned from the focused treatment of specific diseases to the management of the social and interpersonal dimensions of illness.[29] As a "psychodynamic" discipline, aimed at strengthening what Michel Foucault called "productive power," power that works "not from the outside but from within," analysis became integral to the so-called golden age of capitalism, that is, the flourishing of the Keynesian welfare states— large-scale, organized, state-led capitalism—between 1945 and 1975.

The maturity ethic was the public face of this new era. From its place in the established order, psychoanalysis stood for a new ethic of "responsibility," and "adulthood," supposedly linked to a new maturity in America's global role, but also geared to the family-based, mass consumption societies then created in England, France, and Germany. The most important component of the maturity ethic was the rejection of radical politics and the insistence that freedom resided primarily in the private realm. Bruno Bettelheim's "Individual and Mass Behavior in Extreme Situations" argued that what made the first concentration camps so terrible was that there was no retreat from the guards. Stanley Elkins's *Slavery* portrayed the absence of private space for slaves, such as a garden, as the root of the special virulence of American racism. Hannah Arendt's *Origins of Totalitarianism* distinguished the "totalitarian" subversion of the private sphere from "tyranny," which was supposedly restricted to the public realm. The private sphere supplied the terrain on which the maturity ethic flourished, but "maturity" also underlay a changing conception of the public realm. During World War II, Talcott Parsons urged Franklin Roosevelt not to react to antiwar protests "hysterically," but rather to model himself on the psychoanalyst who "de-confirms" neurotic perceptions by refusing to respond to them. George Kennan argued that, if the U.S. remained firm and did not respond impulsively, Soviet paranoia would disintegrate from within. In the 1956 *Man with the Grey Flannel Suit,* the heroine overcomes her wounded narcissism and accepts her husband's war baby, thus symbolizing the Marshall Plan's postwar responsibility for Europe. In the words of Erik Erikson, the mature person was "tolerant of differences, cautious and methodical in evaluation, just in judgment, circumspect in action, and capable of faith and indignation."[30]

Postwar psychoanalysis, then, exemplified the dialectic of absorption and marginality or sectarianism. Central to cold war ideology through its stress on private life, integral to the normalizing project of the Keynesian welfare state, analysts propounded the new emphasis on productive power, power that worked from inside the individual and not from above or outside. Thus absorbed, ego psychology functioned as a form of social control. Challenging the definition of homosexuality as a crime, psychoanalysts redefined it as an "illness," thereby intensifying the shame that too many homosexuals felt. Validating women's sexuality in theory, some analysts, though by no means all, wielded terms like *femininity, the mother,* and *vaginal orgasm* as weapons against assertive women. Claiming the high ground "above" politics, some, perhaps many, analysts cooperated enthusiastically with Defense Department and CIA initiatives that funded analytic research for cold war ends.[31] To be sure, the experience of fascism and militarism produced profound self-reflections to which analytic thought contributed. Among these were Masao Murayama's theory of the "modern ego" in Japan, Alexander and Margarete Mitscherlich's account of "the inability to mourn" in postwar Germany, and Richard

Hofstadter's "The Paranoid Style in American Politics" in the U.S.[32] Still, this mode of thought was not pursued among American analysts. Far from lending themselves to such projects, analysts facilitated the recruitment of Germany and Japan into the cold war order and explicitly condoned McCarthyism.[33]

Nevertheless, even as postwar American psychoanalysis—ego psychology—was absorbed into the cold war welfare state, it retained its link to its charismatic, anti-institutional origins, partly through "the aura of close association with the founding fathers," partly through its relations to art and religious experience, but especially through its associations with sexual love, that "gate into the most irrational and thereby real kernel of life."[34] During the 1950s, analysts drew on these associations to resanctify the heterosexual family, investing domesticity with deep personal, ethical, and sexual meanings previously attached to extrafamilial forms of personal life. In so doing, however, they were invoking charismatic forces they could not always contain. By the 1960s, antinomian upsurges inspired by a Freudian spirit would overflow the boundaries of the analytic profession, the heterosexual family, and the welfare state. Simultaneously normalizing and fueled by charismatic sources, then, analysis was at the center of *both* the growing rationalization of personal life unfolding in the 1950s *and* the looming critique of rationalization, the charismatic rejection of the mundane that came to the fore in the 1960s.

4.

By its nature, a period of self-exploration, such as the one spawned by psychoanalysis, will be short-lived. The normal direction of the mind is outward. Hence, it is no surprise that new scientific theories, therapies, and folk psychologies emerged to challenge the analytic focus on self-reflection, nor that the New Left and the women's movement rejected "the maturity ethic," effectively destroying analysis's institutional charisma. A fuller account of the "postanalytic" world that emerged in the sixties is given in chapter 5, but there is one last point to be made in this chapter: the way the attacks on analysis contributed to a final mutation in the spirit of capitalism.

The last stage in the relations of psychoanalysis and capitalism saw the transformation of restraint into release and the accompanying "obsolescence" of psychoanalysis. This stage reflected "The Keynesian Revolution," the triumph of a consumer economy during the "thirty glorious years" (1940s–1970s) as well as the shift toward a new "post-Fordist" spirit of decentralized, service-oriented, credit-based, network and globally organized neoliberal capitalism, which followed the demise of the Keynesian model in the 1970s. Like the rise of mass production, post-Fordist neoliberalism entailed a change in the nature of the family: the shift toward the two-earner family, the valorization of married women's and mother's employment, and the destigmatization of "atypical" forms of family life, such as homosexuality in both sexes, divorced couples, and the female-headed Black family. As much cultural and psychological as sociological, this shift involved the crumbling of traditional restraints on both sexuality and aggression. Because psychoanalysis had been integral to the Keynesian-era family system, and because any successor system had to incorporate new understandings of personal life, a challenge to the authority of analysts proved central. In fact, the ascent of a full-blown consumerist spirit of capitalism coincided with the decline of psychoanalysis.

The deepest grounds for Freud's mass appeal had always rested on his insistence that civilization made excessive demands upon the individual. At the same time, Freud did not advocate *releasing* the instincts from civilized demands, but rather *sublimating* them, which required "abstinence" or delayed gratification in order to transform sexual energies into desexualized insight or rationality. There *were* individuals in the analytic movement who advocated freedom of the instincts as an end in itself, but they were few. In 1907 Max Weber, using language that might have been used by Freud himself, rejected for publication an article by one of these, Otto Gross—a forerunner of Wilhelm Reich. According to Weber, Gross believed that "*every* suppression of emotion-laden desires and drives leads to 'repression'" and therefore calls for revolution. But ethical life invariably entails repression. Gross, Weber complained, espoused a "psychiatric ethic": "admit to yourself what you are like and what you desire."[35]

Marginal during the early years of psychoanalysis, Gross's approach came into its own as the twentieth century wore on. With the growth of a mass production economy, capitalism's potential to generate a surplus, and therefore to lessen the need for self-restraint and savings, was unmistakable. During the "thirty glorious years" of Keynesian prosperity, this potential was expressed in such terms as *affluence, automation,* and the *triple revolution*. Prosperity also coincided with a demographic revolution, the *baby boom*. Advertisers tapped the vast purchasing power of the new cohort, beginning with the Davy Crockett fad, followed by blue jeans, rock, and recreational drugs. Student enrollments expanded exponentially. Technological change deepened the "generation gap." The youth-centered explosions of rock music and soul projected an imagined eros of instinctual release. New Age psychologies, the New Left, and the women's movement all expressed the new possibilities for release, and all sought to bend psychoanalysis to that purpose.

Three moments, each containing a sharp challenge to psychoanalysis, stand out. First, psychoanalysis purported to study "the durable, unique individual personality," whereas a host of new "intersubjective" theories and practices insisted that no such thing had ever existed.[36] The analytic focus on the individual led to the stigmatization of madness, deviance, and femininity, but in the 1960s stigmatization was rejected as the product of authoritarian labeling. Furthermore, a "relational revolution" insisted that psychotherapy should involve an authentic exchange between "open," socially aware individuals, not the subordination of the individual to a supposedly objective authority. Along with their sometimes salutary therapeutic implications, the new "relational" theories helped advance the new post-Fordist, finance and information-based capitalism, whose imaginary centered on open, indeterminate, shifting networks, rhizomorphic contexts, and deterritorialized flows. The idea of a personal life interior to the individual was repudiated in favor of an emphasis on flexibility, sociality, and sensitivity to difference.

Second, psychoanalysts held a critical attitude toward narcissism, which was regularly contrasted to autonomy, viewed as an obstacle to analysis and as an "optimistic denial . . . of inferiority, real or imaginary," in the words of Karl Abraham.[37] By contrast, thinkers and movements of the sixties embraced a new culture of expressiveness, which validated narcissism. Even within psychoanalysis, Heinz Kohut contemptuously rejected Freud's view that narcissism was a mere "stage" in the development of the ego, castigating analysts' "courageously facing the truth" and "health-and-maturity-morality" and arguing that narcissism had replaced sexuality as the defining issue of the age. Here, too, however, the effects of the critique were not always intended. As it turned out, the validation of narcissism helped facilitate the shift to the "dense interpersonal environment" of postindustrial society, an environment that produces relationships ("networks"), not things, and in which image, personality, and interpersonal skills, not autonomy or knowledge, have the highest commercial value.

Finally, and most importantly, the 1960s marked the culmination in the revolution in the nature of the family that had begun with the second industrial revolution. Benjamin Spock stopped practicing analysis in the 1940s because of his disquiet over an "intensely feministic" female patient who "argued fiercely against every interpretation for over two years."[38] However, Spock's reaction was hardly typical of a time when the family system still presumed a full-time mother. By the sixties, however, life outside the traditional family context, for example, as a single person, as a homosexual, or in a two-earner family, was becoming both feasible and desirable. In that context, a New York analyst told Betty Friedan that for twenty years he had repeatedly found himself "having to superimpose Freud's theory of femininity on the psychic life of my patients" in a way that he was no longer willing to do. He treated one woman for two years before facing "her real problem—that it was not enough for her to be just a housewife and mother. One day she had a dream that she was teaching a class. I could not dismiss the powerful yearning of this housewife's dream as penis envy. . . . I told her: 'I can't analyze this dream away. You must do something about it.'"[39]

Anticipated by the New Left's rejection of psychologization, second-wave feminism translated Freud's intrapsychic theory into a theory of societal oppression. As the women's movement turned to consciousness-raising, "individual explanations" were officially discouraged. What had been forbidden or suspended within psychoanalysis— "acting out"—became privileged. The Oedipus complex was reinterpreted as a "power psychology." Penis envy was actually "power envy."[40] Because she had supposedly seized control of her destiny and rejected psychoanalysis, Dora became a feminist icon.[41] Gayle Rubin redefined psychoanalysis as "feminist theory *manqué*," meaning that feminism supplied the social perspective (the patriarchal organization of kinship) that Freudianism merely reflected.[42] The rebuff of Erica Jong's heroine to her analyst in Jong's 1973 *Fear of Flying* was emblematic: "Don't you see that men have always defined femininity as a means of keeping women in line? Why should I listen to you about what it means to be a woman. Are you a woman? Why shouldn't I listen to myself for once? And to other women? . . . As in a dream (I never would have believed myself capable of it) I got up from the couch (how many years had I been lying there?) picked up my pocketbook, and walked . . . out. . . . I was free!"[43]

Taken together, these three changes—the birth of an ideology of intersubjectivity, the validation of narcissism, and the emergence of feminism as what might be called the Calvinism, or "the psychoanalysis," of the third industrial revolution—helped give birth to a new post-Fordist spirit of capitalism. If we contrast the original spirit of capitalism described by Weber to the new spirit that emerged in the last third of the twentieth century, we might think of psychoanalysis as having supplied a crucial but temporary mediation: asceticism—challenged by the analytic emphasis on the instincts and against repression—had become narcissism; compulsivity—challenged by the Freudian analysis of Puritanical guilt—had become flexibility; finally, hypocrisy— challenged by the Freudian ethic of directness and honesty—had become empowerment. Psychoanalysis, in a sense, had accomplished its historical task as the era in which it had dominated popular consciousness came to an end.

Let me conclude. Psychoanalysis, I have argued, served as the Calvinism of the second industrial revolution. By this I mean it gave individuals the chance to assign personal meaning to a vast social transformation that would otherwise have been merely pragmatic, sociological, or economic. In the last decade of his life, Freud tried to develop a new approach to history, one that emphasized the role of profound upheavals, moments full of emotional intensity with long-lasting effects on tradition, character, and culture. Psychoanalysis itself was such a moment, one in which, to use Weber's language, history "switched tracks." In some ways, it is still too early to understand the long-term implications of that moment. Does it portend, like Calvinism, a higher form of social organization or does it portend increasing antinomianism, anomie, and the decline of leadership? Much depends on the evolution of the new social movements such as feminism and gay liberation, which supplanted psychoanalysis. In any event, we can now appreciate one of the most striking features in the history of analysis: its paradoxical character. Almost instantly recognized as a great force for human emancipation, it eventually became a degraded "pseudoscience" whose survival is today in doubt. This paradox can be explained when we realize that, on the one hand, it gave voice to emancipatory aspirations that served as a critique of the first industrial revolution while, on the other, those aspirations were recuperated within a revised spirit of capitalism corresponding to the second.

# 2

# Beyond the Blues

*The Racial Unconscious and Collective Memory*

The transformation in the self-image of American Blacks between 1902, when *The Souls of Black Folk* appeared, and the 1960 sit-in movement, is dramatic. Early twentieth-century African American society was a ravaged continent, protoliterate and impoverished, still dominated by despots such as Booker T. Washington or white overlords, "philanthropists," and political allies. Two generations later, Black college students shook off all tutelage and boldly extended the civil rights movement into the darkest reaches of Mississippi, Alabama, and Georgia. Most historians appreciate the role played by radical cultural and political movements such as those of the Harlem Renaissance, the Popular Front, and the anti-imperialist tendency that culminates in the idea of the Black Atlantic in bringing about this change. What is less recognized is the contribution of Freudianism.

There were many reasons for the African American interest in Freud, including the wish to understand the irrationality of racism. But one in particular stands out. Africans had been separated from their families, taken from their homelands, kinship and language groups, sold, resold, and sold again, kept in ignorance, beaten, raped, slaughtered at will, and, at best, patronized and condescended to. As they sought to overcome this horrendous legacy, African Americans needed to come to grips with their history through mourning, working through, and the constitution of collective memory. Inevitably this would be painful, at times humiliating, and would typically bring forth great rage. At key moments in this process they drew on Freudianism.

To understand how and why rests on recognizing that slavery was ultimately a patriarchal system; the slave originally was part of the master's household, and, long after the Civil War, African Americans found themselves "in the master's house," especially as they sought to assimilate into American society. Black intellectuals used Freud to struggle with the problem of remembering and reconstituting a patriarchal past in which they were still immersed. To illuminate this process I draw on Hegel's now canonical phenomenological description of how the slave attains freedom.[1]

In the first stage, the slave's consciousness is divided or "doubled" in the sense that the slave is continuously aware of "the other," i.e., the master. In the second, the slave realizes her nature as a free person through a struggle in which she literally risks her life. In a final stage, the relations of slave and master are reversed; the master has become dependent on the slave, and the slave's consciousness exists "for itself." Hegel's schema can illuminate the African American people's *internal* struggle against their psychic masters, which complemented the social and political struggles that unfolded in streets, public squares, churches, and schools. At three moments African American radicals turned to psychoanalysis to forge both memory and identity: the Harlem Renaissance, the Popular Front, and postcolonialism. These correspond to the three moments in the slave's struggle for freedom, as we will see.

What makes the encounter between African American intellectuals and psychoanalysis so salient to the theme of political Freud is that it did not occur through the development of a profession or of an isolated academic tendency, but rather through the engagement of Black intellectuals with an entire people. As a result, psychoanalysis took on a political dimension that was greater than usual. For middle class white America, psychoanalysis served as avatar, interpreter, and authority over private, intimate space. In African American society the line between public and private was more tenuous, breached by racial intimidation, economic victimization, and sexual misuse. The call-and-response tradition of African American music and of the Black church illustrates the differing character of the public/private division. When a blues or gospel or jazz singer shared his pain with an audience, it was a collective pain that was being shared. Analogously, Freud, in the African American community, was not typically the interpreter of personal life per se but had to be political as well. The porosity of the public and the private in the Black community also helps explain why that community has been central to America's political culture. The exploration of the psychic life of Black America was not only a necessary component in building an African American community; it also helped lay bare the collective unconscious of the white middle class.

In the *Souls of Black Folk* W. E. B. Du Bois noted the centrality of music to African American memory. Following his lead, we will situate the African American Freud in the context of music, especially in relation to the blues. The enslaved African captives created spirituals, a sacred music that told them that they were a chosen people and that they would be liberated. The blues, which first emerged in the United States in the late nineteenth century, were a secular descendant of the spirituals, a lower- and working-class response to the African American community's continued history of bondage, exclusion, and violated dignity. As the word suggests, the blues signified pain, but they also signified something new. Descended from collective sources such as ring shouts, work songs, protest songs, and field hollers, the blues were the first explicitly *personal* form in the history of African

American music, an outbreak of sound closely linked to psychoanalysis: not just the emotion-wracked collective voice of an oppressed group but the personal voice of an individual longing for emancipation, including emancipation from the racial community itself.

The traumatic origins of African American society made themselves felt in the anguish of the singer; the mournful humming that so often accompanied the guitar; the prevalence of such themes as blindness, old age, and impotence; and the overall sense of impasse, passivity, and stasis. When Blind Willie Johnson moans, "My mother is dead" or when Fred MacDowell describes himself as lost, humiliated, and unmanned or when Ma Rainey laments betrayal by her man, there is no self-pity. Rather, as Ralph Ellison wrote, "The Blues [was] an impulse to keep the painful details and episodes of a brutal experience alive in one's aching consciousness, to finger its jagged grain, and to transcend it, not by the consolation of philosophy but by squeezing from it a near tragic, near comic lyricism." As a form, Ellison writes, the "Blues [was] an autobiographical chronicle of personal catastrophe expressed lyrically."[2] What this means, however, is that the blues were ultimately affirmative. They affirmed the triumph of the singer over her sorrow—that is, of art over reality. Reflecting the still closely felt presence of a great wrong or harm, blues singers transcended pain through art, music, and humor but offered no path beyond it.

When Ellison described the blues as part of an effort to keep "a brutal experience alive," he was describing the role of the blues in the construction of African American memory. Psychoanalysis contributed to this task because, more than any twentieth-century movement, it placed memory at the center of all human strivings toward freedom. By memory I mean not so much objective knowledge of the past or history but rather the subjective process of mastering the past so that it becomes part of one's identity, a process that goes on for individuals and for groups. African Americans brought psychoanalysis into the collective processes through which they reconstructed their group memory as one of several ways of moving beyond the impasse the blues represented. Other ways included Marxism, pan-Africanism, artistic modernism, and existentialism, all of which interacted with Freudianism as well as with the blues. Still, there was specificity to the Freudian contribution. In trying to bring the violence, discord, and negativity of African American history into consciousness, African Americans experienced similar difficulties—impasses—to those encountered by individuals who undergo psychoanalysis. Attempting to translate a repressed unconscious into conscious collective memory and will formation, they encountered *defenses* or *resistances*, in part reflecting the obdurate intensity of racism and in part reflecting the shame, guilt, and anger of the African American community itself. African Americans learned, accordingly, that the road to the past could never be direct but had to proceed *through* the resistance, through shame, guilt, and anger. It was especially at those most touchy and difficult moments that African Americans drew upon Freudianism.[3]

## Freud and the Harlem Renaissance

The first stage in the movement beyond the blues, the Harlem Renaissance, began with W. E. B. Du Bois's idea of a double consciousness. Du Bois first formulated this idea in 1902 as a consciousness divided between self-consciousness and regard for the gaze of the other. Originally an intersubjective idea—self and other—under the impact of Freudianism double consciousness took on a depth-psychological inflection, that of "the racial unconscious." Consciousness, accordingly, turned inward, albeit at the collective level. Thus a new way of thinking about the self, as having an unconscious, began to develop in tandem with a new way of thinking about memory, that is, as the unconscious resources of a group, such as their folktales, their music, and their habitus.

The idea of a racial unconscious evolved out of a broadly shared notion of culture generated during the democratic revolutions of the eighteenth century. During these revolutions romantic poets and philosophers, such as Johann Herder, counterposed the idea that each "folk," people, nation, or "race," had its own spirit, language, or "culture," against the supposedly rootless cosmopolitanism of aristocratic "civilization." By the late nineteenth century the idea of culture expressed itself in a series of philosophies and theories that defined human beings as symbol-producing animals. Works like W. E. B. Du Bois's *The Souls of Black Folk* (1902) showed that Black Americans had maintained a culture under slavery and thus had a basis on which they could participate in American and world history. It was in this spirit that James Weldon Johnson contended in his 1922 *Book of American Negro Poetry* that "no people that has produced great literature and art has ever been looked upon by the world as distinctly inferior."[4]

Johnson notwithstanding, music provided the deepest sense of historical continuity for the African American community created under slavery. The first slaves already carried small, secreted musical instruments with them. They also remembered and preserved African (pentatonic) rhythms. The centrality of not just music, but *remembered* music, to African American history animates *The Souls of Black Folk*. Writing of the fragments of music that he placed at the start of each chapter, Du Bois recounted: "Ever since I was a child these songs have stirred me strangely. They came out of the South unknown to me, one by one, and yet *at once I knew them as of me and mine*." They descended, he explained, from his "grandfather's grandmother seized by an evil Dutch trader two centuries ago." Passed down through the generations, the melody reached Du Bois in the following form:

Do bana coba, gene me, gene me!
Do bana coba, gene me, gene me!
Ben d'nuli, nuli, nuli, nuli, ben d'le.

Du Bois confessed he had no idea where these fragments came from, but he regarded them as precious gems drawn from the onrushing and often pain-ridden stream of the past.

*The Souls of Black Folk* set the stage for Freud's entry into African American culture. Here is Du Bois's famous passage:

> The Negro is a sort of seventh son, born with a veil, with second-sight in this American world,—a world which yields him no true self-consciousness, but only lets him see himself through the revelation of the other world. It is a peculiar sensation, this sense of always looking at one's self through the eyes of others, of measuring one's soul by the tape of a world that looks on in amused contempt and pity. One ever feels his two-ness,—an American, and a Negro; two souls, two thoughts, two unreconciled strivings; two warring ideals in one dark body, whose dogged strength alone keeps it from being torn asunder.[5]

The evocation of duality lends itself to many readings—Kantian, Emersonian, and Jamesian among them—but what remains most powerful is the problem of defining oneself through the eyes of the other and therefore of having no true self-consciousness. In posing the problem in this way, DuBois placed the master-slave relationship at the center of the race problem.

To be sure, Du Bois's immortal passage already contains powerful suggestions of interiority: "two souls, two thoughts, two unreconciled strivings; two warring ideals in one dark body," along with its self-and-other "two-ness." But the element of internal struggle was strengthened when Freudianism entered African American culture, along with the explosive growth of urban Black racial awareness, during and after World War I. The Harlem Renaissance was an expression of this explosion. Freud was important to the Black cultural milieu of the twenties just as he was to the white, middle-class "jazz age" milieu. Like white flappers and modernist radicals, African Americans deployed Freudianism to counter Victorian sexual repressiveness, expressed in the hygienic advocacy of Booker T. Washington and in the Puritanism of the Black church. Whether or not there were analysts practicing in Harlem, the new Black media were replete with such articles as "The

Psychoanalysis of the Ku Klux Klan," "The Madness of Marcus Garvey," or "The Mirrors of Harlem: Psychoanalyzing New York's Colored First Citizens." Popular African American newspapers like the *Messenger* or the *Crisis* speculated about white people's "repressed" love of blacks.[6] In this context Du Bois's double consciousness took on an increasingly Freudian valence, expressed in the image of a "racial unconscious."

The idea of a racial unconscious emerged in the course of the study of African American folk culture. Zora Neale Hurston's ethnographic journeys into the American South in the 1920s supply the best starting point. A student of Franz Boas and of Edward Sapir (the main figure responsible for introducing psychoanalysis into American anthropology), Hurston at first complained that there was no such thing as African American folk culture, since Southern Blacks were interested only in radio and the movies. Later she discovered a folk culture in "the arts and crafts, the beliefs and customs of our lumber camps, city evangelical storefront churches, back-alley dives, farmer's festivals and fairs, hill frolics, carnivals, firemen's lofts, sailor's cabins, chain gangs, and penitentiaries."[7] According to Hurston, the Black South's dialect, tales, humor, and folk mores constituted a collective, aural catalogue of the past, a past that was still insistently present and that had its own character. "The white man thinks in a written language and the Negro thinks in hieroglyphics," she wrote.

We might already consider folk culture an expression of a Black collective memory, but the Freudian influence helped bring to the fore the element of internal conflict that ran through the African American experience of memory. One indication of this lay in Hurston's interest in dissonance and negativity. Directly referencing Ruth Benedict's Freudian *Patterns of Culture*, Hurston's "Characteristics of Negro Expression" described Black America's unconscious grammar in such terms as lack of reverence, "angularity," redundancy, mimicry, and "restrained ferocity in everything."[8] Hurston's best-known work, *Their Eyes Were Watching God*, traces the efforts of a Black woman to work through her own traumatic experiences by drawing upon the warm, wet tremolos and resonant vibratos of the Deep

South. It was only when Hurston's heroine turned the collective memory of her people—the racial unconscious—into something autonomous, personal, and idiosyncratically hers that she became "a speaking Black subject."[9]

Jean Toomer, the author of *Cane,* also linked the idea of a racial unconscious to a disrupted, fragmented, painful past. In a 1921 review of Eugene O'Neill's *The Emperor Jones,* he wrote: "the contents of the unconscious not only vary with individuals; they are differentiated because of race.... Jones lived through sections of an unconscious which is peculiar to the Negro. Slave ships, whipping posts, and so on.... His fear becomes a Negro's fear, recognizably different from a similar emotion, modified by other racial experience." *The Emperor Jones*, Toomer concluded, is "a section of Negro psychology presented in significant dramatic form."[10] Not just slavery but the Great Migration produced the dissonance and contradictoriness of the racial unconscious, according to Toomer. *Cane* used visual images and musical effects as a literary equivalent for the dislocations "wrought by moving people from soil to pavements, making them ashamed of their traditional folk culture or changing it into commercial entertainment."[11]

Freud's influence on the construction of African American memory persisted long after the Harlem Renaissance. Hurston's *Moses, Man of the Mountain* (1939) inspired by Freud's claim that Moses was both Egyptian and Hebrew, described an invariable element of indeterminacy that went into African American identity as well as the specialness that mysterious birth provokes. Like the spirituals that the slaves sang, and like Du Bois in *Souls,* Hurston identified African Americans as the chosen people. Comparing the long, slow process of African American emancipation to the Hebrews' forty years of wandering in the desert, Hurston insisted that freedom posed internal challenges at least as difficult as those posed by slavery. Freedom, Hurston's Moses repeatedly tells his people after they have fled Egypt, is an inner state, "not a barbecue."[12]

In African America's first encounter with Freud, then, the idea of a divided consciousness gained depth-psychological content. Nonetheless, the encounter remained stamped with a defensive impulse. For all its richness and complexity, the aim of the Harlem Renaissance was to bring out the humanity of the African American past, the sense in which Black lives had not been negated by slavery, not been reduced to mere haulers of wood, tobacco, and cotton, to what Aristotle called *zoon*, mere animal existence. What Du Bois, Toomer, Hurston, and many others showed was that even under the conditions of slavery Blacks had retained their music, history, humor, folk tales, sexual practices, religion, family ties, in a word, their culture. To be sure, Du Bois, Toomer, Hurston, and others described African American consciousness as divided, conflictual, dual: "two warring ideals in one dark body." But what this duality revealed was that African American society had a telos, that of freedom, which remained to be realized. *Soul*, as defined by Du Bois, was similar to the blues: it was the acceptance of an ambiguous, in-between state, an acceptance based upon the unjust, sad (blue) but ultimately comic, in the sense of triumphant, character of the Black experience. The humor and sensuality with which Hurston leavened bitterness, the irony with which Toomer portrayed Black strivings for upward mobility, the enormous spiritual resources in Du Bois's oeuvre: these are all examples of "soul," that is, of the spirit's triumph over adversity. The bittersweet "blue" quality of the triumph is what gives Black literature, music, and visual art its deeply moving quality.

Yet the African American project of cultural reconstruction could not and did not rest content with the ideas of soul, culture, and a racial unconscious, even when inflected by Freudianism, as they were. Du Bois, who had moved toward communism ever since visiting the Soviet Union in 1927, intuited that psychoanalysis offered a deeper picture of human irrationality than the idea of a racial unconscious. In his 1940 autobiography *Dusk of Dawn*, he recalled that as a young man he had thought of the "Negro problem as a matter of systematic investigation and intelligent understanding. The world was thinking wrong about race, because it did not know. The ultimate evil was stupidity, the cure for it was knowledge based on scientific investigation." Then "there cut across this plan which I had as a scientist, a red ray which could not be ignored . . . a poor Negro in central Georgia, Sam Hose, had killed his landlord's wife. I wrote out a careful and reasoned statement concerning the evident facts and started down to the *Atlanta Constitution* office. . . . I did not get there. On the way news met me: Sam Hose had been lynched, and they said that his knuckles were on exhibition at a grocery store . . . I turned back to the university, I began to turn aside from my work." Lynching, DuBois grasped, came from deep inside the twisted white psyche. As he later concluded: "In the fight against race prejudice, we were not facing simply the rational, conscious determination of white folk to oppress us; we were facing age-long complexes stuck now largely to unconscious habit and irrational urge." Criticizing his earlier view that "race prejudice [was] based on wide-spread ignorance," Du Bois concluded that he had not been "sufficiently Freudian to understand how little human action is based on reason."[13] Du Bois's insight, though focused on the racist and not on the race, anticipates the second moment in the African American encounter with Freudianism, the moment when the slave risks his or her life and is thereby launched toward true self-consciousness or freedom. Our discussion of this moment will center on Richard Wright.

## Freud and the Popular Front

Richard Wright was born in 1908 on a plantation near Natchez, Mississippi. His father was a sharecropper who abandoned the family; his mother and her female relatives were religious zealots. To understand the quasi-totalitarian environment of his childhood, consider Orlando Patterson's notion of slavery as social death. Slavery, Patterson argued, was the result of defeat on the field of battle. The slave was incorporated into the society as an internal enemy, a nonbeing; death was not absolved but postponed. Thereafter the slave had no social existence except as mediated by the master; powerlessness and dishonor constituted the main experiences of life.[14] Wright later wrote of his childhood: "I had already grown to feel that there existed men against whom I was powerless, men who would violate my life at will."

"If I was a nigger," a coworker later told him, "I'd kill myself." How would the child of a sharecropper, the grandchild of slaves, respond to this condition?[15] Wright responded by consciously negating every message that society, including his family, directed at him. "In what other way," Wright asked in his autobiography, *Black Boy*, "had the South allowed me to be natural, to be real, to be myself except in rejection, rebellion, and aggression?"[16]

In 1925, at the age of seventeen, Wright left Mississippi for Memphis and then, two years later, moved to Chicago. Responsible for the support of his sick mother, Wright found Chicago reinforced his early experiences of intimate everyday violence. According to one biographer, "His inability to prevent his resentment from registering on his face or in his demeanor result[ed] in his dismissal from various jobs because his employers [did] not like his 'looks.'"[17] On one occasion, Wright was fired for saying "yes sir, I understand," since that showed more self-respect than a Southern Black was meant to possess. "I could not make subservience an *automatic* part of my behavior. I had to feel and think out each tiny item of racial experience in the light of the race problem, and to each item I brought the whole of my life," Wright wrote. Literature alone, he says, allowed him to stay "alive in a negatively vital way." Above all, H. L. Mencken inspired him. As he wrote in *Black Boy*: "this man was fighting, fighting with words. He was using words as a weapon, using them as one would use a club."[18]

In his Depression-era jobs Wright encountered what Ellison later called invisibility. As a hotel bellboy he was summoned to rooms where naked white prostitutes lolled around as if he wasn't there. "Blacks were not considered human beings anyway," Wright observed. "I was a nonman, something that knew vaguely that it was human but felt that it was not . . . I felt doubly cast out."[19] Wright also worked as an orderly in a Chicago medical research institute, an experience that underlined the significance of voice and language to the working through of trauma: "Each Saturday morning I assisted a young Jewish doctor in slitting the vocal cords of a fresh batch of dogs from the city pound. . . . I held each

dog as the doctor injected Nembutal into its veins to make it unconscious; then I held the dog's jaws open as a doctor inserted the scalpel
and severed the vocal cords. Later, when the dogs came to, they would
lift their heads to the ceiling and gape in a soundless wail. The sight
became lodged in my imagination as a symbol of silent suffering."[20]

The Communist Party, more than anything, first gave Wright his
voice. Nor was Wright unusual in this regard. Claude McKay, Coun-
tee Cullen, Langston Hughes, Alain Locke, Paul Robeson, Chester Himes, Ralph Ellison, and W. E. B. Du Bois were only a few of
the African American intellectuals of the time active in or around
the Party.[21] To be sure, American communism had been sparked by
the huge upsurge in strikes involving Blacks, both as workers and as
strikebreakers during World War I. But what attracted Wright and
others to the Party was not primarily its commitment to the struggles
of labor, but its contribution to the construction of African American
memory. Ever since the Russian Revolution, the "labor question" had
been largely subsumed into the "national question," and for a while
Wright's favorite book was Stalin's *Marxism and the National and
Colonial Question*. "Of all the developments in the Soviet Union," he
later recalled,

> the way scores of backward peoples had been led to unity on a
> national scale was what had enthralled me. I had read with awe
> how the Communists had sent phonetic experts into the vast
> regions of Russia. . . . I had made the first total emotional com-
> mitment of my life when I read how the phonetic experts had
> given these tongueless people, a language, newspapers, institu-
> tions. I had read how these forgotten folk had been encouraged
> to keep their old cultures, to see in their ancient customs mean-
> ings and satisfactions as deep as those contained in supposedly
> superior ways of living.[22]

We can see the impact of Communism on African American life,
as well as the way it paved the way for the second African American

Freud, by considering its relation to the blues. In the world that Wright's life encompassed, that of sharecropping in the Mississippi delta and odd jobs in Black Chicago, the blues had been ubiquitous. The reason was that they were integral in overcoming the shame culture that had pervaded slavery and persisted under Jim Crow. Shame is the feeling of personal inadequacy in a group context and is intrinsic to Hegel's first stage in the struggle for freedom. The rejection of shame can be seen in the blues' scatological language and pungent sexuality, their acceptance of weakness, frailty, and bad luck, of failed marriages and failed jobs, their embrace of the simple joys of eating, drinking, and sex, and their acceptance of ambivalence, which was expressed through humor: "I put my head on the lonesome railroad track, but when the train come by, I snatched it back." Reflecting the triumph of narcissism (humor) not only over slavery but also over Jim Crow, the blues were integral to the great step taken by the black middle classes during the Harlem Renaissance: Louis Armstrong, Duke Ellington, Bessie Smith, Ethel Waters, and Ma Rainey (so-called Mother of the Blues) all attained their first great success during the 1920s, while Gershwin's *Rhapsody in Blue*, which demonstrates how the blues and classical music crossed paths, dates to 1924.

Still, the Russian Revolution, which inspired American leftists like Pete Seeger and Alan Lomax, had the impact of redefining the blues, to make explicit their lower-class (proletarian) and, even more, their *folk* meaning. The blues were in fact one of the world's leading examples of a folk art that had successfully made the transition to urban, industrial society, an achievement that lies behind the world supremacy of American popular music. The African American folk traditions, Alain Locke argued, were the American counterparts to the communal and medieval traditions of Europe and thereby invaluable for the modern world. At the same time, beginning in the twenties, blues, jazz, ragtime and the whole panoply of the musical Black past were in danger of being commercialized and losing their political implications. Wright believed this had already happened to African American literature, which, unlike the blues, was being written primarily for white audiences. A class analysis made it possible for him to explain this. In a 1937 essay Wright contrasted the "parasitic and mannered" literature of the Harlem Renaissance's "rising Negro bourgeoisie," which sought to obliterate its roots in the lower-class and slave experience, to the "blues, spirituals and folk tales recounted from mouth to mouth," the Black mother to her Black daughter, the Black father to his Black son, the shared sex experiences of the streets, the "work songs sung under blazing suns."[23] Memory required direct confrontation with authority. Unlike the blues singers, Wright charged, the writers of the Harlem Renaissance had "entered the Court of American Public Opinion dressed in the knee-pants of servility, curtsying to show that the Negro was not inferior, that he was human, and that he had a life comparable to that of other people."[24]

In the context that a left wing movement provided, blues singers were able to capture the anger and pain emanating from the Black community sharply and with emotional depth. An example comes from Robert Johnson's 1937 "Hellhound Blues," which refers to a Mississippi sheriff notorious for sending a trained horse out after fugitives. "I got to keep moving, I got to keep moving / blues falling down like hail / blues falling down like hail . . . and the days keep on worryin' me / there's hellhound on my trail / hellhound on my trail / hellhound on my trail." Wright sought to create a literature capable of a similar emotional impact. His "Long, Black Song," written at the height of the Popular Front, is an example. The story portrays a white traveling salesman, selling phonographs with clocks, who seduces a black woman, Sarah, by playing records of spirituals for her. When Sarah's husband Silas learns what happened, he beats his wife, kills the salesman, and waits for the lynch party so he can kill a few more of his oppressors. In "Long, Black Song" the spirituals are no longer the resource for the race that they were in *The Souls of Black Folk*. Rather, they have been co-opted into a crass commercial culture that rests on racism, violence, and the transformation of the past into kitsch; like Sarah, they have been raped.

The Popular Front's orientation to the working class, the subproletariat, and especially to the idea of a folk, along with an awareness of the ubiquity of violence, made Wright's writing crucial for the construction of an African American past. Many of his subjects were semiliterate and nonintrospective so that his writing took on qualities of oral literature, such as folklore and song. Relying on onomatopoeia—rifles that CRACK!, whips that "whick," steam that goes "Psseeezzzzzzzzzzzzz"—foregrounding lynching, rape, murder, and the fugitive's futile escape, "pressur[ing] the surface of reality (the surface of the text) in order to make it yield the full, true terms of his story," Wright's characters gain access to subjective self-awareness only as the result of committing an act of violence. Here, then, was the significance of *Native Son* (1940), the key text in moving African American consciousness beyond the blues and into the second stage of the master/slave struggle described by Hegel.

Bigger Thomas, who smothers his drunken, communist, female employer because he fears being discovered alone with her, and who blindly rapes his girlfriend during the flight that follows, supplanted the seventh son as the iconic representative of the African American struggle because he exemplified the knot of resistance and negativity at the heart of African American memory. Thomas's situation is truly tragic: an accidental murder puts him in the first situation of his fear-ridden life in which he manages to take moral guilt and responsibility for himself.[25] In the aftermath of the murder, he experiences a profound "lifting of tension and calmness." The reason was "the thought of what he had done, the awful horror of it, the daring associated" with it. "He had murdered and had created a new life for himself. It was something that was all his own, and it was the first time in his life he had anything that others could not take from him. Yes; he could sit here calmly and eat and not be concerned about what his family" or anyone else thought or did. After being convicted and sentenced to die, Bigger had further insight into his crimes. To the dismay of his lawyer, he cried out, "When a man kills it's for something. . . . I didn't know I was really alive in this world until I felt things hard enough to kill for 'em. . . . It's the truth, Mr. Max. I can say it now, 'cause I'm going to die. I know what I'm saying real good and I know how it sounds. But I'm all right. I feel all right when I look at it that way."

After finishing *Native Son,* Wright wrote two autobiographical works: "How Bigger Was Born" and *Black Boy (American Hunger).* In one of his most powerful childhood memories, he recalled a friend, Carlotta: "One day I stood near her on the school ground; we were talking and I was happy. A strong wind blew and lifted the Black curls of her wavy hair and revealed . . . a long, ugly scar." The rawness and violence of the sight never left him.[26] In *Black Boy* Wright reflected on the effects of a traumatic past on Black memory and culture: "After I had outlived the shocks of childhood, after the habit of reflection had been born in me, I used to mull over the strange absence of real kindness in Negroes, how unstable was our tenderness, how lacking in genuine passion we were, how void of great hope, how timid our joy, how bare our traditions, how hollow our memories, how lacking we were in those intangible sentiments that bind man to man, and how shallow was even our despair. After I had learned other ways of life I used to brood upon the unconscious irony of those who felt that Negroes led so passional an existence! I saw that what had been taken for our emotional strength was our negative confusions, our flights, our fears, our frenzy under pressure." Here we have an unprecedented reflection on the costs exacted by a traumatic past, searing in its pain.

Ralph Ellison's review situated *Black Boy* in the context of the blues. In its refusal to offer solutions, Ellison wrote, *Black Boy* shared something with the blues, since the blues "provide no solution, offer no scapegoat but the self." But, to my reading, *Black Boy* expressed elements of defiance and existential rage that moved beyond the blues. Perhaps for the first time, the unbelievable enormity of the crimes that had been committed against African Americans began to rise to the level of consciousness, and men and women began to bear the anguish that the realization of a traumatic past entails: the discovery that one's life could have been different, that one's best potential had been betrayed by the rapacity of others, that the sanctity of one's heart had been violated by the instruments of an enemy, that one's parents, grandparents, and ancestors had had their lives stolen from them. Even Ellison conceded that Wright "has converted the American Negro impulse toward self-annihilation and 'going under-ground' into a will to confront the world."[27]

Communism, which was a fundamentally historical conception of the world, and which therefore fostered collective memory, had played a role in this. Communism, Wright wrote, was "something more recondite than mere political strategy. . . . It was a *life* strategy using political methods as its tools. . . . Its essence was a voluptuous, a deep-going sensuality that took cognizance of fundamental human needs and the answers to those needs. . . . It was a noneconomic conception of existence." Communism helped bring the subterranean violence of African American life into the foreground and give it a systematic and structural focus. But communism had no room for the distinct and idiosyncratic struggle of an individual subjectivity. Like so many others, Wright felt it was necessary to leave communism in order to advance the cause of freedom that communism had itself in part unleashed. Wright wrote in his preface to St. Clair Drake and Horace R. Cayton Jr.'s *Black Metropolis: A Study of Negro Life in a Northern City* (1945), "We know how some of the facts look when seen under the lenses of Marxist concepts but the full weight of the Western mind has yet to bear upon this forgotten jungle of Black life. What would life on Chicago's South Side look like when seen through the eyes of a Freud, a Joyce, a Proust, a Pavlov?" "I'm convinced" he added in his diary, "that the next great area of discovery in the Negro will be the dark, landscape of his own mind, what living in white America has done to him. Boy, what that search will reveal! There's enough there to find to use in transforming the basis of human life on earth."[28]

In seeking to combine Marx with Freud (not to mention Joyce, Proust, and Pavlov) Wright pioneered an important variant of the idea, pervasive in later twentieth-century politics and social thought, that mental states, such as hysteria, "neurosis," or anxiety, as well as antisocial proclivities, such as racism, authoritarianism, or criminality, had a historical and social basis. Wilhem Reich had pioneered this version of political Freudianism in the thirties by explaining "the mass psychology of fascism." Karen Horney, a student of Reich's, applied it to sexism. The Popular Front was suffused with it, under such rubrics as neo-Freudianism, "national character," "culture and personality," and in the widely read writings of such figures as Erich Fromm. To be sure, the confrontation with the Nazis largely decimated hereditarian and eugenic theories of Black "deviance," leading to a deepening appreciation of sociological and cultural explanations of "individual problems" such as E. Franklin Frazier's theory of the "weakness" of the Black family. However, harnessing psychoanalysis to the Popular Front critique of racism had its own distinctive character.

Wright's involvement in this project began with two white, left-liberal Jewish psychiatrists: Benjamin Karpman and Frederick Wertham, as well as with the Black sociologist Horace Cayton. In April 1943 Karpman, a psychiatrist at St. Elizabeth Hospital in Washington, DC, who taught at all-Black Howard University and considered himself "a specialist in minorities," wrote Wright urging him to do an article for *Harper's Magazine* that "might deal with such a topic as 'The Blind Inability of the White Man to Understand the Psychology of the Negro,' which blindness is a defense barrier put up by him, while the negro too, when dealing with white people, is also on the defensive." Among Karpman's "special qualifications" for pursuing a "psychogenetic study on the problems of the negro" he cited his "intimate contact with the people for the past twenty five years, which I doubt that many white people have had an opportunity to have"—a contact that Karpman "sought," "nourished," "cultivated" and to which he "gave all the sunshine [he] could." In his parting words to Wright, Karpman emphasized that he "had met among [his] students Bigger Thomas long before [Wright] ever thought of writing about them." Karpman also told Wright that he "probably would not have gone into Psychiatry were it not for my feeling that neurotics and psychotics are a greatly misunderstood minority. Similarly, the criminal has been misunderstood and abused as well. I found the same situation existing with respect to homosexuals." Wright appealed to various foundations and mayor's committees for funds to publish Karpman's case studies of Black criminals, studies that Karpman hoped would prove the "scientific parallel to *Native Son*."[29]

In addition, Wright formed a relationship with Frederick Wertham, née Wertheimer, a refugee from Germany, director of the Mental Hygiene Clinic at Bellevue and author of a psychoanalytic study of matricide, *Dark Legend*.[30] As in the case of Bigger Thomas, a "violent destructive act seemed to have been a rallying point for the constructive forces of [the hero's] personality." In Germany Wertham had observed the misuse of psychiatry by Kraepelin and others to stigmatize leftists and Jews. Wertham treated Wright, partly to help him avoid service in World War II as well as assisting him in an ill-fated intervention in the New Jersey prison system. In June 1944 Wertham presented "An Unconscious Determinant in Native Son" at the annual meeting of the American Psychopathological Association. According to Wertham, the project was unique since "no psychoanalytic study of a literary creation based on analytic study of its author [had] ever been undertaken."

Horace Cayton, coauthor with St. Clair Drake of *Black Metropolis*, was another figure who sought to wed Freud to leftist sociology. Cayton's honesty about how racism affected him personally endeared him to Wright. Considering *fear* to be the fundamental emotion guiding Negro personality and behavior, Wright wrote, "I like Horace because he's scared and admits it, as I do." According to Wright, "None of us want to believe that fear—a fear that lies so deep within us that we are unaware of it—is the most dominate [*sic*] emotion of the Negro in America. But what if we are afraid and know it and know what caused it, could we not contain it and convert it into useful knowledge? But we are afraid and we do not want to tell ourselves that we are afraid; it wounds if we do; so we hug it, thinking that we have killed it. But it still lives, creeping out in a disguise that is called Negro laughter." Wright called upon his fellow Negroes to face the fear of exploring the psychological and emotional effects of racist oppression. He called this process "The Conquest of Ourselves."

The friendship between Wright and Cayton was marked by an intense interest in the theoretical insights of psychoanalysis for the Negro. "About the whole problem of psychoanalysis," Cayton wrote to Wright, "I would like to talk to you at length. Especially would I like to discuss the question of what constitutes the rock bottom of the Negro's existence & personality structure—his earlier psychological conditioning in the family or his reaction to his subjugation. My notion is that they are curiously blended—one reinforcing the other to produce the most devastating results. However, I would have to talk to you about this at length. It is not in the literature and we could make a real contribution if we could express it." In "A Psychological Approach to Race Relations" Cayton also theorized white Americans' "guilt-hate-fear complex": "The white man suffers then from an oppressor's psychosis—the fear that there will be retribution from those he has humiliated and tortured."[31]

Cayton underwent a long analysis with Dr. Helen V. McLean, a disabled woman and a prominent advocate for the inclusion of psychoanalysis in discussions of American race relations. Through McLean, Cayton arranged for Wright to give a lecture at the Chicago Institute of Psychoanalysis on the utility of psychoanalysis for understanding fear and hate in the American Negro. Speaking of his own analysis, Cayton wrote that beginning with the idea that race was a "convenient catchall," a rationalization for personal inadequacy, a "means of preventing deeper probing," he had concluded that race "ran to the core of [his] personality" and "formed the central focus for [his] insecurity." "I must have drunk it in with my mother's milk," he added.[32]

Psychoanalysis also provided Cayton and Wright with the language and concepts to explore the impact of racism on African Americans' sexuality and family life. The dominant—white, middle-class—ideal of the family was rooted in the "cult of true womanhood." White racism was integral to this cult. Blacks were degraded and associated with the profane, while white women were placed on a pedestal. In Freudian terms this cast the white man as a protector of virginity, while the Black man was hypersexualized and therefore in need of being castrated. Wright felt that Black men internalized this racism, by castrating themselves before they could suffer at the hands of others. In 1943 Wright, traveling with Cayton in the South on a Jim Crow train, insisted that they eat in the dining car. The white steward sat them last, in the least desirable table, pulling a curtain around them so no one could see them. Their waiter, however, was Black. After they ate, Wright queried Cayton about the waiter: "Did you notice that waiter when he talked to the steward? . . . Poor Black devil, his voice went up two octaves and his testicles must have jumped two inches into his stomach. . . . He does that to emasculate himself, to make himself more feminine, less masculine, more acceptable to a white man."[33]

Wright's wish to redeem Black masculinity cannot be reduced to sexism. Rather, it has to be situated in the context of bisexuality in the Freudian sense of the term, which ascribes heterosexual and homosexual currents to both sexes. In Wright's short story "Man of All Work" (1957), the hero, Carl, had been a cook in the army, but he is now busy taking care of a newborn and a sick wife, and the only work available is as a domestic. To feed his family, Carl dresses as a woman and gets a maid's job. Not only is Carl invisible as a Black man but also as a woman, as we learn when the man of the house tries to rape him. The story's high point comes when the wife of his employer forces Carl to give her a bath, thus compelling him to look upon a naked white woman. At its end, Carl's whole family—a newborn, a six year old, and a sick wife—are crying, and Carl joins in: "Aw, Christ, if you all cry like that, you make me cry," and then comes a wail from the blues, "Oooouuwa." As in the case of Tyree, the Southern Black father figure in Wright's last novel *The Long Dream*, the Black father may only appear castrated; we need always appreciate the feminine or maternal elements in his character, which are motivated by love of family and not solely by fear of white intimidation.

In 1945 Wright joined Wertham in opening a low-cost therapy center, the Lafargue Clinic, in Harlem, named for Paul Lafargue, an Afro-Cuban French-born socialist who was also Karl Marx's son-in-law. The clinic, a pioneering experiment in "mass therapy," charged twenty-five cents an hour and did not pay psychiatrists. Ralph Ellison called it the "most successful attempt in the nation to provide psychotherapy for the underprivileged" and "one of the few institutions dedicated to recognizing the total implication of Negro life in the United States." General Omar Bradley, director of the Veterans Administration, recommended it to all veterans, regardless of race. Wright wrote several articles popularizing the clinic, including "Psychiatry Comes to Harlem," in which he spoke of the "artificially made psychological problems" of Blacks.[34] According to Wright, "the powerful personality conflicts engendered in Negroes by the consistent sabotage of their democratic aspirations in housing, jobs, education, and social mobility creates an environment of anxiety and tension which easily tips the normal emotional scales toward neurosis." Embodying a "social psychoanalytic approach professing that change within the social environment can and will affect the black psyche," Wright referred to it as "the extension of the very concept of psychiatry into a new realm, the application of psychiatry to the masses, the turning of Freud upside down." The clinic's location in the basement of St. Philip's Episcopal Church led Wright to imagine it as an "underground" institution.

Ralph Ellison was also closely involved with the clinic. Born in Oklahoma City, Ellison moved to New York in 1937, where he found work as a clerk for the psychoanalyst Harry Stack Sullivan. Sullivan, like Karen Horney and Erich Fromm, was a "neo-Freudian," i.e., someone who followed Wilhelm Reich in insisting that psychoanalysis needed to be situated in the context of social and cultural conditions and, therefore, ultimately in the context of memory and history.[35] Like Wright, Ellison explained the Black psyche in terms of the Great Migration of Blacks to Northern cities. Perceived psychological disorders among African Americans, Ellison wrote, mask deeper intellectual energies that are repressed due to Southern oppression. The Black Southerner who possesses insight into the illogical nature of his inferior position appears to be a hysteric. When he moves north, "his family disintegrates, his church splinters, his folk wisdom is discarded in the mistaken notion that it in no way applies to urban living," but he also experiences a "quick rise in intellect," a spurt in energy that takes the form of nervous tension, anxiety. In September 1944 Ellison wrote Wright: "I did hear the rumour that you were neurotic again; first it was Bigger and now you. 'If you can't control a nigger, call him crazy,' you know the technique."

In "Harlem Is Nowhere" (1948) Ellison expressed his hopes that the Lafargue Clinic could give shape to the overall project of African American emancipation. The Harlem streetscape, he wrote, resembled the devastated inner world of many African Americans: "a ruin—many of its ordinary aspects (its crimes, its casual violence, its crumbling buildings with littered area-ways, ill-smelling halls and vermin-invaded rooms) are indistinguishable from the distorted images that appear in dreams, and which, like muggers haunting a lonely hall, quiver in the waking mind with hidden and threatening significance." Harlem's citizens inhabit a social, geographic, and psychological no-man's-land where they "feel alienated and their whole lives have become a search for answers to the questions, Who am I, What am I, Why am I, and Where? Significantly, in Harlem the reply to the greeting 'How are you?' is often, 'Oh man, I'm nowhere'—a phrase so revealing an attitude so common that is has been reduced to a gesture, a seemingly trivial word." According to Ellison, "the phrase 'I'm nowhere' expresses the feeling borne in upon many Negroes that they have no stable, recognized place in society. One's identity drifts in a capricious reality in which even the most commonly held assumptions are questionable. One 'is' literally, but one is nowhere; one wanders dazed in a ghetto maze, a 'displaced person' of American democracy." In contrast to the devastation Ellison found in Harlem's streets, he claimed the clinic's "importance transcends even its great value as a center for psychotherapy; it represents an underground extension of democracy."

The Lafargue Clinic had a long reach. Conducting individual interviews, mosaic tests, and group observation, psychiatrists at the clinic found that segregation resulted in Black children having feelings of inferiority, insecurity, and alienation and bred sentiments of racism and prejudice among white children. After the study, Wertham concluded that segregation was "a massive public health problem," creating "in the mind of the child an unsolvable conflict."[36] Joined with the research of Drs. Kenneth Clark and Mamie Clark, the study was later instrumental for the NAACP attorneys who relied heavily on psychological evidence in Brown v. the Board of Education. In a more long-term sense, the experience of the clinic, linked as it was to the Supreme Court integration decision, provides an indelible moment situating Freudianism in African American memory as it exists today.

The Popular Front, then, provided the context for the second great political Freud in African American history. While the New Negro of the 1920s still contained elements of proving oneself, the Popular Front insistence on the integrity, and even moral superiority, of lower-class culture encouraged a new sense of equality not as something bestowed but as always already present. This changed the emphasis of African American memory, from the cultural achievements of the past to the devastation that slavery and racism had wrought. A shift in the class basis of the freedom struggle was the key to this change. The inclusion of the lower classes and of *folk* culture not only grounded African American identity more widely than before; it also deepened it. This deepening, which reflected a kind of popular sociological and political Freudianism, can be seen in terms of sex and aggression. On the one hand, the African American struggle for a fully sexual life and for a family life in the context of racism was validated; on the other hand, the centrality of aggression, conflict, and even violence in African American history was admitted into consciousness. Unlike the Freud of the Harlem Renaissance, then, who was always aware of his "twoness," the Freud of the Popular Front helped inspire a life-and-death struggle against the dominant culture. Indeed, so important was psychoanalysis to left-wing African American culture of the forties that the later Popular Front should be thought of as Marxo-Freudian and not merely Marxist.

As we have already seen, the blues helps clarify the context in which the project of African American memory germinated. In particular, attention to the blues demonstrates the way in which Popular Front collectivism, almost in spite of itself, was generating a new and potentially radical focus on individual subjectivity, and not just on group consciousness. Blues historians often say there is no such thing as the blues, only Ma Rainey blues, Blind Lemon blues, Willie Johnson blues.[37] During the Popular Front, the new and increasingly refined focus on the individual voice, along with the single harmonica, banjo, or guitar, expressed the incomparable qualities of the idiosyncratic individual, as did the sliding between scales (pentatonic and heptatonic), the slurring, vocal leaps, and falsettos, the syncopation, which accented the weak or offbeat notes, the dark introversions of the minor keys, and the improvised, informal, spontaneous performance, impossible to reproduce for a mass public. A new consciousness, centered on jazz, abstract expressionism, and existentialism, along with psychoanalysis, was in the process of being born, and Wright pursued it by moving to Paris in 1946, where the third African American and now Afro-Caribbean Freud was also germinating.

## The Freud of the Black Atlantic

In *Black Jacobins* (1938) C. L. R. James struggled to understand how Toussaint L'Ouverture, perhaps the greatest liberator of the Age of Revolution, had lost the support of his people. "Knowing the race question for the political and social question that it was," James wrote, "he tried to deal with it in a purely political and social way." Toussaint's failure to appreciate the passions of the ex-slaves "was a grave error," James continued, a "failure of enlightenment, not of darkness."[38] Behind James's wrestling with Toussaint lay the self-inflicted tragedy of the Russian Revolution. A leading figure in the Fourth (Trotskyist) International, James believed the revolution had disintegrated into Stalinism because the Bolsheviks lost touch with the subjective experiences of the Soviet peoples.

A deepening awareness of subjectivity, and indeed of freedom, also lies behind the third incarnation of Freud in African American history: the anticolonial Freud or—the term I will eventually suggest—the Freud of the Black Atlantic. Even more than his two great predecessors—the Freud of the Harlem Renaissance and the Freud of the Popular Front—the anticolonial Freud was a transnational figure, issuing from a diverse community of left-wing African, African American, and Caribbean insurgents and intellectuals, formed in Paris after the Second World War, and including Richard Wright, Chester Himes, James Baldwin, Frantz Fanon, and C. L. R. James, as well as French intellectuals such as Jean-Paul Sartre, Simone de Beauvoir, Albert Memmi, and Octave Mannoni. Also important were pan-Africanist intellectuals in London, notably George Padmore, South Africans like Peter Abrahams, and exponents of *Négritude* like Amilcar Cabral and Leopold Senghor. Deeply influenced by existentialism, these thinkers externalized the psychoanalytic idea of an unconscious, turning it into an account of projection, projective identification, and intersubjective conflicts and defenses. Diverse though they were, the long-term result of their labors was one of the great paradigms of the postwar world: the antagonistic self/other relations of domination exemplified by the anti-Semite and the Jew (Sartre), colonizer/colonized (Fanon, Memmi, Mannoni), sexism (Beauvoir), knowing subject/object of knowledge (Foucault), racism (Stuart Hall), and orientalism (Edward Said).

The anticolonial Freud emerged against the background of a powerful leftist social and historical concept, that of imperialism. In 1935 the Italian invasion of Ethiopia encouraged African Americans to think of U.S. racism as one building block in a worldwide system of racialized colonialism. In 1936 the Spanish Civil War brought the fascist boot down in Spain's North African colonies. World War II was waged mostly by two self-proclaimed anticolonial powers, the United States and the Soviet Union, against expansionist empires: Nazi Germany, fascist Italy, and imperial Japan. As the war was ending, President Roosevelt sought to dismantle the French and British empires. As a result, many African Americans expected that the postwar era would also lead to the end of Jim Crow. When the leaders of India's independence movement refused to fight the Nazis without the promise of independence, when African and Caribbean national liberation movements exploded, or when the British suspended Nigerian press freedoms, these were huge stories in the African American community, closely linked to expectations of an end to the American racial divide. Equally powerful, if less conscious among African Americans, was the awareness of a contemporaneous expression of racial hatred, the murder of six million European Jews.

The Allied victory did see the beginnings of the end for colonialism, but it also saw the outbreak of the cold war. Instead of defining the postwar world through the liberation of long-oppressed and racially stigmatized peoples, American elites defined it as a struggle between communism and freedom. According to modernization theory, the dominant paradigm in cold war America, racism, Nazism, and communism were coequal forms of immaturity, symptoms of individual or cultural backwardness or "pathology" on the path toward rational, self-interested, market-oriented behavior. In particular, a new academic language of "prejudice," "stereotypes," "intergroup relations," and "self-esteem" sprang up to describe racism. Judaism was subsumed in a new "Judeo-Christian" or "axial" synthesis, counterposed to "godless" Nazism and communism, as explored in the next chapter. Freud was recruited into the cold war synthesis as a supposed critic of utopian ideas and advocate of "maturity." Jazz, bebop, and the blues became glittering jewels in the armor of cold war anticommunism as Louis Armstrong toured the Gold Coast on behalf of the Voice of America and Dizzy Gillespie toured the Middle East with an interracial orchestra. "We are expected to be the model," Secretary of State Dean Rusk explained.

Meanwhile, the most promising challenge to cold war consumerism did not come from an already largely discredited communism, nor from psychoanalysis, but rather from artistic radicalism, including music such as the blues, jazz, and bebop and—the seedbed of the third African American Freud—from existentialism. A theory of human freedom, choice, and contingency, existentialism had emerged against the background of France's defeat, resistance, and collaboration. Sartre called existentialism an "individualism of the Left," reflecting the way in which leftist thought had shifted, albeit subtly, from the Popular Front's preoccupation with equality to the postwar preoccupation with freedom. Existentialism drew on the French conception of the subject or *cogito*, which had originated with Montaigne, Pascal, and Descartes, a conception that was weak or absent in Anglo-American philosophical thought. With this legacy in mind, Sartre criticized Freudianism because it seemed to analyze consciousness from the outside, as if it were an objective "thing," and not from within. Still, Sartre's reading of Freud was ambiguous, hovering between outright rejection and phenomenological restatement. What Freudianism brought to existentialism, as it had brought it to the Harlem Renaissance and to the Popular Front, was a sense of the weight of the past, which is to say depth psychology. Frantz Fanon, our main example of this third moment in the relations of Freudianism and African American memory, saw this, and so he sought to synthesize the existentialist subject and the Freudian unconscious in his historically framed conception of a "racial complex."

Termed by Edward Said "Freud's most disputatious heir," Fanon came of age in the wake of the war's terrible violence. Born in 1925 into a middle-class black Martinican family in the French West Indies, he was intensely conscious of his race, but also deeply grounded in French (Alsatian) identity by virtue of his class and education. His first overt experiences of bigotry came from Vichy troops in Martinique after the fall of France in 1940. Fanon responded to these experiences by enlisting in the Free French forces, although he found the latter racist too. At the same time, he fell under the spell of his lycée instructor and mentor in Martinique, Aimé Césaire, a founder of the *Négritude* movement. After the war, Fanon trained as a psychiatrist at Lyons and later practiced in Algeria, in whose revolution he participated. Reflecting the extraordinary jangle to which world history subjected postwar colonials like Fanon, throughout his short life he changed identities regularly, from French Martinican to Algerian to Pan-African to a new universalist humanist, but never lost his almost preternatural sensitivity to racial insult.

The original psychoanalytic element in Fanon's thought was the idea that the unconscious could serve as a revolutionary force. This idea drew on Freud's *Interpretation of Dreams* and ignored the later complexities in Freud's theory of memory, such as Freud's elaboration of a theory of psychic structure. In fact, Fanon derived his original idea of the unconscious less from his analytical training than from surrealism, artistic radicalism, the blues and jazz, and from his *Négritude* background. Though influenced by the Harlem Renaissance, *Négritude* rested on the conviction that the achievement of genuine subjectivity on the part of an oppressed race had to pass through the recognition of degradation, an insight we have already seen in Wright. In his great 1939 poem *Retour d'un pays natal,* Césaire describes the Caribbean sun as venereal and diseased and portrays Martinique as "scrofulous," still echoing with the groans of despair in the hulls of the slave ships. Recalling monstrous sodomies, prostitutions, hypocrisies, petty cowardice, and "wheezing enthusiasms," the poet describes the Martinicans as a race of "worthless dishwashers" who have "never invented anything." In his final line, repeated by Fanon, Césaire describes the Afro-Caribbean past as "the great black hole" (*le grand trou noir*) into which the poet expects to drown (*noyer*).

Surrealism, which Césaire called "a weapon that exploded the French language," rested on the idea that unconscious traces of the past, which could take the form of physical sites, even of urban neighborhoods, but also of subaltern behaviors and practices, had revolutionary potential. In 1941 André Breton, interned in Martinique by the Vichy government, discovered Césaire's poem and praised it for revitalizing surrealism after Stalinism had dealt it a near-mortal blow. Surrealism, Breton wrote, "is allied with people of color . . . because it has sided with them against all forms of imperialism and white brigandage. . . . Both envision the abolition of the hegemony of the conscious and the everyday." Césaire, in turn, termed surrealism "a process of disalienation," able to awaken the tortured Baudelairean albatross of the colonized self, sick from "fear, inferiority complexes, trepidation, servility, despair, abasement," yet capable of poetic sublimity. Fanon quoted Césaire's words at the start of *Black Skin, White Masks* (1952), his first book, and described his own project too as "disalienation."[39] Surrealism, though, was similar to the blues in that it provided access to unconscious or primary process thinking, but had no means of turning primary process material into speech acts, social theory, and political action, in other words into memory in the sense of a subjective, structured, collective account of the past.

Sartre's thought, though not explicitly concerned with memory, provided Fanon with a model of agonistic struggle. Most important was Sartre's 1946 essay *Anti-Semite and Jew,* a response not just to French anti-Semitism but also to Nazism and to the camps. In Sartre's searing account of the intersubjective character of anti-Semitism, which Fanon applied to racism, "We experience our inapprehensible being-for-others in the form of a *possession.* I am possessed by the Other; the Other's look fashions my body in its nakedness, causes it to be born, sculptures it, produces it as it *is,* sees it as I shall never see it."[40] Freud's work suggested that the origins of this experience of being taken possession of by the other lay in infancy, but also in the lingering effects of traumatic experiences of prehistory. Fanon grasped this point, but substituted the *history* of slavery and colonialism for Freud's prehistory. For Fanon, as for Freud, then, both individual and collective memory included earlier strata, byways, tunnels, and burrows that had not disappeared in the course of time, even though new structures had been built so that the earlier ones were no longer available to consciousness. Both Fanon and Freud saw themselves as historically minded archaeologists unearthing the remains of these early strata, which were the remains not so much of primitive civilizations as of primitive catastrophes—catastrophes that remained "at one and the same moment actively vital and . . . incapable of resolution."[41] For Fanon, though, these catastrophes were the French invasion, capture, and brutal sexual and economic violation of the Caribbean islands. Unearthing these early catastrophes, Fanon believed, was the key to transforming what Wright had called negative confusions, flights, and frenzy into the ordered authority of a mastered past. Because Freudianism provided a sense of how this could be achieved, Fanon insisted, in *Black Skin, White Masks,* that "only a psychoanalytical interpretation of the black problem can lay bare the anomalies of affect that are responsible for the structure of the [racial] complex."

The changing character of psychoanalysis during the thirties and forties also facilitated Fanon's reconstruction of racial memory. The experience of the war, and the shocking discovery of the concentration camps along with that of new nations discovering their own origins in the midst of imperial holocausts and the capture of slaves, seemed to have more in common with a primal murder than with the social contract promoted by postwar modernization theorists. Writing in the wake of World War II, Fanon registered the traumatic impact of the Holocaust when he described the colonial world as "one vast concentration camp."[42] Equally poignant was the Freudian-inflected resonance between the patriarchal slave owner and the modern dictator. Psychoanalysis had much to say about the ways in which individual minds can be subjugated, reduced to villeinage and servility, not just through economic deprivation or foreign conquest, but also from within, as had occurred in Nazi Germany and the Soviet Union, as well as among colonials and, as some claimed, in middle-class white America itself. Finally, a subgroup among psychiatrists were identifying with inmates, patients, and other subordinated groups, anticipating the antipsychiatry movements of the sixties associated with such figures as R. D. Laing and David Cooper. Fanon was one of these. After qualifying as a psychiatrist in 1951, he worked at Saint-Alban Hospital in Southern France, a famed center of the resistance, under the Catalan psychiatrist François Tosquelles, a leading advocate of "socio-analysis," which enlisted patients and staff in a struggle against institutional psychiatry, again highlighting the role that power struggles played in the excavation of the unconscious.

The transformation of psychoanalysis into a theory of the mother/infant relationship during the 1930s also contributed to the project of memory by encouraging the rethinking of the relevance of Freudianism to non-Western settings where many believed the Oedipus complex was absent. In its place the preoedipal mother appeared, often represented by the natal group. Marie Cécile and Edmund Ortigues's *Oedipe Africain,* published in 1962 but reflecting several decades of work, held that in Senegal "guilt does not appear as such . . . but rather under the form of an anxiety at being abandoned by the group, of a loss of object."[43] The Ortigues's work suggested that the relationship to the mother underlay such anticolonial preoccupations as origins, roots, and beginnings, as suggested by the term *motherland.* Such themes fused in Fanon's inspired 1952 leap, *Black Skin, White Masks,* which relied on *La névrose d'abandon,* the 1950 work of a Swiss psychoanalyst, Germaine Guex, to illuminate the catastrophic effects of the earliest traumata, the racialization of one's earliest attachments, the drive for a homeland or identity, and the role of the natal group in "healing" the deformations wrought by colonialism. The heart of the abandonment syndrome described by Guex was the feeling that one had never been truly wanted as a child. According to Fanon, the resulting sense of disappointment, betrayal, and devaluation of self perfectly described the colonial for whom France was a beloved mother who had shown no interest in her accursed progeny.

Fanon's sense of the colonial power as a negligent and often cruel mother lies behind the pathos of his entire contribution to African American and Afro-Caribbean memory. Echoing Horace Cayton, who described racism as lacing his "mother's milk," Fanon described the Black colonial's longing to be white, or to possess whiteness, as "lactification," a wish to be finally, adequately nursed by the warm white liquid. Later, in *The Wretched of the Earth* (1961), he likened the French colonial power that tells the Algerians that they will never be able to govern themselves to an intrusive, malevolent mother who pretends to help by "protecting" her perverse offspring from giving free rein to its instincts. "The colonial mother," Fanon wrote ironically, "is protecting the child from itself, from its ego, its physiology, its biology, and its ontological misfortune." The result is the double bind reported by a patient: "All it took for me was to come of age and go and serve my adopted motherland in the country of my ancestors to make me wonder whether I hadn't been betrayed by everything around me, white folk refusing to accept me as one of their own and black folk virtually repudiating me." In Fanon's summary, "Others have betrayed and thwarted him and yet it is only from these others that he expects any improvement in his lot."

Fanon's evocation of the mother in explaining the colonial experience of abandonment and neglect drew on the preoedipal moment in Freudianism, but Fanon also drew on Freud's oedipalization of Hegel's portrait of the master/slave relationship to evoke the threat of "castration" omnipresent in the colonial order. The theme of castration was not only important because it pervades sexuality but also because it shows how colonialism entailed an *internal* submission to the looming, threatening French father. Yet just as the oedipal rests on the preoedipal, so the colonial subject's fear of castration rested on the prior experience of being abandoned and unloved. The white child's awful "'Dirty nigger!' or simply, 'Look a Negro,'" seals the Black man into a "crushing object-hood" in part because it reverberated with an earlier wound.[44] Speaking autobiographically of the Antillean who goes to France for study, Fanon evoked the weight of an unmastered past: "I had to meet the white man's eyes. An unfamiliar weight burdened me. In the white world the man of color encounters difficulties in the development of his bodily schema. . . . I was battered down by tom-toms, cannibalism, intellectual deficiency, fetishism, racial defects. . . . I took myself far off from my own presence. . . . What else could it be for me but an amputation, an excision, a hemorrhage that spattered my whole body with black blood? . . . I am over-determined from without . . . I am fixed."[45]

Fanon's recollection echoes Toomer's account of the racial unconscious, Sartre's account of the gaze, but also Freud's account of primal catastrophe. For Fanon, however, Freud's account also evoked the importance of race to sex, which is fundamental to the postcolonial Freud. As in Freud's description of the girl's discovery of sexual difference, so with Fanon's description of the colonial's discovery of race, a sudden shocking—often but not always visual—experience creates a new life-world pervaded by a hierarchical dichotomy: black/white as well as man/woman.[46] In Freud the discovery of sexual difference follows different paths in boys and in girls; so, with Fanon, race has different meanings for whites and for Blacks. The *white* discovery of race is analogous to the *boy's* discovery of sexual difference: race is not a sudden discovery but is rather an insidious process that disturbs and distorts the white person's humanity. By contrast, the Black's discovery of race is a shock—"Look a Negro"—analogous to the girl's discovery of sexual difference, resulting in permanent (i.e., ontological) anxiety. The horrors of the colonial order translate into psychic devastation. In Albert Memmi's summary of Fanon's thought, "the war waged by the White against the Black also brings about a war of the Black against himself, a war that is perhaps even more destructive, for it is waged unremittingly from within."[47] The results of this insight are some of the most moving passages in Fanon, passages that resonate with the sea change in African American memory that occurred in the 1930s and 1940s. For example: "Shame. Shame and self-contempt. Nausea. When people like me, they tell me it is in spite of my color. When they dislike me, they point out that it is not because of my color. Either way, I am locked into the infernal circle."[48]

By drawing on Freudianism then, Fanon, like Wright, placed both race and sexuality at the center of the colonial past. For Fanon, there was no sexual relationship in the colonial world that was not disfigured by race. On the one hand, the Black male's thwarted struggle for masculinity and self-respect led him to demand that black women deliver a "love that will strengthen [the black man] by endorsing [his] assumption of manhood." As Françoise Vergès has written, Black women sometimes served as "a degraded mirror for the Black man" in Fanon's work. "The recovery of . . . wounded masculinity is done at the expense of women's own desires."[49] Analogously, the black man who desires the white woman thinks: "I marry white culture, white beauty, white whiteness." "When my restless hands caress those white breasts, they grasp white civilization and dignity and make them mine." Since Fanon saw colonial memory as pervaded by racialized sexuality, his blind spot toward sexism is striking, especially since Simone de Beauvoir's *The Second Sex* had been published in 1949, three years before *Black Skin, White Masks,* and based on the same Sartrean model of asymmetric domination. It would not be until the publication of Juliet Mitchell's *Psychoanalysis and Feminism* in 1974 that the Freudian model Fanon wielded so deftly against racial oppression would be applied to sexual domination.[50]

Fanon's understanding of the pervasiveness of shame and guilt in the master/slave relationship went so far beyond Wright's that we are perhaps justified in describing it as a new—third—stage in the construction of memory. Most important, the third Freud broadened the scope of African American memory from slavery to colonialism, from the United States to the Americas as a whole, and from "the West" to Asia and Africa, transforming historical thought by placing the struggles against slavery and colonialism at the center of modern radicalism, not displacing but rather explaining the labor struggles that consumed the Popular Front. Still, this third stage does not conform to Hegel's optimistic dialectic. For Fanon, there is no transcendence or reconciliation, as there was for Hegel. For one thing, the racial complex has inflicted each individual with "narcissistic scars," claims and reproaches that interfere with the possibilities of love. According to Fanon, "authentic love"—i.e., object love in the psychoanalytic sense, the achievement of the oedipal stage—"will remain unattainable [until] one has purged oneself of that feeling of inferiority." For example, a Black woman laments, "I should have liked to be married, but to a white man. But a woman of color is never altogether respectable in a white man's eyes. Even when he loves her." Fanon also speaks of "the fear, the timorousness, the humility of the black man in his relations with the white woman, or in any case with a woman whiter than he."

The inability of colonial subjects to experience genuine object love reflects the intense weight of an unmastered past. Speaking of a Black character in a novel by René Maran, Fanon wrote, "Jean Veneuse would like to be a man like the rest, but he knows that this position is a false one. He is a beggar. He looks for appeasement, for permission in the white man's eyes. For to him there is"—Fanon here both echoes and deepens Du Bois—"'the Other.'"[51] "The Negro wants to be like the master," Fanon continued. "Therefore he is less independent than the Hegelian slave. In Hegel the slave turns away from the master and turns toward the object [i.e., toward labor and ultimately toward revolution]. Here the slave turns toward the master and abandons the object." "In the man of color there is a constant effort to run away from his own individuality, to annihilate his own presence," Fanon added, in obvious pain. Writing of the power of the past to intrude upon the present, Fanon recalled, "out of the blackest part of my soul across the zebra striping of my mind, surges this desire to be suddenly white."[52] As James Baldwin, who know both Fanon and Wright in Paris, wrote, "Perhaps . . . we have no idea what history is, or are in flight from the demon we have summoned. Perhaps history is not to be found in our mirrors, but in our repudiations; perhaps the other is ourselves."[53]

Unmasterable though the past is, Fanon's generation was successful in weaving existentialism, cosmopolitanism, and the postcolonial perspective into a deepening account of African American memory. In 1953, the year after finishing *Black Skin, White Masks*, Fanon wrote to Wright that he was "working on a study bearing on the human breadth (*portée*) of your works."[54] Although the work was never completed, the two men were in dialogue throughout the fifties. In 1942 Wright had propounded a generalized symbol for African American identity, "the Outsider," based on the experiences of guilt, stigmatization, and exclusion ubiquitous to the construction of nations and races. The outsider was a figure for *homo sacer,* the banned but unmourned victim in ancient Rome. Jews in Germany, like runaway slaves or victims of lynching in the United States, were regularly hunted down and slaughtered—slaughtered but not sacrificed, because they had not attained the free status that characterized the human. Yet in the modern world there was also a possibility of transcendence since the Outsider lives "in one life, many lifetimes," and, though "born in the Western world, is not quite of it."[55]

Wright's "The Man Who Lived Underground," the story of a Black man falsely accused of murder, living in an underground sewer, observing reality from "below," is a brilliant example of the Outsider. The Outsider is persecuted and excluded, but this works in part because of the effects of a primal catastrophe. Thus, although the police have framed Wright's hero, he accuses himself, "always trying to remember a gigantic shock that had left a haunting impression upon one's body which one could not forget or shake off, but which had been forgotten by the conscious mind." Even so, the struggle for memory gives the Outsider what Du Bois called the second sight of the seventh son.

"Negroes, as they enter our culture," Wright's character explains, "are going to inherit the problems we have, but with a difference. They are outsiders and they are going to *know* that they have these problems. They are going to be self-conscious; they are going to be gifted with a double vision, for, being Negroes, they are going to be both *inside* and *outside* of our culture at the same time. . . . They will become psychological men, like the Jews."[56]

Wright's conception of a double vision builds on Du Bois's awareness of being a minority in a white-dominated land, but the image has become both more global and more psychological. Not just otherness but internal conflict, repression, and absence have become the problem that lies behind memory. This can be seen in Wright's 1955 description of the elites of Asia and Africa at the Bandung Conference of Non-Aligned States as

> men without language. . . . It is psychological language that I speak of. For these men there is a "hole" in history, a storm in their hearts that they cannot describe, a stretch of centuries whose content has been interpreted only by white Westerners: the seizure of his country, its subjugation, the introduction of military rule, another language, another religion—all of these events existed without his interpretation of them. . . . The elite has no vocabulary of history. What has happened to him is something about which he has yet to speak.

How, Wright asked, did previously traumatized peoples learn to speak? Calvin and Luther—"two bold European insurgents"—found their voices, Wright wrote, by "a stupendous introjection of the religious symbol by which the men of their time lived." Wright's hope was that an "irrational Western world . . . unconsciously and unintentionally to be sure" had precipitated a similar introjection in Asia and Africa.[57]

Both Wright and Fanon agreed that *Négritude* was only a stopgap measure in the recovery of African American memory. Speaking in Paris at the First Congress of Black Writers and Artists in 1956, with those in the audience including Aimé Césaire, Léopold Senghor, James Baldwin, Jean-Paul Sartre, Claude Lévi-Strauss, and Fanon, Wright confessed, "I have the feeling, uneasy, almost bordering upon dread, that there was a fateful historic complement between a militant, white Christian Europe and an ancestral cult religion in Africa." Whereas Sartre had complained that the new black elites had to communicate through the language of the colonialists, Wright welcomed the fact that the condemnations of the West he heard at Bandung "were uttered in the languages of the cultures that the delegates were denouncing! . . . By this means English was coming to contain a new extension of feeling, of moral knowledge."[58]

In Fanon's work the painful search for a homeland gives a lyrical quality to the writing, breaking it into a series of short, anguished cries. Wright, by contrast, refused to use the term *African American,* embracing instead the diaspora identity that goes back to Hurston's *Moses, Man of the Mountain* and that Paul Gilroy later linked to the Black Atlantic.[59] In a 1954 work Wright described *Pagan Spain* as a border region, somewhat akin to Afro-America, neither wholly of the West and yet not non-Western either. Influenced by Américo Castro's *The Structure of Spanish History,* which stressed the hybrid, "impure," multicultural—pagan, Catholic, Jewish, Muslim, African, Moorish, *converso, morisco, marrano*—strands of Spanish memory, Wright invented the term *white Negroes* (later associated with Norman Mailer) to describe the Spaniards.[60] Nor was Wright unaware that Spain had been the center of the slave trade. In *Pagan Spain* he likened the ritualized violence of the bullfight to a lynching: "That starting Black hair, that madly slashing tail, that bunched and flexed mountain of neck and shoulder muscles, that almost hog-like distension of the wet and inflated and dripping nostrils, that defiant and careless lack of control of the anal passage, that continuous throbbing of the thin, trembling flanks, that open-mouthed panting that was so rapid that it resembled a prolonged shivering."[61]

Wright contacted dysentery in Africa in 1957 and died in 1960 at the age of fifty-two. Fanon died of leukemia in a CIA hospital in 1961 at the age of thirty-six. Du Bois died in Africa at the age of ninety-five, one day before the 1963 March on Washington. As these three great pioneers perished, the activist movements of the 1960s were born.

One expression of the new mood was the attempt to historicize the blues, a watershed moment in the achievement of African American memory. In 1960 Paul Oliver, a British architect who had never visited the United States, published the first history of the blues, *Blues Fell This Morning*. As Wright lay dying, he wrote a forward to the book in which he praised the idea that an outsider should have written the history of the blues, but challenged the "passivity, almost masochistic in quality, and seemingly allied to sex in origin, that appears as part of the meaning of the blues. Could this emotional stance," he asked, "have been derived from a protracted inability to act, of a fear of acting?"[62] Fanon, too, saw the need to move beyond the blues. In *The Wretched of the Earth* he argued that during the anticolonial liberation struggle the colonialists "become the defenders of the native style." As an example, he rejected what he called the "despairing, broken down nostalgia of an old Negro," trapped between whiskey and racial hatred in favor of the new intellectual jazz of bebop infused, as it was, with contempt for mainstream "square" culture.[63] In 1963 Amira Baraka (then LeRoi Jones) published *Blues People*, still the best account of the place of the blues in African American memory. The next year, in *The Dutchman*, Baraka's buttoned-down, uptight "Negro" finally explodes, claiming that "Ofays" say "I love Bessie Smith and don't even understand that Bessie Smith is saying, 'Kiss my ass, kiss my black, unruly ass.'" We can take Baraka's dialogue as an interpretation of the surreal and unconscious content always latent in the blues.

Because the whole project of recovering African American memory was in so many ways launched by Du Bois, it is striking that in 1954, when his 1896 doctoral dissertation, *The Suppression of the African Slave Trade* was reprinted, Du Bois wrote an "Apologia": "The work of Freud and his companions and their epoch making contribution to science was not generally known when I was writing this book, and consequently I did not realize the psychological reasons behind the trends of human action which the African slave trade involved. Trained in the New England ethic of life as a series of conscious moral judgments, I was continually thrown back on what men 'ought' to have done."[64] In repudiating freestanding, abstract moral condemnation and exploring the "psychological reasons" behind the slave trade, Du Bois was insisting on that the concrete history of slavery needed to be infused with the Freudian sensitivity to the unconscious. In other words, he was advocating political Freudianism. In any event, no apologia was needed.

In his great "I have a dream" speech at the 1963 March on Washington, Martin Luther King turned from memory to history, thanking the conveners in his first sentence and then turning to the Emancipation Proclamation, promulgated "Five score years ago." The sixties witnessed a dramatic revolution in the writing of American history, from a white Southerner-centered account that viewed the Civil War as a "tragic era" to the slavery- and abolition-centered account that prevails today.[65] History records few historiographical revolutions more complete and more morally significant than that accomplished in the 1960s and 1970s, through the introduction of African American history into American historiography. But the record also shows that alongside the objective history wrested from the records by innumerable working historians stood the monumental subjective struggle to rescue African American memory initiated by blues singers and pushed forward not only by writers and artists but by political Freudians like Wright and Fanon. That this project never ended is suggested by Toni Morrison's description of her project in *Beloved* as excavating "something that the characters don't want to remember, I don't want to remember, black people don't want to remember, white people won't want to remember."[66]

Finally, just as African Americans uncovered deep intersubjective and structural forms of domination, byways of resistance, and countless twists and turns in their struggle for memory, so the blues evolved into new and complex musical structures. In a way that parallels the struggle for memory, African American musicians explored dissonance, diminished thirds, fifths, and sevenths, minor scales, tragic modes, semiquavers, deceptive cadences, caesuras, dominants, negras, contras, dirges, minstrelsy, rags, flats, taps, scats, and silences. The blues gave rise to jazz, gospel, bebop, soul, rap, rock and roll, as well as "rhythm and blues," as "race records" for the "Negro market" were renamed under the impact of the Popular Front. Later, the explosive entry of rhythm and blues into mainstream American popular music created a new intimacy between the performer and the audience, unleashing the sexuality of the preteen, largely female, audience. Ultimately, the blues became the "most important single influence on the development of Western popular music," giving it that quality of "soul" that Du Bois first identified, but also absorbing much of its radical content.[67] As this chapter shows, the struggle for memory is never unilinear or straightforwardly progressive. As soul triumphed, the United States took its turn toward the war in Vietnam and toward a whole new level of inequality based not only on race but also on class. Hence the need to engage the dark, dissonant side of modernity has no final movement.

# 3

## In the Shadow of the Holocaust

### *Rereading Freud's Moses*

Texts that are inertly of their time stay there: those which brush
up unstintingly against historical constraints are the ones we
keep with us, generation after generation.

—EDWARD SAID

Of the enduring books of the twentieth century, *Moses and Monotheism* remains one of the most difficult to interpret. Written while
Freud was old, sick, and in the shadow of the Nazi terror, based on
scant historical research, the book describes Moses as an Egyptian and
the Jews as the bearers of an "archaic heritage" that includes their collective but unconscious memory of murdering Moses. But while the
book has spawned endless controversy, nearly all commentators agree
that its subject is Jewish identity. Writing in the wake of the Holocaust,
the earliest interpreters, such as Gershom Scholem, Leo Strauss, and
Paul Ricouer criticized the book for denying the Jewish people their
national ideals. After a long hiatus, interest in the book revived when
Jacques Derrida and Yosef Hayim Yerushalmi described it as "a psychological document of Freud's inner life," focused on Freud's own Judaism. Most recently Edward Said, representing a third, "postcolonial"

generation, praised Freud's conviction that Moses was an Egyptian for demonstrating that no identity can "constitute or even imagine itself without [a] radical originary break or flaw which will not be repressed."

Freud himself reinforced the view that the book essentially concerns Jewish identity. He wrote that the subject of the book was "what has really created the particular character of the Jew?" and how has the Jew "in view of the renewed persecutions . . . drawn upon himself this undying hatred?"[1] But at a deeper and perhaps largely unconscious level the driving force behind the book was Freud's worry concerning the survival of psychoanalysis. Writing the book while dying, and in the course of being driven into exile, Freud was well aware that psychoanalysis could be stamped out just as quickly and surprisingly as monotheism had been stamped out in ancient Egypt. For Freud the survival of the values he associated with the discovery of the unconscious was far more important than the survival of the Jewish religion, which he considered of little value, and even of Jewish ethnicity, to which he was deeply attached, although differently from the way he was attached to psychoanalysis. Of course, it must be said that Freud, like everyone else, had no idea that he was facing the attempted destruction of the Jewish people, a fact we know now that has profoundly shaped our perceptions.

Furthermore, Freud didn't consider the question of the survival of psychoanalysis alone but posed the question of the survival of spiritual or intellectual advances in general. For that reason, the book should be read as a meditation on the overall crisis of the Western world in the light of the rise of Nazism, comparable to contemporaneous works, also largely written in exile, such as Erich Auerbach's *Mimesis,* Erwin Panofsky's work on perspective, and Hans Baron's *Crisis of the Italian Renaissance.* Nazism demonstrated, as perhaps no other current of the twentieth century did, why something like Freud's hypothesis of the unconscious was necessary. That so horrific and primitive an example of sustained hate and destructiveness could arise in the country of Bach and Goethe showed how deluded our sense of ourselves as progressive and enlightened could be. Freud's idea of the unconscious, implicitly defended in *Moses and Monotheism,* is analogous to Auerbach's idea of

realism, Panofsky's idea of perspective, or Baron's idea of civic humanism: a tentative and fragile advance in our understanding of subjectivity. In posing the question of the survival of psychoanalysis, Freud
joined a group of scholars and thinkers concerned with the question of
the survival of core human values overall.

Nor did Freud restrict himself to the thought that the discovery
of the unconscious could be wiped out by brutality and violence—it
already had been in Germany and Austria while he was writing the
book! In addition, Freud feared disintegration from within, as had
occurred in ancient tribal societies such as the Hebrews, among whom
an unparalleled spiritual breakthrough degenerated into empty ritual
and legalism, and in Christianity, where monotheism disintegrated
into a cult of martyrs and saints. Analogously, Freud feared that in the
United States, where analysis had sparked a pullulating therapeutic
industry and become integral to advertising, film, and mass culture, the
"gold" of psychoanalysis was being lost in the "dross" of adaptations.
For Freud, Judaic monotheism had an *affinity* with psychoanalysis, not
in the sense that Freud incorporated "Jewish ideas" into analysis, but in
the sense that both were difficult and even ascetic practices subject to
vulgarization and distortion as they took a popular form.

What monotheism and psychoanalysis had in common Freud
called *Geistigkeit*. Often translated as intellectuality or spirituality,
the best English equivalent for *Geistigkeit* may be inwardness or subjectivity. Freud believed that the invention of monotheism had been a
world-historical event, not because it created the Hebrew people, but
rather because of the prohibition on graven images, which forced the
Hebrews into envisioning a God they could not see or feel or touch.
For Freud, *Geistigkeit* was a difficult human achievement, which went
against the instinctive drive for sensory satisfaction as well as against
the mind's unconscious propensity to relive libidinal satisfactions from
infancy. *Geistigkeit* was related to the ancient Hebrew idea of holiness
(*kedushah*), but it was also related to the German idealist philosophical
tradition that had taken shape as a critical response to Anglo-American
empiricism and that informed Freud's education and scientific milieu.

In both meanings—spiritual and philosophical—*Geistigkeit* was integral to the idea of the unconscious. Just as the Hebrews could not represent God, and just as Kant could not empirically demonstrate the transcendental subject he hypothesized, so Freud could only infer, not demonstrate, the existence of unconscious mental processes,[2]

The sense in which *Moses and Monotheism* is centered on the survival of the idea of the unconscious will be apparent when we summarize the book's argument. One man, Freud tells us, created Judaism: Moses. He did so by choosing a circle of followers and initiating them into a difficult practice based on instinctual renunciation rather than sensory gratification. His followers, after some enthusiasm, rejected his practice as too demanding, effectively returning to the idol worship from which Moses had rescued them. Eventually his followers killed Moses, and a debased Judaism triumphed. Nonetheless, the repressed memory of Moses' ascetic doctrine survived and was rediscovered centuries later by the prophets.

Now let us make the obvious substitutions. One man created psychoanalysis: Sigmund Freud. He did so by choosing a circle of followers and initiating them into a difficult practice based on instinctual renunciation rather than sensory gratification. His followers, after some enthusiasm, rejected his practice as too demanding, returning to the idol worship from which Freud had rescued them. Eventually his followers killed Freud and a debased psychoanalysis triumphed. Nonetheless, the repressed memory of Freud's ascetic doctrine survived, and its secrets too would be rediscovered centuries later.

*Moses and Monotheism*, then, should be read in two different but complementary ways. If, at one level, Freud was using psychoanalysis to illuminate the history of Judaism, at another he was using the history of Judaism to illuminate the history of psychoanalysis. Let us start with the latter. Freud's conception of Jewish history has an underlying narrative structure that consists in five parts. In the first the Jews are presented with the monotheistic idea of God, which affords freedom from subordination to the senses and in that way deepens the inner world of the Hebrews; in the second they experience a sense of chosenness, of possessing a special treasure that raises them above those who are still immured in sensory and empirical knowledge; in the third they struggle with guilt at not being able to live up to the new ethical ideals associated with having a conscience and being a chosen people; in the fourth they are tempted to abandon their difficult standards and revert to the sensuous polytheism of the Egyptians as well as to the mother gods of the ancient Near East; and in the fifth they rediscover the original monotheistic message. In what follows I will identify five analogous stages in the history of psychoanalysis, stages that also reflect the extent to which psychoanalysis was the product of Jewish history. In a conclusion I return to situate *Moses and Monotheism* in the context of the Second World War and ask what light it sheds on the place that Judaism and anti-Semitism occupied in that war.

## Stage One: The Hebrew God, the Unconscious, and the Father Complex

In all religions, Freud believed, as in all delusions, there was invariably a bit of historical truth. The historical truth behind Judaism, he speculated, was the destruction of the monotheistic cult at the court of Ikhnaton. When Moses, an Egyptian prince or high court official fearing persecution, fled the court and came to the Jews with the message of a single God, the message had terrific force because it was a repetition. It reminded the Jews of the archaic age during which they had been under the spell of the primal father. In *Totem and Taboo* (1912) Freud described the murder of the primal father as a single event, but in *Moses and Monotheism* (1939) he essentially apologized for this, writing "the story is told in a very condensed way, as if what in reality took centuries to achieve, and during that long time was repeated innumerably, had only happened once." Because Moses was himself a great patriarchal figure, he reminded the Hebrews of the primal father, and they found his presence dangerous and unsettling. The Jewish murder of Moses, then, *repeated* the primal slaying of the father, thereby intensifying a preexisting sense of guilt.

The monotheistic message was also a repetition in a second sense, this time of the cultural advance that occurred in the murder's wake. Egypt's earlier religions were polytheistic and oriented toward nature gods. They abounded in pictorial and symbolic representations of spiritual entities and promised life after death. In the monotheism developed at the court of Ikhnaton, by contrast, "all myth, magic and sorcery" were excluded. Instead of the pyramid and the falcon of the earlier Egyptian religion, the sun god was symbolized by "a round disc from which emanate rays terminating in human hands," a symbol Freud called "almost rational." Strikingly, the new religion had no mention of life after death. Of special importance, for Freud, was the *Bilderverbot*, the prohibition on graven images of the deity. The injunction against visualizing or otherwise representing God, he believed, forced a leap from the material and sensual world to the conceptual or intelligible. In Freud's words, "ideas, memories, and inferences became decisive in contrast to the lower psychical activity which had direct perceptions by the sense-organs as its content." This shift from sensory knowledge to conceptual thought, in Freud's view, was an instinctual renunciation, by which Freud meant sublimation, not repression. As such it brought about a rise in self-esteem.

Freud's account of the birth of monotheism parallels the birth of psychoanalysis. Sigmund Freud's father Jacob Freud came from a Hasidic community in Galicia, and at an early age Freud was made familiar with the family Bible. As Freud later wrote, "My deep engrossment in the Bible story (almost as soon as I had learnt the art of reading) had, as I recognized much later, an enduring effect upon the direction of my interest." A patriarchal God and a foundational crime against that God were central to the book of Genesis. In the 1890s, when Freud was developing psychoanalysis, he grappled continually with the question of paternal authority. Although Freud interpreted a dream of his own for the first time in July 1895 and wrote out a draft of *The Interpretation of Dreams*, he could not complete the book for three more years.[3] He explained the delay as the result of his "self-analysis," the introspection and mourning precipitated by his father's death. The death uprooted him, awakening his past and prompting him to surmise that the death of the father was invariably the most significant event in men's lives. The process of completing *The Interpretation of Dreams* and of coming to grips with his father's death went on together. The parts of the book Freud had difficulty finishing were his debts to his predecessors and the formulation of his most original idea, the primary process or unconscious.

For Freud, the formulation of the idea of the unconscious was not the result of an empirical discovery but of a conceptual breakthrough. Blocked from access to consciousness by what Freud was at that point calling the censor, neither the form nor the content of the unconscious could be directly represented. Rather, Freud would free associate to each of his dream fragments, then interpret his associations, and only after interpretation would he *infer* the contents of his unconscious. The proper starting point for analytic introspection, therefore, was the recognition that one *could not know directly* but rather had to infer the contents of one's mind. In this regard Freud echoed Kant, "Just as Kant warned us not to overlook the fact that our perception . . . must not be regarded as identical with the phenomena perceived but never really discerned, so psychoanalysis bids us not to set conscious perception [that is, our conscious thoughts] in the place of the unconscious mental process which is [their] object."[4]

To be sure, the Hebrew sense of the sacred and unapproachable—all that is connoted by the Hebrew term *kedushah*—and the Greek discovery of philosophy, mathematics, and of a conceptually grounded science, are very different.[5] But they have in common a turn toward the inner life, whether seen as spiritual, intellectual, or both, and the Greek and Hebrew strands were mingled in the Hellenistic, Roman, and early Christian eras, becoming part of a common thread of Western civilization. Freud's education had been "neo-Kantian," meaning that the innate or a priori categories of the mind posited by Kant were being redefined as evolutionary products. In a deep sense, however, Freud inflected the Kantian and neo-Kantian thought in which he had been trained with the ancient Hebrew connotations of *kedushah*. The unconscious, as Freud envisioned it, is not merely unknowable as the metaphysical world is, meaning not directly accessible to the senses; it is unknowable because that is where the dead parents, the memories of childhood, including the unconscious memory of the primal murder, lie not wholly buried.[6] Thus, although Freud described the theory of the unconscious as "an extension of the corrections begun by Kant," Freud's core conception around 1900 was that of repression, a concept unknown to Kant and the ultimate source of the dream images that kept the memories of childhood buried. When Freud insisted in *The Interpretation of Dreams* that the *Ur*-image—the dream—be turned into words, he promulgated a new *Bilderverbot*. Freud's insistence— the so-called single rule in psychoanalysis, namely to free associate— bespeaks his identification with Moses. Moses emancipated the Jews from the graven images of Egypt; Freud may have seen himself as emancipating humanity from dream images, opening up not the unconscious but the *repressed* unconscious, the incestuous and murderous wishes of infancy.

Like Moses, Freud needed to share his discovery, a need that initiates stage 2 in our history. As he formulated the idea of the unconscious, he drew closer to the Jewish community, effectively "choosing" his followers from among them. After returning from Paris in 1885, he had begun working as a private doctor for nervous diseases, primarily with Jewish and immigrant patients. Defiantly opening his first office on Easter Sunday, he presented himself as a convert to the "French" school, often a code word in Vienna for Jewish. He delivered a paper, "On Male Hysteria," supposedly a Jewish disease, before the Viennese Society of Physicians. As anticapitalist and anti-Semitic feeling mounted in late nineteenth-century Vienna, only the emperor prevented the seating of the populist and anti-Semitic Karl Lueger as mayor, and that only until 1897.[7] Freud responded to Lueger's ascent, as well as to the Dreyfus affair, by joining B'nai B'rith. In so doing he stepped down the social ladder from the medical and academic intelligentsia to a stratum of ordinary Jewish doctors and businessmen who, "if they could not assist or further his scientific pursuits, did not threaten or discourage him."[8]

It was from this relatively meager stratum of self-employed Jewish doctors that Freud "chose" his earliest followers.

Among these followers, Freud became a father figure himself, someone—as he wrote of Moses—"in whom one of the human impulsions has found its strongest and purest, and therefore often its most one-sided, expression," although the impulsion for which he stood was subjectivity and rational thought rather than monotheism. Like Moses, Freud eventually became a great cultural superego, a whole "climate of opinion," as Auden wrote in a wonderful poem.[9] Like the Moses of Freud's imagination, many of Freud's followers sought to slay him, at least figuratively. But, unlike Moses, Freud sought to thwart his detractors by telling his own story—in *Moses and Monotheism*. Thus the first stage in the history of psychoanalysis, the founding, was embedded with Judaic meanings, and so later Freud was able to tell the history of the Jews in way that illuminated the first stage in the history of analysis.

## Stage Two: Narcissism and the Chosen People

When the British Zionist analyst David Eder died in 1936, Freud recalled their meeting decades earlier: "We were both Jews and knew of each other that we carried in us that miraculous thing in common which, inaccessible to any analysis so far, makes the Jew." Through writing *Moses and Monotheism*, Freud believed he had discovered the origins of the "miraculous thing" that Jews have in common. It was their "secret treasure," their intellectuality, which gave them their self-confidence and sense of superiority in regard to pagan cultures that had remained "under the spell of sensuality."[10] Characteristically, Freud traced this "miraculous" feeling to the Hebrew people's childlike relation to Moses. He wrote,

> The conception of a god suddenly "choosing" a people, making it "his" people and himself its own god is astonishing. . . . I believe it is the only case in the history of human religions. In other

cases the people and their god belong inseparably together; they are one from the beginning. Sometimes, it is true, we hear of a people adopting another god, but never of a god choosing a new people. Perhaps we approach an understanding of this unique happening when we reflect on the connection between Moses and the Jewish people. Moses had stooped to the Jews, had made them his people; they were his "chosen people."

Being chosen was not without difficulties. When Moses presented the idea of one god to the Hebrew people, they seized upon it because it was a revival of the earlier submission to the primal father. But they also seized upon monotheism because it reproduced the gain made when, after the murder of the father, the brothers renounced their aggression and founded law, ethics, and religion. Like those who accomplished the first advances of civilization, the early Hebrews achieved the "triumph of spirituality (*Geistigkeit*) over the senses; more precisely an instinctual renunciation."[11] The same triumph, however, brought the Hebrews closer to the memory of the "prehistoric tragedy," the murder of the primal father or fathers. Thus, while the Jews after Moses felt "superior to those who have remained in the bondage of the senses," they also felt burdened by a guilt that "clamored for recognition." Ambivalence, then, was inseparable from chosenness.

Once again, an episode in the history of psychoanalysis provided an uncanny repetition of an episode in Jewish history. The original Hebrews had chafed when they discovered that chosenness did not simply bestow a sense of superiority, but rather brought with it a gnawing sense of not living up to one's responsibilities. So, too, beginning around 1906, Freud was caught in the crossfire between two figures who sought a more affirmative psychology than Freud had provided. On the one hand, Carl Jung supported the idea of a psychoanalysis rooted in man's "higher"—i.e., religious—self. On the other hand, Alfred Adler challenged Freud on behalf of the secular ideals of equal status and self-esteem. In retrospect one can see that Jung and Adler represented the two great movements that challenged psychoanalysis throughout its history: Christianity and socialism. These were also movements of enormous consequence for the Jews of Freud's time.

For Freud what was at stake both in ancient Judaism and in the conflicts that swirled around psychoanalysis was the subjectivity or inwardness of *Geistigkeit,* through which the mind rose above the clash of instincts and encompassed its own ambivalence. In his conflicts with Adler and Jung, Freud advanced this value by arguing that narcissism or chosenness was a bivalent or Janus-faced phenomenon that could not be approached in a one-sidedly affirmative way. In *Moses and Monotheism* he described the Christian and socialist faiths as shortcuts seeking to resolve ambivalence by bypassing guilt. For Christians, he wrote, the sacrifice of a son—"It had to be a Son, for the sin had been murder of the Father"—expiated the original murder. Paul, whom Freud called a Jew "with a gift for religion. . . . Dark traces of the past lay in his soul, ready to break through into the regions of consciousness," had intuited the truth of the primal murder, but only in the delusional form of "glad tidings." By contrast, the Jewish refusal of the "good news" of Christ's sacrifice was taken to contain an underlying message: "*We* did not kill the father, *you* did." Hence the Jews' rejection of salvation brought down an unending series of reproaches against them, as if they couldn't let the primal father remain buried, even after the crucifixion.

After the birth of Christianity, then, anti-Semitism changed its character. From a prejudice against a people perceived as alien, clannish, and stubborn, it became a prejudice against a people who reminded others of the fatal inevitability of guilt. When Freud met Jung, the eminently respectable son of a pastor, he hoped he saw a way beyond the anti-Semitism psychoanalysts faced. He "chose" Jung to become the "savior" of analysis, even urging his Jewish associates who did not like Jung to "cultivate a little masochism." Jung helped teach Freud the importance of the anthropology of early myth and ritual, and it was under the spell of his relationship with Jung that Freud wrote *Totem and Taboo.* The two men differed, however, in their interpretations of the unconscious. Jung, in the tradition of German idealism, believed that just as Kant had discovered the laws that governed conscious thought

Freud had discovered the laws of the unconscious. Freud, by contrast, went back to *kedushah*—the law of the Father—in his discovery of the unconscious. His ultimate concern was with the individual soul and not with such anonymous, impersonal regulative principles as condensation, displacement, and considerations of representability, which Jung believed organized the collective unconscious of symbol and myth.

Sandor Ferenczi, one of Freud's closest associates, captured the difference between the two men. Jung's concern was the salvation of the community, not the analysis of the individual, Ferenczi wrote. Of course, it was Christ's sacrifice that laid the basis for the community's salvation. Thus Jung "identifies confession with psychoanalysis and evidently doesn't know that the confession of sins is the lesser task of therapy: the greater one is the demolition of the father imago"—the unconscious image of the father—"which is completely absent in confession." Jung sought to bring the patient to forgiveness and reconciliation, not self-knowledge; this in turn reflected on Jung. Jung doesn't want to be analyzed, Ferenczi wrote, but rather wants to remain to his patients "the *savior* who suns himself in his Godlike nature!" Being analyzed would entail exposing "his hidden homosexuality," that is, his identification with the band of brothers and refusal to recognize his ambivalence toward the father, Ferenczi continued. The band of brothers appears in Jung's writings as the "Christian community" or "brotherhood." Rather than make his own "homosexuality"—his "brotherly love"—clear to himself, Jung prefers to "'despise' sexuality" and praise "the 'progressive function of the [unconscious].'"[12] A few months later, Ferenczi reiterated: "The *father* plays almost no role . . . the *Christian community of brothers* takes up all the more room."[13]

The conflict between Freud and Jung forced into the open the Jewish composition of psychoanalysis. The reason psychoanalysis had emerged among Jews, in Freud's view, was that the Jews were a people "especially sensitive to the repressed historical material that is their tradition," meaning, above all, guilt for the murder of the primal father.[14] Christians, by contrast, evaded the feeling of guilt, since Jesus's crucifixion redeemed the murder. Because, in Freud's thinking, self-knowledge necessitated an inner—personal—awareness of guilt and responsibility, it was harder for the Christian to engage in introspection than it was for the Jew. Thus Freud explained to Abraham, "Racial relationship brings you closer to my intellectual constitution, whereas [Jung], being a Christian and the son of a pastor, can only find his way . . . against great inner resistances. His adherence is therefore all the more valuable"[15]

In these and similar remarks Freud revealed himself to be a member of a parochial, still persecuted minority. For example, he seems to have known nothing of such great Christian thinkers as Augustine, Pascal, and Jonathan Edwards, whose critique of self-love or sense of the power of guilt are in every way the match of Freud's or the superior. Nonetheless, Freud's conceptualization of the unconscious as linked to the capacity to work with an analyst whom one could not see, touch, or feel also offered a riposte of sorts to Protestant philosophers like Hegel who called Judaism the religion of sublimity, meaning that Jews viewed God as all-powerful and man as nothing. For Christians, the passion, suffering, crucifixion, and resurrection of Christ plunged the absolute into history and thus supplied the mediation through which humanity could touch and hear and feel God. Freud, by contrast, conceived of the analytic space as one in which patients could encounter what sometimes seemed to them a remote authority figure, someone whom they could not see and who offered no solace, no advice, no consolation, no relief from guilt. In working through a personal relationship to such a figure, Freud hoped that patients would reproduce infantile fantasies about the father and turn them into insight—what Ferenczi called "demolition of the paternal imago." Ironically, then, it was not the Jew but the Christian who, by substituting confession for analysis, left unanalyzed the transcendent, remote, sublime Godhead that Freud first called the primal father and later called the superego.

Adler's social-democratic and egalitarian critique of psychoanalysis complemented Jung's religiosity. Like the Hebrews who revolted against Moses, Adler sought an affirmative approach to narcissism. Thus, if Christians avoided the difficulties of self-knowledge by insisting

that Christ had already saved humanity, socialists held that the abolition of capitalism would produce universal benignity. Assuming
that individuals had an innate sense of dignity and self-respect, Adler
explained "neuroses" as arising from an insult or affront, such as the
affront of poverty or discrimination or what is known today as status-
injury. Sensitivity to slights, he reasoned, was the real basis for class
consciousness.[16] Any physician, he continued, can observe this sensitivity in the transference. When the neurotic loves or needs, he or she
feels "I am a slave." What Adler called the "masculine protest" was the
revolt against this feeling of enslavement in both sexes. In 1911 Adler
summarized his view: "There is no principle more generally valid for all
human relationships than 'on top of' and 'underneath.'"[17]

Freud called his 1914 "On Narcissism" "the scientific settling of
accounts with Adler," meaning that he had situated narcissism within
what would soon be called the structural theory of the mind. In letters written at the same time, Freud charged that Adler "tries to force
the wonderful diversity of psychology into the narrow bed of a single
aggressive 'masculine' ego-current," as if a child "had no other thought
than to be 'on top' and play the man."[18] The view of life reflected in
the Adlerian system, he added, "was founded exclusively on the aggressive impulse; there is no room in it for love."[19] Adler and Jung complemented one another. For Adler status was everything. Jung, by contrast, despised the ego's petty hurts, its "oversensitivity," prickliness,
its obsession with its standing in the world, traits that he eventually
associated with the Jewish character of psychoanalysis.[20] Both men,
however, sought to affirm narcissism without recognizing ambivalence. Neither man accepted the difficult path toward self-knowledge
that Freud espoused in psychoanalysis, just as Moses had espoused an
equally difficult path in the form of monotheism.

There was a further analogue between Judaism and psychoanalysis, especially significant for understanding America. Visiting New
York, Jung developed a theory of the "Negro complex," which par-
alleled Freud's theory of anti-Semitism. The Negro's example, Jung
believed, posed a threat to the "laboriously subjugated instincts of the

white races," just as the Hebrew rejection of Christ's sacrifice reminded Christians of their guilt.[21] The Negro, in other words, flaunted his or her sensuality, just as the Jews seemed to Christians to flaunt the primal murder. Ferenczi elaborated on this idea: "the persecution of blacks in America" occurs because blacks "represent the 'unconscious' of the Americans. Thus the hate, the reaction formation against one's own vices. . . . The free, 'fresh' behavior of the Jew, his 'shameless' flaunting of his interest in money, evokes hatred as a reaction formation in Christians, who are ethical not for logical reasons but out of repression. It is only since my analysis that I have understood the widespread Hungarian saying: '*I hate him like my sins.*'"[22]

The early conflicts in the history of psychoanalysis, then, parallel the early conflicts in the history of the Jews. Both pivot on the discovery that the "miraculous feeling," the "secret treasure," associated with chosenness was inseparable from an internal struggle over guilt and ambivalence. Jung sought to bypass that struggle by defining therapy in terms of the interpretation of a symbolic world that accompanied Kant's conception of reason. Adler, by contrast, anticipated the demand for recognition, which is the common sense of democratic societies today. Meanwhile, for Freud, the passage beyond the feeling of being chosen had to take place through recognition of the tragic weight of guilt, the subject of the next stage in Freud's schema.[23]

## Stage Three: The Fatal Inevitability of Guilt

In *Moses and Monotheism* Freud explained the inseparability of guilt from the Jewish love of God. "Ambivalence is a part of the essence of the relation to the father: in the course of time the hostility could not fail to stir [again], which had once driven the sons into killing their admired and dreaded father. There was no place in the framework of the religion of Moses for a direct expression of the murderous hatred of the father. All that could come to light was a mighty reaction against it—a sense of guilt on account of that hostility, a bad conscience for having sinned against God and for not ceasing to sin."[24]

Christianity, by sacrificing a son, had offered a one-sided—affirmative—solution to the problem of the Jewish bad conscience. The weakness of this solution revealed itself in the Christian inability to leave the Jews in peace. Instead, the church fathers adopted the Hebrew Bible as their own "Old Testament," rewrote the Hebrew stories so that they foretold the coming of Jesus, insisted that the Jews be preserved as an example of error, and predicted that the second coming would be known by the conversion of the Jews. The radical character of *modern* anti-Semitism, culminating in Nazism, lay in its attempt to destroy the long-standing Christian dependence on Judaism, an aim symbolized by the Nazis' public burnings of the "Old Testament," a sacred text for Christians after all. For many Germans in particular the attempt to build a modern nation-state hinged on the effort to build a world without finance capitalism and without Bolshevism, in other words a "world without Jews."[25]

The weight that guilt plays in Jewish culture was also a problem for young Jews. Before the rise of the Nazis obscured everything else, emancipation implied freedom not just from Christian strictures but from Jewish strictures as well. World War I seemed a turning point. In 1917 the Balfour Declaration promised a Jewish homeland in Palestine. In the same year, the Russian Revolution ended the hated Romanov dynasty, originator of the modern pogrom and inventor of the greatest anti-Semitic lie of the modern world, *The Protocols of the Elders of Zion*. A great revolution swept the German-speaking Jewish world provoking complex rethinkings of Judaism such as those of Gershom Scholem, Martin Buber, and Franz Rosenzweig. Franz Kafka, who died in 1924, was increasingly read as a Jewish thinker as well as a Jewish writer. In the twenties, too, the correspondence between Freud and Einstein, encouraged by the League of Nations, symbolized the way the modern Jewish intellectual was becoming exemplary of Enlightenment values in general.

Freud's writings concerning the uniqueness of the Mosaic moment, the particular contribution of the Jews to world history, and the way in which modern scientific thought, including psychoanalysis, had transcended not just Judaism but all religion, were produced in this context, within which he saw Mosaic Judaism as providing a touchstone through which to interpret psychoanalysis. As the biblical text records, when Moses returned from Mount Sinai he discovered that Aaron had led the Hebrews in building a golden calf. "Make us gods, which shall go before us," meaning gods we can see, touch, and feel, the Hebrew people had cried out. That cry so betrayed Moses' messages that he ordered the sacrifice of three thousand Hebrew men and women who refused to follow him, all the while begging God to allow him, Moses, one look (Exodus 33–34). The insistence that one believe in a God that one cannot see and that thereby offered no sensual relief and consolation eventually led, according to Freud, to the murder of Moses. Just as the early Hebrews rejected monotheism, so in the 1920s two great alternatives to psychoanalysis beckoned: Communism and America. Both appeared as salvation religions, offering powerful and appealing escapes from psychic conflict.

The charismatic and influential Wilhelm Reich represented the Communist alternative. Terming matriarchy the familial system of "natural society," Reich praised "the natural self-regulation of sexuality that it entails."[26] By contrast, the creation of patriarchy, private property and the state constituted the Ur-repression from which all neuroses flowed. Working in "Red Vienna" with its working-class schools, libraries, community centers, and apartment blocks (one of them subsequently named for Freud), all aimed at creating *neue Menschen,* Reich urged the politicization of analysis. Attacking Red Vienna's "sexual abstinence" literature, he called for the sexual liberation of youth and women. The feminist psychoanalyst Karen Horney was among Reich's most devoted followers.[27]

The United States offered an alternative vision: individual rather than collective redemption. There the idea of mental healing, "mind cure," or "positive thinking" was close to a national religion, central to Christian Science, self-help ideologies, salesmanship and career manuals, and movements for racial uplift, such as that of Father Divine. Mind cure preached "mind over matter," not in the sense of *Geistigkeit,* but in the sense of wishful thinking. In analysis the search for quick, affirmative shortcuts came from Sandor Ferenczi and Otto Rank, who suggested an "active therapy" in which the analyst prohibited activities such as masturbation or enjoined patients to fantasize, even suggesting the content of their fantasies.[28] Freud's goal of insight, Ferenczi and Rank explained, was "entirely different from the healing factor. . . . We see the process of sublimation, which in ordinary life requires years of education, take place before our eyes."[29]

Freud was not immune to the appeal of either communism or emigration to the United States. On the one hand, he described himself as sympathetic to the "great experiment" unfolding in Russia while rejecting Reich's view that human beings are benign except insofar as they have been corrupted by property.[30] On the other hand, he called the works of Rank and Ferenczi, "children of their time . . . conceived under the stress of the contrast between the postwar misery of Europe and the 'prosperity' of America, and designed to adapt the tempo of analytic therapy to the haste of American life."[31] In his late seventies and suffering from cancer since 1923, Freud responded to these challenges by deepening his stress on the role of guilt.

Freud didn't believe that patients came to analysts to get well; they came, rather, to satisfy powerful instinctual wishes that had been formed in infancy. For this reason, Freud insisted on "abstinence," meaning no consolation in the form of advice, sympathy, or recognition. In refusing to palliate the patient's situation, Freud's hope was that the instinctual need would be frustrated, intensified, and brought into sharper focus. Eventually, the need itself would become the object of observation and the result would be insight or self-awareness, in other words, *Geistigkeit*. However, the path to *Geistigkeit* was through the resistance: "no stronger impression arises from the resistances during the work of analysis than of there being a force which is defending itself by every possible means against recovery and which is absolutely resolved to hold on to illness and suffering."[32] The key, then, was not to rest content with the *positive* transference, the desire for insight, but to also force the *negative* transference into consciousness. Only analysis did that.[33]

In the 1930s, two powerful forces converged to further focus Freud's imagination on the destructive drives: the difficulties analysts faced in gaining cures and the rise of new, radical forms of anti-Semitism, expressed in the German elections of 1930 in which the Nazis won the second largest number of votes. After Adolf Hitler became chancellor on January 31, 1933, Germany began a series of careful, legalistic efforts to purge the Jews from cultural and economic life. In April 1933 the government ordered that no Jews could serve in an executive function in a medical organization. By 1934 over half the Berlin Psychoanalytic Institute's former members had fled. Increasingly, the Nazi cataclysm threatened to swallow up the whole of Judaism, reducing psychoanalysis to a footnote in a larger tragic history. That was the context in which *Moses and Monotheism* was written.

One great idea pervades the book: the power of the command emanating from the law of the father and passed on unconsciously through evolution and history. In the course of development, Freud wrote, "a standard is created in the Ego which opposes the other faculties by observation, criticism and prohibition. We call this new standard the superego. . . . The superego is the successor and representative of the parents (and educators), who superintended the actions of the individual in his first years of life. . . . The Ego is concerned, just as it was in childhood, to retain the love of its master, and it feels his appreciation as a relief and satisfaction, his reproaches as pricks of conscience." Judaism, then, was a superego religion, an expression of the omnipotent, ubiquitous father. "What seems to us so grandiose about ethics, so mysterious and, in a mystical fashion, so self-evident, owes these characteristics to its connection with religion, its origins from the will of the father . . . which sets out to work compulsively and which refuses any conscious motivation."[34] For still obscure historical reasons, psychoanalysis had inherited both the burden and the opportunity of the Jewish relation to the father, as was shown in its focus on "abstinence" or sublimation. "While instinctual renunciation for external reasons is only painful, renunciation for internal reasons, in obedience to the demands of the superego [brings] a substitutive satisfaction. The Ego feels uplifted; it is proud of the renunciation as of a valuable achievement." Yet "the feeling of guilt is [also] created by the renunciation of aggression." I consider this [idea] the most important progress in analysis," Freud added.[35]

In February 1938 Adolf Hitler summoned the Austrian chancellor, Kurt von Schuschnigg, to Berchtesgaden, the resort town where *The Interpretation of Dreams* had largely been written. On March 11 the Germans marched without opposition across Austria's northern border and into Vienna, shattering Freud's fantasy that Hitler would be stopped at the city gates. Two days later, the board of the Vienna Psychoanalytic Society decided that all members should flee the country and establish the future headquarters of the society wherever Freud went. After disbanding the Vienna Psychoanalytic Society, Freud invoked the memory of Rabbi Jochanan Ben Zakkai who, after Titus's destruction of the second Jewish temple, fled to begin a school of Torah studies.[36] He did not publish *Moses and Monotheism* until he migrated to England. With the destruction of analysis on the continent of Europe, and its rebirth in England and America, the fourth stage in Freud's schema unfolded: assimilation.

## Stage Four: Assimilation and the Matriarchal Impulse

In *Moses and Monotheism* Freud used the transformation of Judaism into Christianity to illustrate the dilution and vulgarization that occurs when a difficult elite doctrine assumes a popular form. The new Christian religion, he wrote, "meant a cultural regression as compared with the old, Jewish one, as regularly happens when a new mass of people break their way in or are given admission. The Christian religion did not maintain the high level in things of the mind to which Judaism had soared. It was no longer strictly monotheist, [and] it took over numerous symbolic rituals from surrounding peoples." Unlike Judaism, too, Christianity "re-established the great mother-goddess and found room to introduce many of the divine figures of polytheism only lightly veiled."[37]

Here, too, Freud's account of the fate of the Mosaic religion reflects his experience of psychoanalysis. The question of matriarchy or mother goddesses had arisen among analysts, along with the question of the role of the mother in psychic development, as a result of the rise of feminism, reflected in women's large and growing role within the analytic movement. Psychoanalysis was arguably the most woman-friendly profession in the world in the twenties and thirties, and Freud played a role in making this happen. For him, however, what psychoanalysis had in common with the Mosaic religion was not *patriarchy,* a word that came into use in the 1970s to signify female subordination, nor *misogyny,* a concept used in psychoanalysis in Freud's time but not at stake here, but rather the stress on *paternity.* Recognition of the father's role in procreation, Freud thought, had been a *cultural* advance, an aspect of the *Geistige* revolution that accompanied monotheism, insofar as the recognition of paternity had no clear instinctual or biological basis, as the mother-child relationship seemed to him to have. The idea of the Oedipus complex, the significance of sexual difference, and the exploration of the unconscious all presumed that prior moment of cultural advance. The stress on paternity did not deny the existence of a matriarchal or mother-centered phase in human history, but it did presume that the movement from matriarchy to what Freud called "the father-headed family" had meant the expansion of the role of culture and law. Analogously, for Freud, the movement in childhood to the recognition of the father's role represented an intellectual advance, one centered on the knowledge of sexual difference. The question, then, was not whether to integrate the matriarchal hypothesis into *Moses and Monotheism* but how.

Historically, furthermore, there were two different currents to the matriarchal impulse, which is to say two different ways of understanding the role of the mother. One derived from the romantic response to the Enlightenment and had a strong tie to the *Völkish* nationalisms that eventually sanctioned the destruction of the Jews of Europe. Johan Jakob Bachofen's 1861 *Das Mütterrecht,* which linked Mother-right to agriculture and the land, represents the best example. For Bachofen, the Mother "feeds" her favored *Völk*. Within psychoanalysis, Jung had represented this Völk-centered current, citing against Freud the "early, cultureless period" in human history when incest prevailed and the father's role was "purely fortuitous."[38] Drawing upon Aryan solar myths, Jung described the earliest societies as mother centered and polytheistic. The purpose of analysis, he urged, should be to "revivify among intellectuals a feeling for symbol and myth, ever so gently to transform Christ back into the [premonotheistic] soothsaying god of the vine, which he was."[39]

A second current in matriarchal thought was social democratic as opposed to Völkish. Here the source was the archaeological excavations in Sumer, Mesopotamia, Egypt, and Southern Europe, which occurred during Freud's lifetime. Freud was particularly struck by the excavations of Minoan-Mycenean civilization in Crete, which led to the remaking of our understanding of classical Greece, in part through James Frazer's twelve-volume compilation of fertility myths, *The Golden Bough*, and in part through Jane Harrison's reinterpretations of Greek tragedy as portraying a conflict between chthonic mother goddesses and patriarchal militarized invaders.[40] This current was bolstered after World War I when Bronislaw Malinowski, a Polish emigré to England, returned from the Trobriand Islands claiming he could not locate a single myth of origin in which the father was assigned a role in procreation. Others argued that social organization arose from the need for prolonged maternal care or portrayed the maternal village as the forerunner of the paternal town.[41] These currents of matriarchal thought influenced Melanie Klein's work and were also linked to social democracy and the welfare state, as discussed in the following chapter.

Both the German Völkish and the Anglo-American social-democratic currents of matriarchal thought depended on the sense of belonging to a common nation or people. Nonetheless, anti-Semitism was central to the Völk-based nationalisms and irrelevant to, and sometimes even opposed by, the Anglo-American variants, even granted the ubiquity of eugenics. The reason was the strength and character of feminism in the Anglo-American context. After World

War I, the women's movement had been transformed by the impact of Freudianism and modernism. With its new democratic ideals of youth and the sexual couple, it rejected the Puritanism of the prewar women's movement and supported social democracy. In the German-speaking world, by contrast, those who exalted the pastoral community advocated the Bismarckian welfare state but were critical of the young sexual couple, praising "masculine society," and attacking the Jewish man for his "hypertrophied" attachment to the family. The Jew, wrote Jung, because of his "extraordinary fixation to the family" was trapped at the level of "uncontrolled incestuous feeling" and thus lacked the "communal" sentiment embodied in the life of the sons or brothers. The Jew, Hans Blüher, editor of the homosexual newspaper *Der Eigene,* elaborated, was "weak in male-bonding."

In envisioning a transition from the "great mother" religions of tribes, in which men were only loosely attached to family life, to "father-headed" or pair-bonded families, *Moses and Monotheism* was closer to the Anglo-American version of matriarchy than to the German-speaking Völkish version. Like Jung, Freud believed there had been a transition from matriarchies to father-headed societies, but in Freud's view this was no loss. Rather, the transition accomplished an intellectual and spiritual gain. In his reasoning, while the father was not known in "primal hordes," one knew one's mother through direct sensory perception. Only after the murder of the primal father led to the creation of kinship relations, law, and the state—in short to the institutionalization of the oedipal order—did the cognitive, extrasensual recognition of one's father become institutionalized. The creation of two-sex families in place of mother-centered tribes signified the "victory of intellectuality [*Geistigkeit*] over sensuality [*Sinnlichkeit*]," in other words, the advance of reflective thought over sensory perception. In making this argument Freud was in line with much subsequent anthropology, such as the work of Meyer Fortes, who wrote, "Institutionalized fatherhood, unlike motherhood, comes into being not by virtue of a biological . . . event, but by ultimately juridical, societal provision, that is by rule. Fatherhood is a creation of society."[42]

Characteristically, Freud emphasized the cognitive gain involved in the recognition of the father's role in procreation, but in connecting this gain to a historical event—the emergence of monotheism in ancient Egypt—Freud was also grappling toward a social, cultural, and, indeed, historical grounding for psychoanalysis. This point is important for understanding political Freudianism. While the nineteenth century self-characterization of historians was narrowly empirical (archive based), and while many contemporary historians describe Freud as "ahistorical" or even antihistorical, Freud's way of thinking is very close to that of the working historian. This can be seen in his focus on concrete, particular events, especially turning points, in the geologically derived idea of strata that underlie both the historical and analytic professions, in the understanding that in any historical era currents from many different moments are in play, and in the skeptical approach to sources, so prominent in *Moses and Monotheism*. Combining evolution with the study of written sources to which historical writing has traditionally been confined is also familiar today.

Given these changes in our approach to history, Freud's idea of a transition to "father-headed families" can be better understood. The "pair-bond" created by recognition of the father's procreative contribution is a distinguishing mark of our species for two reasons. First, recognition of paternity made posible the sexual division of labor and thereby the prolongation of infancy, which led to the growth of the brain. Second, recognition of paternity is linked to social cooperation because it makes genealogy and kinship transparent and thereby useful for social organization, not half-hidden as they were when only the mother's role was apparent.[43]

For Freud, the Hebrew Bible reflected an important historical moment in this evolutionary past. The shift from the mother-centered fertility goddesses of polytheistic Sumeria, Babylon, Canaan, and Egypt to Mosaic monotheism involved what might be called paternalization, involving multiple changes at the levels of family life, genealogy, communal order, and political authority.[44] When Freud used such phrases as "the rule of the father," he generally had in mind not only the evolutionary past but also the Hebrew sense of a pervasive law or order having the family at its center. This was not the patriarchal family invented in ancient Rome and molded by the Christian focus on original sin, the condemnation of "concupiscence" (sexual desire) as an expression of love of self, and the exaltation of female virginity, but rather the patriarchal family of the Hebrew nomads.

Viewed historically, Freud's conception of monotheism as an intellectual or spiritual advance was also linked to the "dual-sphere" family, which became so important in the nineteenth century and was the family system in which Freud grew up. In Jewish history the dual spheres were the religious center (ultimately the synagogue) and the home; in Freud's day these had become work and the home. The underlying idea was of respect for the autonomy of each sex in his or her sphere. As the *complement* to the home, the synagogue is not equivalent to all-male institutions, such as men's lodges, premised on the derogation of family life. In contrast to such systems, Freud's emphasis on dual-sphere families reflected his view that the sexes had the same early aims and objects and yet diverged essentially through the recognition of sexual difference in the course of the oedipal transition. He equated this recognition of sexual complementarity and difference with *Geistigkeit* and placed it at the center of human development.

*Moses and Monotheism* also provided an evolutionary and historical counterpart to the discovery of the mother's role in psychoanalytic clinical practice. Just as Freud had turned the primal father into the superego, so he integrated the matriarchal archaeological discoveries into psychoanalysis. In 1931 he likened the psychic discovery of a preoedipal or matricentric stage of psychic development to the archaeological discovery of Minoan (i.e., pre-Mycenean) Greece. Everything, he wrote, "in the sphere of this first attachment to the mother seemed so difficult to grasp in analysis—so grey with age and shadowy . . . that it was as if it had succumbed to an especially inexorable repression."[45] During the preoedipal stage, Freud argued, psychic development was the same in both sexes. Later, however, during the oedipal stage, sexual difference became important, indeed, inescapable. At the same time, the early common path was critical to his reconceptualization of the oedipal stage. In the course of development, he wrote, "something which both sexes have in common [was] forced ... into different forms of expression." This common current Freud called the "repudiation of femininity," meaning the defensive repudiation of vulnerability in relation to the father.

At around the same time as Freud wrote *Moses and Monotheism*, he posited that the mother was the "child's first erotic object," "the first and strongest love-object," "the prototype of all later love-relations— for both sexes."[46] Freud did not, however, take this as evidence of a primal matriarchy whose overthrow constituted the "world historical defeat of the female sex," as did, for example, Wilhelm Reich or, in a somewhat different sense, Friedrich Engels.[47] Rather, the recognition of the role of the mother informed the democratic welfare state, which, in the context of World War II, included an enormous psychoanalytic component aimed at specifying and securing the psychological prerequisites of a democratic citizenry. To be sure, the idea that the recognition of paternity represented a cultural advance could and did lead to sexist conclusions, such as the hypostatization of the mother's role in early childhood, which occurred in postwar U.S. and Britain. But these were not inevitable given Freud's emphasis on the psychic as opposed to biologically given character of sexual difference. This emphasis on the psychical also found an echo in Freud's approach to Jewish identity.

According to the anthropologists and psychiatrists of Freud's time, the Jews were a tribe (*Stamm*) or a race (*Rasse*), which implied they were marked by a positive—in the sense of external or manifest— identity. It was thought, therefore, that the empirical sciences could identify the nature of the Jew through observation, measurement, or genetic tracking, a project on which the Nazis were already embarked when *Moses and Monotheism* was being written. Freud, by contrast, rejected the idea of direct, sensuous, concrete recognition of descent or racial identity, just as he linked the family and kinship to a

cognitive advance, In effect, he was insisting that one could no longer know directly what it meant to be Jewish, just as one could not
know directly who one's parents were. Of course, this is true of all
identity; there is always a cognitive or *Geistige* element that makes
it impossible to know identity directly. This *Geistige* element can be
linked to cosmopolitanism or civilization, the unifying spirit and
recognition of diversity the world has known at least since Alexander.
In the late nineteenth century, however, the way in which our common humanity exceeds our empirical identity was posed as an accusation against the Jews. Richard Wagner, for example, reputedly called
the Jews "the plastic demon of the decline of mankind."[48] To many
misogynistic and anti-Semitic minds, this accusation linked the Jews,
who supposedly could take on so many different national attributes,
to the new woman, who supposedly had no fixed sexual identity. Thus
Otto Weininger called the Jews "pervasively feminine," meaning that
they lacked the autonomous Kantian ego that Weininger equated with
masculinity.[49] As these examples show, there was a connection between
Jewish identity and gender identity, not because Jewish men were pervasively feminized, as some have recently argued, but rather because both
Jews and women were questioning the derogation of their ascribed biologically given identities.[50]

In any event, there were grounds for Freud's intuitions concerning
the resonance between some forms of maternalism and the dilution or
vulgarization of psychoanalysis. In England, where a brilliant Freudian offshoot had developed around Melanie Klein, Ian Suttie's 1935
*The Origins of Love and Hate* described Christianity as a "system of
psychotherapy" in which matriarchal elements were central. Emphasizing the social over the individual, the external over the internal,
and the altruistic over the selfish, Suttie called the Freudian emphasis
on the father "a disease." In the United States, where a market society
encouraged a narrow empiricism, and where the Calvinist heritage
enfeebled explorations of the problem of guilt, the emphasis on the
mother became linked to a deemphasis of the unconscious. Gertrude
Stein looked forward to an un-Freudian twenty-first century, "when

everybody forgets to be a father or to have one." She broke with her brother Leo as a result of his decision to be analyzed, insisting that "if you write about yourself for anybody it sounds as if you are unhappy but generally speaking everybody . . . has a fairly cheerful time in living."[51] In the 1970s, psychoanalysis took the so-called relational turn, which was based on the idea that the mother-child relationship was itself always already intersubjective, thereby cultural and not in need of the recognition of paternity in the form of the Oedipus complex, which had been so important to classical analysis. These developments were already underway when Freud wrote *Moses and Monotheism* as a contribution to what he hoped would be an eventual return of the repressed—the recovery of the original discoveries of psychoanalysis.

Soon after finishing the book, Freud died. With his death the question arises: will there be an analogue to the fifth stage in Freud's schema, in which the repressed tradition is rediscovered and reclaimed? Or would psychoanalysis become of merely historical interest? *Moses and Monotheism* itself addressed this question. There Freud wrote, "it would be wrong to break off the chain of causation with Moses and to neglect what his successors, the Jewish prophets, achieved. Monotheism had not taken root in Egypt. The same failure might have happened in Israel. . . . From the mass of the Jewish people, however, there arose again and again men who lent new color to the fading tradition, renewed the admonishments and demands of Moses and did not rest until the lost cause was once more regained."[52] Is there an analogy to the prophetic tradition within psychoanalysis, for example in figures like Herbert Marcuse or Juliet Mitchell, who discovered radical trends in what others had taken as conservative, or in Jacques Lacan, who called for a "return to Freud?" Or has psychoanalysis already been decisively absorbed in a new popular, eclectic mix of cybernetics, neuroscience, behaviorism, relational analysis, feminist therapy and culture criticism, just as Judaism was absorbed into Christianity? Whatever we say about that, another question arises: How can we understand *Moses and Monotheism* so that it sheds light not only on the history of psychoanalysis but also on World War II?

*Moses and Monotheism* and the Meaning of World War I I

While writing *Moses and Monotheism,* Freud peered into the looming abyss of the Second World War almost as a dying person might look into an open grave. At the preconscious level he interwove strands from ancient Egypt, the Hebrews, personal memories and the Jews of Europe with his own anxieties concerning the future of psychoanalysis. The result is a seminal text for understanding the war, comparable to works by exiles such as Erich Auerbach and Hannah Arendt and survivors like Primo Levi and Paul Celan. As I have argued, viewed as a meditation on the coming war, the book's central concern is the survival of *Geistigkeit* or spirit. Having endured the expulsion of the Jews from German and Austrian cultural and social life and the destruction of continental European psychoanalysis, Freud questioned whether self-knowledge would continue to be valued and whether the space in which self-reflective thought could unfold would be salvaged.

Simultaneously Freud saw himself as historicizing psychoanalysis, not only by seeking out its evolutionary and historical roots but also by situating it in the context of what was then called "Western" thought. He took the endangered state of psychoanalysis as a metaphor for the endangered state of Western civilization. In this sense the book effectively sought to define the values for which the war was about to be fought, even if Freud himself was only dimly aware of this. As we have seen, this gives the book its place in a family that includes Erich Auerbach's *Mimesis* (1946), Erwin Panofsky's "Renaissance and Renascences" (1944), Hans Baron's *Crisis of the Early Italian Renaissance* (1952), Karl Polanyi's *The Great Transformation* (1944), and Hannah Arendt's *The Origins of Totalitarianism* (1948). All these works pinpoint a transcendent value such as realism, single-point perspective, republicanism, or societal collectivity, identified with the ideals of subjectivity and democracy, which the war brought into crisis.

At the same time, *Moses and Monotheism* is a Jewish work: it belongs to the tradition of Jewish thought and is a product of the persecution of the Jews on the eve of World War II. Perhaps the best way to grasp this is by reference to Franz Kafka. Kafka was born, like Freud, in Moravia, one generation after Freud, and died another generation before Freud did. In both authors we have the vision of an all-powerful God or primal father, impossible to locate empirically, and an all-pervasive but fraying law (*Gesetz*), a patriarchal order, or even tradition, which cannot be directly accessed, whose claims are beyond rationality, and that leaves no place for the individual to hide. Kafka's writings represent the real-world external literary complement to the Freudian inner world, the unconscious turned inside out. Gregor Samsa actually wakes up as an insect, right in his own bed, an ego's defensive maneuvers dig out an underground burrow, the "instincts" take the form of speaking animals, bisexuality becomes a brother and a sister, and Joseph K. is not only irrationally guilty, he is also "shot like a dog." For both writers, the essential relationship is between "man" and God, or "man" and the Father, and is not the I-thou relationship so favored in the Christian imaginary. Gershom Scholem captured the Jewish vision that the two authors share in a 1931 letter to Walter Benjamin that likened *The Trial* to the Book of Job: "Here for once a world is expressed in which redemption cannot be anticipated—go and explain this to the *goyim*!"[53]

Freud's retelling of the biblical Moses story so that it centers on survival and transmission also belongs to such Jewish traditions as Talmud (commentary), *Zohar* (exegesis), and Haggadah (telling), especially because there is a strong paternal voice running through it. Auerbach's famous opening chapter in *Mimesis* describes the Hebrew mode of exposition as shaped by God's entry from some vast heights or depths, some "undetermined dark place," from which He or She calls: "Abraham!" So, too, did Moses enter Jewish life from some dark, undetermined place, leaving behind trails—archives for Jacques Derrida—of tradition, ritual, and law. Thus Freud argued that if a religious tradition were based only on conscious or explicit communication "it would be listened to, judged, and perhaps dismissed, like any other piece of information from outside; it would never attain the privilege of being liberated from the constraint of logical thought. It must have undergone the fate of being repressed, the condition of lingering in the unconscious, before it is able to display such powerful effects on its return, to bring the masses under its spell." Religious texts such as the Bible showed evidence of this long process of unconscious transmission and reworking. Thus Freud argued that Exodus—like all codifications of memory—had been "subjected to revisions which have falsified it . . . mutilated and amplified it and have even changed it into its reverse" while simultaneously expressing a "solicitous piety [that] sought to preserve everything as it was."[54]

*Moses and Monotheism* is also a work of Jewish testimony, written by a political refugee. While the Jews occupied a territorial kingdom for several centuries, they were *displaced*—in exile—when Moses found them and for most of the time afterward. That helps give the story of Moses its untoward power. The Hebrew people were both the "founders" of Western culture—the originators of the idea of a single God, from which the whole of Christianity and Islam descend—but also "the Other" to the very culture they unwittingly founded. Their role as founders is crucial to understanding why anti-Semitism had the scope, power, even—for its progenitors, as well as for its enemies—the majesty that it did, as we shall see. But the Jewish role as "Other" also anticipates the way the vortex of World War II's hurricane moved from Western Europe to the regions that Timothy Snyder has called "Bloodlands," such as Poland, the Ukraine, Byelorussia, and Western Russia, and then again to the struggles against colonization in Asia, Africa, and the Middle East and the postwar search for a new, extra-Western world order.[55]

Exile, longing, and memory had been the locus of Jewish identity since the destruction of the Temple. The Hebrew liturgy states, "A fire kindles within me as I recall—when I left Egypt, but I mourn as I remember—when I left Jerusalem." The Haggadah enjoins, "In each and every generation let each person regard himself as though he had emerged from Egypt." Freud was himself an exile at both the beginning and end of his life. He made his childhood situation as an exile clear in an early dream discussed in *The Interpretation of Dreams* (1900). In

the dream he saw himself almost in tears: "a female figure—an atten-
dant or nun—brought two boys out and handed them over to their
father, who was not myself." The dream, Freud wrote, concerned "the
Jewish problem, concern about the future of one's children, to whom
one cannot give a country of their own, concern about educating them
in such a way that they can move freely across frontiers."[56] In associations to the dream, Freud recalled a Jewish asylum director who had
been dismissed for confessional reasons, cousins able to flee Moravia
for England during Freud's infancy, and a performance of Theodor
Herzl's (1894) *The New Ghetto*. He saw himself sitting at the side of a
fountain in Rome weeping and recalled Psalm 137, the Israelite lament
from the Babylonian captivity, "By the waters of Babylon we sat down
and wept."

Because they were in exile, Ashkenazi Jews like Freud faced east-
ward. Just as in the anti-Semitic discourse of Freud's times, the Jews
were "Asiatics," so many Jewish intellectuals believed that the spiritual
center of Judaism lay in Poland, the Ukraine, and in the Russian Pale,
as well as among the Sephardim and Mizrahim, rather than among the
assimilated Jews of Germany and Austro-Hungary. Assimilated German Jewish homes were often filled with tallises, yarmulkes, tefillin, sid-
durim, and kashruth dishes from the East; Kafka's breakthrough writing came after he saw an East European Yiddish theater troupe perform
in Prague. At the same time, the Jews poured into the modern universities, modern business, science, and literature. This posed a conflict in
regard to Jewish identity. We can understand the conflict by contrasting
Martin Buber's writings on the Hasidim, and his "I-Thou" philosophy,
which originated during World War I, with Gershom Scholem's *Major
Trends of Jewish Mysticism* (1941). Both Buber and Scholem believed
that the renewal of Jewish life would come from the *Ostjuden*—from
the East—but they had opposing views as to how this would happen.
Buber used the Hasidic tales to stress the universality of the Jewish
experience, especially its resonance with enlightened Christian themes
such as the existentialist encounter. By contrast, Scholem drew on
the Hasidim, and especially on their mystical currents, to emphasize

Jewish difference, chosenness, and unassimilability. Freud was certainly closer to Scholem than to Buber on this divide, but he was even more radical in that he moved the *topos* of Jewish spirituality back in time and further East in space—to Egypt, the one Arab country of Freud's time that had a continuous history with the biblical era.

Egypt was a special passion for Freud. Although he had grown up in the shadow of the statue of Athena that stood in the Ringstrasse in Vienna, Freud was convinced that Athena was the descendant of the Egyptian phallic mother goddess Neith of Sais, the goddess of war. Isis, Osiris, and Horus were among his favorite antiquities, and when he visited London in 1908 he refused most invitations to tour, spending his evenings reading up for the next day's visit to the Egyptian rooms of the British Museum. When Freud first met Karl Abraham, he slipped two Egyptian figurines into Abraham's briefcase as a going away present. When Abraham wrote on Ikhnaton five years later, Freud called the essay a new "orientation" for psychoanalysis, intending the pun. Like his contemporaries, Freud was especially struck by the discoveries of mother goddess figurines at the palace at Knossos (Crete), which many archaeologists believed was an Egyptian colony. In Freud's view, ancient Egypt was the most bisexual of all civilizations, and bisexuality for Freud laid the strongest basis for intellectual and artistic advance.[57]

The mystery of origins lies behind *kedushah*, which is as important as reason to *Geistigkeit*. Freud described Moses as a "Great Stranger." In fact, the Jews were "strangers" in Canaan before being enslaved in Egypt. When the Torah was written, the "other" was Babylonia. The God of the Midrash was fashioned against the backdrop of the Byzantine Empire, and that of the Kabbalah against the backdrop of Muslim Spain. In *Freud and the Non-European* (2003) Edward Said wrote, "Freud was deeply gripped by what stands outside the limits of reason, convention and, of course, consciousness: his whole work in that sense is about the Other." According to Said, by locating Egypt *in* Israel rather than outside it, Freud was suggesting that there was something unknown, uncanny and unconscious, at the center of Jewish identity.[58] There is truth in this—the truth of of postcolonialism—but it is not the whole truth. Freud was not so much trying to put Egypt at the center of Jewish history as putting universality (*Geistigkeit*) at the center of all history, including that of the Jews. In that sense, *Moses and Monotheism* was exemplary of the Popular Front, the Marxist-inspired struggle against fascism. The Popular Front defined World War II as a conflict between those nations that descended from the Enlightenment, including the Soviet Union, and those that rejected the Enlightenment, led by Nazi Germany. For Freud, psychoanalysis was a child of the Enlightenment from which the concept of *Geistigkeit* derived.

Seen in that context, the attack on the Jews was not only an attack on the Jews as a people; it was also an attack on the civic republicanism of the Renaissance (Hans Baron, Erwin Panofsky), on the age of democratic revolutions (Karl Polanyi, Hannah Arendt), and on what Erich Auerbach called the tribal-democratic mode of representing everyday reality, which had begun with the ancient Hebrews. Freud, like almost all European analysts of the time, was a social democrat, not a classic free-market liberal, as he has so often been (mis)described, for example, by Peter Gay.[59] Still, it would be more precise to describe him as an important figure *for* the Popular Front than an advocate *of* it. In *Moses and Monotheism* he criticized the idea that consciousness can be traced back to so-called material factors and stressed instead the force of tradition, charisma, and "the personal influence upon world-history of individual great men." Whatever the relation of Freudianism to the Popular Front, leftism had implications for Jewish identity. The Polish Jewish Trotskyist Isaac Deutscher grasped this in 1954 when he described Freud as a "non-Jewish Jew." Praising "the Jewish heretic who transcends Jewry," Deutscher connected Freud to Heine, Marx, and Rosa Luxemburg, all figures who "were born and brought up on the borderlines of various epochs . . . where the most diverse cultural influences crossed and fertilized each other. . . . They were each in society and yet not in it, of it and yet not of it. It was this that enabled them to rise in thought above their societies, above their nations, above their times and generations, and to strike out mentally into wide new horizons and far into the future."

In *Moses and Monotheism* Freud was trying to understand Jewish history, as well as Jewish identity, but he was also trying to understand anti-Semitism, not only in its ancient national and religious forms, but in its modern forms as well. The Judeocide, to be sure, took place after Freud died, but the psychology that created and tolerated it was in place throughout the 1930s, certainly in the German-speaking world. According to Mark Mazower, "National Socialism . . . fits into the mainstream not only of German but also of European history far more comfortably than most people like to admit."[60] Mazower had in mind especially Nazism's racial-nationalist welfare system and its attempt to create a common European market, but Nazism was also close to the European mainstream in its attempt to free European Christianity from its dependence on the Jews. Richard Evans provides a clue to the centrality of anti-Semitism to World War II in his review of Timothy Snyder's *Bloodlands*. As Snyder argues, the Jews were killed along with Poles, Ukrainians, Byelorussians, Roma, and many other peoples. Yet, according to Evans, "There was something peculiarly sadistic in the Nazi's desire not just to torture, maim and kill the Jews, but also to humiliate them. . . . The Slavs, in the end, were a regional obstacle to be removed; the Jews were a 'world enemy' to be ground into the dust."[61]

Freud's book on Moses suggests how the idea of the Jews as "world enemy" and the project of excluding them from the German nation and then exterminating them could have gained such force. Judaism gave meaning to Nazism in a way that the German struggle for continental hegemony, the *drang nach Osten* (Eastern Europe and the Ukraine) in search of land, oil, and wheat, or even the struggle for racial purity, did not and could not. Moses brought *the law* to the Jewish people, especially the *Bilderverbot*; he thereby launched the world on its first reliable step toward conceptual thought. Insofar as that step concerned struggles with authority, tradition, and guilt, and not only with metaphysics, it was not intellectual alone. From the modern Jewish point of view, reflected in such figures as Kafka and Freud, it was not Christ's sacrifice that gave meaning to history, but rather the covenant between a single people and God, a modus operandi that began the long process of emancipating humanity from the rule of the father. Nor were Jewish thinkers like Freud alone in this view. For the Nazi revolution to be something more than a social revolution or a ploy in Great Power politics—for it really to accomplish its revolutionary, thousand-year aims—it needed to accomplish a new founding of and for itself, one freed of the "unclean," "diseased," "foreign" "element that had "contaminated" the German effort at transcendence until then. For this reason the cleansing of every German institution of *Judentum* to the point of exterminating the Jews was even more important than winning the war. Pursued in the manner of an open secret, mingling frisson with cold calculation, the "secret treasure" of the Chosen People had to be appropriated while its bearers were ground into dust. Yet so powerful was the "existential threat" of this "world enemy" that Nazis preserved the ashes of synagogues, cemeteries, and bits of Torah so they could be folded into the history of a new redeemed Germany.

The concern for the spiritual stakes supposedly involved in political and military conflicts survived even the Holocaust. In works such as Henry Luce's *The American Century* (1943), with an alacrity that still amazes, the struggle of the allies against fascism became a struggle against Communism. The ensuing cold war was, to a great extent, a cultural and even spiritual war, especially in the forties and fifties. Just as antifascism had required a new spirit, so anti-Communism required a new spirit when it conquered postwar Europe. The new spirit was Anglo-American liberalism. Jazz, abstract expressionism, and a new, ethnic, especially Jewish American literature were all incorporated into this spirit, as such figures as Saul Bellow realized. Nonetheless, religion retained its extralogical power. The U.S. claim to moral superiority over Communism rested less on its economic performance than on its insistence that freedom required spiritual foundations. The second of the "Four Freedoms" articulated by President Roosevelt in his 1941 State of the Union Address was freedom of religion. The cold war, like World War II, was waged against the supposedly atheistic or "godless" Communist enemy. Nor was the Mosaic keystone neglected. Rather, the

Jews, whom the Nazis tried so desperately to reduce to history, were accorded a place within a new, liberal "Judeo-Christian" synthesis.

The cold war effort to transform Anglo-American liberalism into a universal ideology involved a search to locate the spiritual origins of "the West." Since so much of the cold war unfolded in Asia, Africa, the Middle East, and Latin America, this search took place in non-Western and extra-Western locales. To be sure, for some former fascists like Mircea Eliade and Georges Dumézil, as well as reactionaries like Henry Corbin, the search for new spiritual origins involved marginalizing or excluding the Jews, as it had for the Nazis. Arnold Toynbee's *Study of History* (1934–64) and T. S. Eliot's "Notes Toward a Definition of Culture" (1948) both argued that only a Christian response—meaning Christian as opposed to Jewish—could be adequate to the catastrophe of World War II. But of all the postwar efforts to establish a new anti-Communist and anticolonial spiritual basis for the West, the most influential was Karl Jaspers's 1948 adaptation of an idea originally formulated by Alfred Weber: the Axial Age. Understood as a response to the great central Asian migrations of the first millennium BCE, the thinkers of the Axial Age, such as Confucius, Lao-Tse, Buddha, Socrates, the Hebrew prophets, and, in some readings, Zoroaster, were supposedly the first to experience the "limitless vastness of the world" and the first for whom man became a question for himself.[62] The Axial Age thesis, like its successor, "multiple modernities," first formulated by the Israeli American sociologist Shmuel Eisenstadt—the heir to Martin Buber at Hebrew University in Jerusalem—was a way of assimilating "Western civilization" to the great religions of everyday life and of the family such as Confucianism, Mahayana Buddhism, and Hinduism. Like Freud, the thinkers who formulated the Axial Age hypothesis were centered on the breakthrough to a conceptual and universal realm. Nonetheless, there are profound differences between the Axial Age thesis and *Moses and Monotheism*.

Whereas the Axial Age thesis presumed unilinear progress, *Moses and Monotheism* rests on the idea of regression, which interrupts and reverses historical flows, but also allows for historical depth. The Axial

Age thinkers placed morality or justice at the center of their conception of human nature; Freud did not dispute the importance of morality and justice, but complicated our understanding of their place in the psyche by distinguishing ego and superego. The Axial Age theorists stressed the contribution of a universal morality to the rise of states and empires; Freud viewed monotheism as an insurgency, which took shape "in deliberate hostility to the popular [religion]," an insurgency that the prevailing authorities opposed. Axial Age thinkers viewed the Axial Age breakthrough as a mass breakthrough; Freud stressed the difficulty of preserving spiritual and intellectual gains when they were translated into mass forms. Freud's approach is critical while the Axial Age thinkers are affirmative. That is why Freud's concern with the survival of difficult, challenging ways of thought remains so relevant in today's post–cold war "end of history" framework and why the "obsolescence" of psychoanalysis is important to so much more than the history of psychiatry.

Finally, let us return to the question of Jewish survival. World War II led to the triumph of the affirmative sense of Jewish identity implicit in the Axial Age hypothesis. American Jews rejected the themes of exile, minority status, or stigmatization, redefining the meaning of Judaism to conform to American ideals of pluralism. The founding of Israel in 1948 complemented the "Judeo-Christian" solution to the Jewish problem. Israelis rejected what Freud had called the Hebrew preference for "spiritual endeavor," which "helped build a dyke against brutality and the inclination to violence" and affirmed David Ben-Gurion when he boasted, "We are not Yeshiva students debating the finer points of self-improvement. We are conquerors of the land."[63] Does *Moses and Monotheism* offer any insight for those who reject the American Century and Zionist versions of Judaism but still call themselves Jews?

We might approach this question by contrasting the problem of Jewish survival to the problem of African American history discussed in the previous chapter. In both cases the core problem was one of memory, but this problem took opposing forms for the two peoples. In the African American case, the problem was too little memory;

memory had to be forged out of fragments like "Do bana coba, gene me, gene me," pentatonic beats, and the aching undertow of the blues. In the case of the Jews, there had been too much memory—almost nothing but memory in the sense of the overwhelming presence of the Bible, the tradition, the law, the chosenness. As a Jew of his time, Freud tried to clear away the brambles that underlay the refractory, conflict-ridden persistence of the Jews under conditions of exile, foreign occupation, persecution, and even genocide. In returning in a deeply personal, essentially autobiographical, way, to the encounter between the Hebrew people and Moses, Freud was posing the enigma *of* the Jews as an enigma *for* the Jews. Writing when the question of Jewish survival itself was at stake, this reclaiming of the question of Jewish identity is among the book's enduring contributions.

# 4

## The Ego at War

*From the Death Instinct to Precarious Life*

Psychoanalysis and the Spirit of War

Like capitalism, racism, and anti-Semitism, the problem of war has spawned a substantial body of political Freudian reflection. The main reason for this has been that twentieth-century wars have been "total wars," which blurred the boundaries between battlegrounds and home fronts and forced governments to motivate the masses to lay down their lives. This required a new spirit of war that might be likened to the new spirit of capitalism discussed in chapter 1. In participating in these wars, and in seeking to understand them psychoanalytically, something like a theory not just of war but of the twentieth-century subject emerged.

As the century began, an older aristocratic, honor-based way of life still supplied war with its "spirit" or animating ethos. The unexpected horror and bloodletting of World War I, along with the impotence of the political and military elites, made such motivations as "honor," "glory," and "sacrifice" seem empty. The mass outbreak of "shell shock," the first large-scale expression of what we call today post-traumatic stress disorder, helped bring the antiwar sentiment to a head. Not only did the older honor code begin to seem obsolete; so too did the nineteenth-century liberal ideals of optimism, rationality, and progress.

Psychoanalysis provided a counterpoint to earlier ideals. As if tailor-made for a theory of the unconscious, the outbreak of shell shock brought to light the existence of traumatic shocks or stimuli that overwhelm the mind and force individuals (and peoples as well) to remain fixated on an unmastered past. Because they could not be handled through the normal mechanisms of the unconscious, manifested in dreams, neurotic symptoms, or wishful fantasies, such stimuli forced a revision of psychoanalytic theory. Earlier, Freud saw the unconscious as repressed; now he saw it as exerting *permanent* or *structural* demands on the conscious mind, taking such forms as impulses, self-criticisms, or aspects of character itself. The effect was to spur his thinking about the ego, which he saw as able to mobilize unconscious forces, but also as self-protective, on guard against being overwhelmed. Above all, Freud saw the ego's Achilles heel in its defensive denial of vulnerability, which he called a "preference for the active role" and saw as implicated in shell shock. Thus the shell shock outbreak confirmed Freud's view that the obstacles to reason and progress were "structural," in other words, internal to the ego or consciousness, the site of reason and progress.

Developed in the aftermath of World War I, the Freudian idea of the ego was displaced in a second historic encounter between psychoanalysis and war centered on World War II. This encounter drew on explorations of early childhood, and especially of the role of the mother in development, which had begun in the 1920s. These investigations produced a new tendency in psychoanalysis—object relations—that became central to the social-democratic welfare state. When Britain went to war against Nazi Germany, object relations theorists like Melanie Klein helped reconstruct an ancestral justification of war, which to some extent served as a new spirit of war. The earliest relation to the mother, they argued, laid the basis for ethical responsibility: in other words, soldiers fought to protect those who were close to them and vulnerable, especially women and children. In emphasizing the role of the mother, object relations theorists were deepening the Freudian idea of the ego by making explicit its basis in primary family relations and its relation to gender. At the same time, they minimized or ignored the role of the ego as the site of reason and self-reflection, thereby paving the way for today's psychoanalysis, which replaced the concept of the ego with the concept of the self, as in such terms as *self-image* or *self-esteem.*

The concept of the self was central to a third historic encounter of psychoanalysis with war, which centered on "the war on terror" in the early twenty-first century. The backdrop to this encounter included the social movements of the 1960s and their successors, such as feminism and poststructuralist philosophy, which precipitated the full-scale shift from ego to self. An important contributing figure was Jacques Lacan, who launched a tendentious attack on "ego psychology" in the 1950s and 1960s. The resulting poststructuralist reading of psychoanalysis generated this third approach to war, best exemplified in the philosopher Judith Butler's 2004 work *Precarious Life.* According to Butler, the American invasion of Iraq should be understood as a defensive reaction to a catastrophic humiliation, the breaching of vulnerable narcissistic boundaries, both individual and national. In her view, American narcissism, or "exceptionalism," had dissimulated our underlying "sociality of the self . . . the fact that we are not bounded beings . . . but also constituted in relation to others." What form, Butler asks, might political reflection take if we take injurability as our point of departure for political life, rather than independence and self-mastery?

The evolution of a political Freudian tradition centered on war can therefore be situated in the context of the shift from the classical Cartesian or Kantian view of the rational, independent, "bounded" ego—which stands at the cusp of the modern world—to today's view that the ego is formed through recognition, object relations, and language. At the center of this shift, as Butler's work suggests, is the place of vulnerability in our conception of the human subject. For Freud, as we shall see, vulnerability was ontological and genetic in the sense that it arises from our prolonged infancy and is constitutive of human development. For Butler, by contrast, vulnerability has become normative, in the sense that its recognition constitutes the central ethical imperative of political life. This difference has an important consequence. Freud's aim in exposing what he termed our "preference for the active role" was to *strengthen* the ego, not unveil its illusions of self-mastery. By the time we get to Butler, however, the point of drawing on psychoanalysis is to dispel the very idea of an individual ego and to bring to light instead the underlying network of unconscious relations and dependencies, which are seen as constituting our humanity. In moving from the ego to the self, from autonomy to recognition, and from an ontological to a normative approach to vulnerability, have we advanced or weakened our understanding of war, of politics, and of the human psyche? That is the question this chapter poses.

## World War I and the Collapse of the Warrior Ethic

Before the rise of the modern nation, the men who fought wars were either aristocrats, bred for war, or serfs or peasants, conscripted regardless of their will. The rise of mass democracy changed that by creating mass civilian armies, and total wars, meaning wars in which the warrior/civilian distinction was eroded or eliminated. Early examples of total wars include the Napoleonic Wars, the American Civil War, and the Franco-Prussian War. Since these wars involved conscript armies, a problem emerged. How could free men, and later women, be persuaded to lay down their lives, often in their earliest youth?

The nineteenth century gave an answer to this question, namely, that in dying one does not *lose* one's life but rather *sacrifices* it for one's nation. This answer connected modern nationalism to an older warrior ethic ultimately rooted in sacrificial religions. Sacrifice lends dignity to peoples, nations, or causes, unifies the past and present under a common sign, and makes a claim on future generations. Identifying soldiers' deaths as a series of meaningful and consecrated events gives the nation its incomparable reality.[1] Sacrifice also channels male heroism, drawing on ritual, race, tribalism, and the idea of a national founding. During World War I the warrior ethic, romantic nationalism, and the ideals of martyrdom and self-sacrifice began to come into question.

After an initial burst of enthusiasm, World War I turned out to be a matter of mass, insensate violence rather than heroism and sacrifice. The unprecedented scale of catastrophe, the defensive stalemate symbolized by the trenches, the new landscape of mines and no-man's-land, the fear of being buried alive, the deafening sound and vibration, the insidiousness of gas, the disappearance of the distinction between night and day, identification with the enemy, and the narrowing of consciousness all upended nineteenth-century expectations. The new Freudian mind picture, which included such notions as resistance, defenses, cathexis (i.e., *Besetzung* or occupation), trauma (wound), repression, and *Zwangsneurose* (stalemate) seemed more pertinent than the search for glory and honor. Shell shock, then, provided the first occasion for the encounter between psychoanalysis and war.

Within a year of the outbreak of war, hundreds of thousands of cases appeared on both sides. Although originally explained as an impairment of the nervous system resulting from an explosion, psychiatrists increasingly turned toward psychological explanations, especially after the symptoms of shell shock were successfully removed by hypnosis. Even then the persistence of the older warrior ethic revealed itself in such diagnoses as "greed neurosis" and "pension-struggle neurosis," which suggested malingering. Psychoanalysis cast the matter in a different light. Ernst Simmel, a young German student of Freud's, wrote: "It is not only the bloody war which leaves such devastating traces . . . it is also the difficult conflict in which the personality finds itself. . . . Whatever in a person's experience is too powerful or horrible for his conscious mind to grasp and work through filters down to the unconscious levels of his psyche. There it lies like a mine, waiting to explode."[2]

What distinguished the new approach was the observation that shell shock was precipitated by the unnerving experience of passive waiting, rather than by the fear of death per se. By 1916 the psychiatrists' favored explanation for shell shock became the enforced "passivity" of the trenches. According to one chaplain, a "high degree of nervous tension is commonest among men who have . . . to remain inactive while being shelled. For the man with ordinary self-control this soon become a matter of listening with strained attention for each approaching shell, and speculating how near it will explode. . . . An hour or two . . . is more than most men can stand."[3] The British War Office also concluded that the primary cause of shell shock was "prolonged danger in a static position." Such explanations seemed vindicated when the incidence of shell shock plummeted after the German offensives of 1918.[4]

Analysts developed the link between passivity or passive suffering and shell shock by noting a second characteristic of shell shock, namely repetition. Far from *repressing* their battlefield experiences, as Freudians would have expected, the victims of shell shock *repeated* them in dreams, symptoms, and anxiety attacks. How could the repetition of a painful experience be explained? Freud had already addressed this problem. In the clinical situation, he argued, patients feared being in a passive, vulnerable position. They expressed their "resistance" to analysis by refusing to *remember* their experiences; instead they *repeated* them. To illustrate this point, he described his grandson's behavior when his mother left him. The child invented a game in which he alternately hid and produced a ball, saying *da/fort*, here/gone. "At the outset," Freud wrote, his grandson "was in a *passive* situation—he was overpowered by the experience; but, by repeating it, unpleasurable though it was . . . he took on an *active* part."[5] By analogy, shell shock appeared as a misguided attempt to master the experience of passively waiting in the trenches by repeating the experience of being bombed.

The observation of shell shock in war, along with resistance in the consulting room, led Freud to a revised theory (or "mythology," as he called it) of the instincts, namely the conflict between life and death, or between order and disorder, or between an open, homeostatic system and entropy. Shell shock also led Freud to formulate his theory of the ego. Infused with the life instincts, the ego is a binding force, but it is also subject to the conservative or regressive pull of the instincts toward lesser organization and ultimately toward death. Sexuality, which Freud formerly thought of as a disruptive force, he now thought of it as part of the life instincts or eros and therefore aimed at cohesion and binding. Critical to Freud's emerging theory of the ego is the transition from instinctual life to something like reason, insight, or subjectivity, which he would later call *Geistigkeit*, the product of sublimation or "instinctual renunciation." In light of the rebellion against passivity evident in both the shell shock outbreak and in his own therapeutic work, Freud began to speak of the ego's "preference for the active role"—in both sexes. But in no sense did Freud valorize passive wishes, rather, he sought to bring them into consciousness or the ego.

As the war was ending, psychoanalysis increasingly became an ego psychology. This was shown by Freud's famous formula, where id was there shall be ego. But this was no longer the Cartesian or transcendental ego, which was reason supposedly emancipated from the instincts. Rather the Freudian ego was the precipitate of inclinations, drives, love objects, and identifications. Its task was not to gain access to "clear and direct ideas," as in Descartes, but rather to mediate between different and conflicting instinctually driven demands, including cravings emanating from the id, self-criticisms coming from the superego, and competing representations of the social world. Freud now rejected his own prewar view that the basic conflict in the mind was between consciousness and the repressed unconscious. That view implied that the repressed was "afraid to be discovered."[6] But the fact of repetition, evident in shell shock and in analytic work, suggested that the repressed was continuously trying to break through to consciousness. Since it was the ego that prevented it from doing so, a great deal of psychoanalysis thenceforth was directed at analyzing the ego's defenses rather than interpreting unconscious wishes directly.

Freud's emerging theory of the ego was accompanied by a comprehensive transformation in the understanding of gender, one that psychoanalysis both reflected and advanced. Because of its emphasis on the defensive denial of vulnerability, the analytic understanding of shell shock brought with it a new picture of manhood, one that reflected the decline of the warrior ethic. Garfield Powell, a British army diarist incensed by antiwar talk during the Somme offensive, exclaimed: "Shellshock! Do they know what it means? Men become like weak children, crying and waving their arms madly, clinging to the nearest man and praying not to be left alone."[7] Captain McKechnie, in Ford Madox Ford's *Parade's End,* pleaded: "Why isn't one a beastly girl and privileged to shriek." In a fictionalized treatment of a historic episode, the novelist Pat Barker reconstructed the English doctor W. H. R. Rivers's reflections as he began to apply analytic methods to shell shock patients:

> In leading his patients to understand that breakdown was nothing to be ashamed of, that horror and fear were inevitable responses to the trauma of war, and were better acknowledged than suppressed, that feelings of tenderness for other men were natural and right, that tears were an acceptable and helpful part of grieving, [Rivers] was setting himself against the whole tenor of their upbringing. They had been trained to identify emotional repression as the essence of manliness. Men who broke down, or cried, or admitted to feeling fear, were sissies, weaklings, failures. Not *men.* And yet he himself was a product of the same system. . . . In advising his young patients to abandon the attempt at repression and to let themselves *feel* the pity and terror their war experience inevitably evoked, he was excavating the ground he stood on.[8]

Rivers treated the British poet Siegfried Sassoon for shell shock. Sassoon, wounded, deranged, later recalled Rivers walking into his hospital room: "Without a word he sat down by the bed; and his smile was benediction enough for all I'd been through. 'Oh Rivers, I've had such a funny time since I saw you last!' I exclaimed. And I understood that this is what I had been waiting for."[9]

The new awareness of male vulnerability was accompanied by a transformation in women's relations to men, especially their sexual relations. When Vera Brittain began nursing at the front in 1915, she had "never looked upon the nude body of an adult male." But "from the constant handling of their lean, muscular bodies," she not only found herself at home with physical love, but also was led "to think of the male of the species not as some barbaric, destructive creature who could not control his most violent instincts but as a hurt, pathetic, vulnerable, patient, childlike victim of circumstances far beyond his control."[10] The older identification of men with the warrior ethic persisted, as in Virginia Woolf's 1938 claim that the cause of war lay in men's desire for "other people's fields and goods," their insistence on making "frontiers and flags, battleships and poison gas," and their willingness to "offer up their own lives and their children's lives."[11] But for most other women, a new awareness of male vulnerability fostered interpersonal tenderness and responsiveness. The result was a conflict between the prewar suffragist mothers who had spoken regularly of the "sex war" and called marriage "legalized prostitution," and the postwar, jazz age, Freudian-influenced flappers who, the *New York Times* noted, could "take a man's view as her mother never could."[12] In short, a tendency toward reconciliation between the sexes began to emerge, based on each sex's awareness of its own and the other sex's vulnerabilities.

After the war, young men and women turned against the earlier honor code and the aristocratic society on which it had rested. Thomas Mann, reading a 1921 newspaper review of *Beyond the Pleasure Principle,* wrote in his diary that the book signaled the "end of Romanticism."[13] By this Mann meant to signal the role that romantic ideas of the warrior self and heroic sacrifice could play in bringing reactionary, ultimately fascist forces to power in Germany. In the hope of finding an alternative to romanticism, he turned to Freud's account of the fragile contingent ego, which stood in a force field "of destructive torrents and explosions," both internal and external.[14] Even the still distant

United States felt the force of the wartime revelations. In 1895 Oliver Wendell Holmes, a member of the Civil War generation, could still tell the Harvard graduating class that only in war could men pursue "the divine folly of honor."[15] In 1929 Ernest Hemingway wrote that words like *honor* and *glory* had become obscene.[16]

Postwar social democracy developed as the alternative to the older, honor-based aristocratic societies for three related reasons. It recognized and accepted human vulnerability, it recognized the new, more egalitarian, relations between men and women, and it sought to integrate the lower classes into an organic conception of democracy. Postwar European psychoanalytic culture was overwhelmingly social democratic in this sense. The first postwar psychoanalytic convention, held in Communist Budapest in 1918, passed a resolution urging analytic societies to prepare for "mass," i.e., publically financed, therapy. Freud explained: "the poor man should have just as much right to assistance for his mind as he now has to the life-saving help offered by surgery . . . the neuroses threaten public health no less than tuberculosis."[17] During the twenties and thirties most European analytic societies offered large numbers of low-cost analyses aimed at workers and their families. Analytic institutes offered public lectures targeted at the working classes, while the term *applied analysis* emerged to describe analytic work in nursery schools, child guidance clinics, teenage consultations, and social work. "Red Vienna," which donated a building to the analytic society, was especially supportive of what Elizabeth Danto called "Freud's free clinics."[18]

Postwar social democracy and reform was also infused with antiwar sentiment. The League of Nations was founded in 1919 with great hopes, and its covenant included such reforms as compulsory arbitration for international disputes, sanctions, and arms reduction. Maternalist feminists like Jane Addams and Helene Stöcker turned support for motherhood toward the antiwar cause. Nonviolence emerged to supplement civil disobedience as a serious philosophy on the left. Tolstoy's Christian anarchism was revived, as was his belief that it was the "masses of men" who were truly responsible for the crimes of the era and not their ostensible leaders, whom he compared to "the brooms fixed in front of the locomotive to clear the snow from the rails," meaning that the politicians called out empty moral slogans and *casus belli* in order to divert the masses from their own destructive passions. *Time* magazine made Gandhi their Man of the Year in 1930. In 1933 students began signing the "Oxford Pledge," which announced that under no circumstances would they support the "government in any war it may conduct."[19]

Prodded by the League of Nations, Freud and Albert Einstein exchanged letters over the question of war. In 1932 Freud asked Einstein, "How long shall we have to wait before the rest of mankind become pacifists too?" adding, "whatever fosters the growth of civilization works at the same time against war."[20] If we unpack this statement, we can understand Freud's thinking concerning war. As the product of the nineteenth-century classical education, Freud took "civilization" to mean political order and justice; Rome was the paradigmatic case. But by "civilization" he also meant, psychoanalytically, eros or the work of binding. Viewed psychoanalytically, vulnerability is the core of the human situation; the ego is important because it is the only part of the mind that can shed light into the darkness of the depths. In a 1926 work, Freud evoked the "biological factor" that underlay the dangers faced by the ego and the reasons for conflict in the mind:

> the long period of time during which the young of the human species is in a condition of helplessness and dependence. Its intra-uterine existence seems to be short in comparison with that of most animals, and it is sent into the world in a less finished state. As a result, the influence of the real external world upon it is intensified and an early differentiation between the ego and the id is promoted. Moreover, the dangers of the external world have a greater importance for it, so that the value of the object which can alone protect it against them and take the place of its former intra-uterine life is enormously enhanced. The biological factor, then, establishes the earliest situations of danger and creates the need to be loved which will accompany the child through the rest of its life.[21]

The political point here is that object love and family life, as well as education, psychotherapy, and political leadership (*virtu* in the classical sense of the term), can serve as binding forces that work to strengthen the ego and thereby extend the range of justice, peace, and political order against the destructiveness set off by helplessness.

Given the intense antiwar feeling of the time and the strength of social democratic and leftist sentiment, the basic question faced by antiwar forces was the extent to which capitalism had been the cause of World War I. Woodrow Wilson, following Montesquieu and John Stuart Mill, answered that question in a classically liberal way by insisting that commerce was an alternative to war and ultimately fostered international cooperation. Against Wilson, Vladimir Lenin held that war was intrinsic to capitalism, as industrial states seeking to expand into undeveloped agrarian parts of the world competed against one another. In *Civilization and Its Discontents* (1930), Freud challenged the assumption underlying Lenin's argument, namely that human beings are intrinsically good and that only "private property has corrupted his nature." Aggression, Freud wrote, "did not arise as the result of property . . . it shows itself already in the nursery." But in this challenge Freud was in no sense siding with Wilson. Rather he distinguished aggression, which can serve as a binding force, from the entropic, conservative, and repetitive forces within the mind that foster destruction and which can express themselves through commercial interactions, insofar as they are exploitative, as well as through their misguided abolition.

In Freud's late essay "Analysis Terminable and Interminable" we find the chilling words, provoked by the failures of analysts to achieve cures as well as by the impending world catastrophe,

> No stronger impression arises from the resistances during the work of analysis than of there being a force which is defending itself by every possible means against recovery and which is absolutely resolved to hold on to illness and suffering. . . . If we take into consideration the total picture made up of the phenomenon

of masochism immanent in so many people, the negative therapeutic reaction and the sense of guilt found in so many neurotics,
we shall no longer be able to adhere to the belief that mental
events are governed exclusively by pleasure. These phenomena
are unmistakable indications of the presence of a power in mental life which we will call the instinct of aggression or of destruction according to its aims, and which we trace back to the original death instinct of living matter.[22]

These words suggest a pessimism that the coming repetition of the horrors of the First World War, but on a much grander and more terrible
scale, validated.

## The London Blitz and the "Munich Complex"

The decline of the warrior ethic opened the problem of motivating a
democratic citizenry for war. During World War II this problem was
solved for Britain and the United States in the most efficient manner, namely through an attack from the outside. For the British, the
1939–40 German bombing of London, one observer wrote, was experienced as "a natural disaster, which fosters a single spirit of unity binding the whole people together."[23] Similarly, the Japanese bombing of
Pearl Harbor on December 7, 1941, a day "that will live in infamy," in
Franklin Roosevelt's famous phrase, had such a powerful effect that
in the year 2000, a full year before 9/11, the neoconservative Project
for a New American Century, directed by William Kristol and Robert
Kagan, was already ruminating on "some catastrophic and catalyz-
ing event—like a new Pearl Harbor" that could motivate Americans
for military action in the Middle East as they had been motivated for
action in the Far East and Europe earlier.[24]

Important as an attack from the outside was in motivating British and American support for World War II, there was also a new
basis for national solidarity, namely social democracy. Underlying
social democracy was a powerful new sense of the early mother-infant

relationship, exemplified by the terms *homeland* and *motherland*. During the First World War, Freud called the mother's body "the former *Heim* of all human beings," adding "whenever a man dreams of a place or a country and says to himself, while he is still dreaming: this place is familiar to me, I've been here before,' we may interpret the place as being his mother's genitals or her body."[25] In the United States, James Steinbeck's *Grapes of Wrath* (1939) ends with a young mother breast-feeding a starving vagrant, a symbol for nurturance, peace, and security. In turning toward the mother, psychoanalysis was both reflecting and advancing the maternalist iconography of social-democratic nationhood. This iconography shaped America and Britain's participation in World War II.

In building the welfare state, some believed that an entire nation could share a common project, as during the New Deal, or even that international relations could be solidaristic, as Popular Front Bolsheviks urged. For most people, however, as Robert Westbrook has shown, such universal ideals were too thin to justify the sacrifice of young men and women in war. In 1942 Norman Rockwell, asked by the *Saturday Evening Post* to illustrate what Rockwell regarded as Roosevelt's highfalutin rhetoric of the "four freedoms," intuited that modern citizenship rested on immediate, particularistic, and family-centered loyalties, not on dreams of universal brotherhood. Accordingly, Rockwell sought to render the Four Freedoms "in simple everyday scenes. Freedom of Speech—a New England town meeting. Freedom from Want—a Thanksgiving dinner." Freedom of religion became an older couple praying at a local church. Freedom from fear became a husband and wife tucking their children in at night. Aiming to express democratic ideals "in terms everybody can understand," Rockwell created a sense of the modern American nation as rooted in concrete particularistic experiences.[26]

Psychoanalysis, increasingly cast as a familial and mother-centered ideology in the 1930s and 1940s, spoke to that sense and thus played an important role in World War II. In the U.S., every doctor in the military was taught the basic principles of analysis; psychoanalytic theories of morale and group psychology informed estimations of the effects of civilian bombing; psychoanalytic theories of culture were used to design the occupations of Germany and Japan.[27] However, the fullest development of the psychoanalytic theory of the ego or, as it now appeared, *subject* occurred in Britain. There the stronger communal, class-conscious background, the passionate—Bloomsbury-inspired—interest in the new middle-class currents of personal life, and the large number of female analysts turned Freud's conception of the ego as reflecting the defensive denial of vulnerability into a full-fledged theory of the mother-infant relationship. Melanie Klein was the central figure in this transformation.

Klein's thought rested on the idea that the original basis of human society was matriarchal. After World War I, Bronislaw Malinowski, a Polish emigré to England, had returned from the Trobriand Islands claiming he could not locate a single myth of origin in which the father was assigned a role in procreation. In 1924 Robert Briffault's *The Mothers* argued that all forms of social organization arose from the need for prolonged maternal care. Lewis Mumford's *Technics and Civilization* (1934) portrayed the maternal village as the precursor of the paternal town. Based on the excavations of Minoan-Mycenean civilization in Crete, Jane Harrison reinterpreted Greek tragedies as reflecting the conflict between earth mother goddesses and patriarchal, militarized invaders, symbolized by Zeus. According to Harrison the "archpatriarchal *bourgeois*" (Zeus) imposed the heterosexual family on a matriarchal, chthonic, woman-centered order.[28]

With this matricentric paradigm in her background, Klein rethought psychoanalysis so that the psyche was understood to arise from, and never lose the connection to, the mother. This resulted in key differences from Freud. For Freud the main problem was strengthening the ego so as to give the individual freedom from impulses, from social pressures, and from impersonal representations of internalized authority. For Klein the problem was to forge and sustain personal relations, beginning with the relation to the mother. For both thinkers, the individual struggled to achieve goodness, but for Freud the struggle was Kantian and moral, whereas for Klein it was concrete and relational. For Freud, the internal world was dominated by the duty to respect

universal norms; for Klein, it was dominated by responsibility to particular others to whom one had incurred obligations resulting from
specific relations and circumstances. For Freud, the moral core of the
person was formed in conflicts deriving from the "laws" that constitute
our humanity, such as the incest taboo; for Klein, the core conflicts
reflected frustrations in obtaining basic needs, such as milk or attention, from immediate others and in the context of real or imagined
rivals or enemies. British analysts used this Kleinian or "relational" perspective to develop a "feminine" alternative to Freud—an ethic of care
instead of an ethic of justice. Largely, although not entirely, encompassing women, the Kleinian circle elaborated a new, mother-daughter,
mother-son, and sister-sister discourse that influenced Britain's self-
understanding during World War II.

In June, 1940, while the Battle of Britain raged, psychoanalyst Joan
Riviere wrote to Melanie Klein,

> When the first official mention of invasion began, the possibility
> of our work all coming to an end seemed so near, I felt we should
> all have to keep it in our hearts . . . as the only way to save it for
> the future. . . . Of course, I was constantly thinking of the psycho-
> logical causes of such terrible loss and destruction as may happen
> to mankind. So, I had the idea of your telling me (and then a
> group of us) everything you think about these causes. . . . First
> what you think about the causes of the German psychological
> situation, and secondly, of that of the rest of Europe and mainly
> the Allies, since the last war. To me the apathy and denial of the
> Allies, especially England, is not clear. (I never shared it.) How
> is it connected with what I call the "Munich" complex, the son's
> incapacity to fight for mother and country? . . . One great ques-
> tion is why it is so important to be brave and to be able to bear
> whatever happens. Everything in *reality* depends on this.[29]

In this letter Riviere cast Klein in the role of the mother. Thus she
asks Klein to instruct, and, in so doing, to protect her children in the

face of the emergency. Correspondingly, the most significant male role is not that of the husband or father but that of the son. The key question is whether the son has the capacity to fight for his mother, his sisters, and their children, which is to say, for those who are vulnerable. In her response Klein argued that the son should have learned from his own vulnerability in childhood, that is, from his relation to his mother, to feel responsibility for others. But the English sons are "absent," "plotting and scheming with the destructive father," supine in relation to phallic, "hard," and dangerous males, as the Nazis portrayed themselves. The same weakness that leads to what Klein saw as British men's unconscious complicity with fascism prevents them from recognizing their responsibilities to women and children. For her, accordingly, the relation to the mother means recognizing vulnerability and dependence. The relation to the mother is the key to ethical responsibility.

Klein's rethinking of the theory of the ego found expression in the British welfare state, which began to be constructed during the war, on the model of the famous Beveridge Report, which highlighted the mother-child relationship. The precipitating event behind the welfare state was the bombing of the working-class East End of London in 1942. After the bombing, the queen announced her support for socialized medicine, remarking, "The people have suffered so much."[30] The bombing resulted in the evacuation of approximately 3.5 million people to the countryside. Many of the evacuees were children, many of them poor, many separated from their mothers and fathers who remained behind to do war-related work.[31] The event helped the British to see themselves as a community organized around the need to protect vulnerable children.

This sense of the nation as a child-centered communal project was apparent in the sculptures of Henry Moore. The most celebrated work of art produced during the war, Moore's *Madonna and Child*, was unveiled in 1943. The sculpture resulted from the initiative of Reverend Walter Hussey, who wanted to see the Church of England retake its leading role in the arts. Hussey turned to Moore because of Moore's drawings of individuals and families who had occupied the London tubes, against official orders, during the Blitz. Moore's drawings symbolized the mingling of public and private in a city under siege, as well as the attempt to care for children in a semicommunal environment. The drawings, Hussey wrote, "possess a spiritual quality and a deep humanity as well as being monumental and suggestive of timelessness." At the dedication of the sculpture, Hussey told the congregation: "The Holy Child is the centre of the work, and yet the subject speaks of the Incarnation—the fact that the Christ was born of a human mother— and so the Blessed Virgin is conceived as any small child would in essence think of his mother, not as small and frail, but as the one large, secure, solid background to life."[32]

England's quasi-Christian idea of national unity based on a common relation to the mother also inspired an almost mythic sense of identification with core Western or European values. Whereas during World War I German music had been frowned upon and even banned, during World War II, the allied symbol for victory was the opening bars of Beethoven's Fifth Symphony (*V* in Morse code). Lunchtime concerts were held at the National Gallery (emptied of paintings), bombs sometimes exploding overhead. During one of the most famous concerts, filmed by the documentary filmmaker Humphrey Jennings, the pianist Myra Hess played Beethoven's *Appassionata* sonata followed by Bach's "Jesu, Joy of Man's Desiring." In Kenneth Clark's reminiscence, "in common with half the audience, I was in tears. This is what we had all been waiting for—an assertion of eternal values."[33]

George Orwell's essay "Socialism and the English Genius," written in London at the height of the bombardment, was a bit more skeptical about the feeling of familial solidarity, but affirmed it nonetheless. Orwell called Britain

> a family with the wrong members in control. A rather stuffy Victorian family . . . its cupboards bursting with skeletons. It has rich relations who have to be kowtowed to and poor relations who are horribly sat upon, and there is a deep conspiracy of silence about the source of the family income [the British Empire]. It is

a family in which the young are generally thwarted and most of the power is in the hands of irresponsible uncles and bedridden aunts. Still, it is a family. It has its private language and its common memories, and at the approach of an enemy it closes ranks.

What was needed, Orwell concluded, was a democratic revolution that would "break the grip of the monied class."[34] While a fully democratic revolution was not to be, to some extent Orwell's hopes were achieved in 1948 when Britain became the first Western country to provide free health care to the entire population, the first based not on the insurance principle, in which entitlement follows contribution, but on the principle of social citizenship, and the first to pay for psychological counseling, thanks to the lobbying of the British analysts.[35]

   In the course of advancing a new spirit of war based on concrete obligations to others, first British psychoanalysis, and then American, was remade as a theory of the mother-infant relationship. However, this object relations theory, as I have suggested, was ambiguous in its implications. On the one hand, by demonstrating the depth at which human beings are connected, it highlighted their struggle to create what Klein called "whole objects" in personal relations, art, and democratic social organization. In that sense it gave psychological depth to social democracy. At the same time, it began to lose the idea that reason or rationality was at the core of the individual, an idea espoused by such thinkers as Descartes, Spinoza, Locke, and Kant and profoundly extended by Freud. In that sense it weakened the ties between psychoanalysis and critical thought, spawning a therapeutic culture, but not one devoted to justice. Klein's successors, such as D. W. Winnicott, Harry Guntrip, and Ronald Fairbairn, resolved the ambiguity implicit in object relations by reducing the psyche to its intersubjective relations, in other words, to the demand for recognition. The result was a declining importance of the idea of the ego. As Peter Homans has written, "under the impress of . . . social structural change and augmented by national mourning over the losses inflicted by a terrible war . . . clinical and theoretical concerns with attachment, loss and the social world

of patients" replaced the analysis of the ego.[36] The fact that we find ourselves in a wholly different psychoanalytic landscape today is clear in
our third case study of the interplay between psychoanalysis and war,
Judith Butler's analysis of the U.S. response to 9/11.

## September Eleventh and the Problem
## of Burying the Dead

On September 11, 2001, nineteen radical Islamists hijacked four U.S.
airplanes and used three of them to attack the World Trade Center
and the Pentagon. The immediate response of people throughout the
world was one of sympathy and identification with the United States,
exemplified by the famous *Le Monde* headline, "We are all Americans."
The Bush administration, however, used the opportunity to pursue a
misguided war in Iraq, which turned much of the world against the
U.S. After the attacks, the U.S. began to use torture against suspected
terrorists, and Americans became accustomed to living in a heightened
atmosphere of fear. Barack Obama gained the Democratic presidential
nomination in 2008 largely by promising to reverse the Bush policies,
but on the fundamentals he perpetuated them. What, if anything, has
psychoanalysis to teach us about this event?

For an answer, I propose to examine the arguments made by the
philosopher Judith Butler in her 2003 book *Precarious Life*. Written in
almost immediate "response to conditions of heightened vulnerability
and aggression" that followed 9/11, Butler's book evokes a period when
"US boundaries were breached [and] an unbearable vulnerability was
exposed." Why, Butler asked, did vulnerability lead to military action
and aggression, rather than to the higher level of global communication that seemed possible in the immediate aftermath of the attack? As
we shall see, Butler's answer reflects the interweaving of contemporary
psychoanalysis with poststructuralism, feminism, and phenomenol-
ogy, especially the view that the ego is formed through recognition,
object relations, and language. In addition, I will draw on recent work

by the historian John Dower, which compares the American response to Pearl Harbor with the response to September 11.

Butler situates the American response to the attacks in the broad and familiar context of trauma. Firemen rushing into buildings that were already beginning to collapse, the confusion of New York City street life, the replaying of images, the towers in flames, the towers collapsing, the compulsive visits to "ground zero"—these are all responses to trauma. The mind is unprepared for the event, does not have the means to process it and is overwhelmed. Afterward, the mind goes back to the event, reliving it as if preparing to encounter it again. The aim is to master the event through repetition and thereby assimilate it to everyday consciousness.

As a trauma, the psychological essence of the attack lay in the breaching of boundaries. The wound or *piercing* (which is the Greek root for trauma) became a *site* for the reactivation of unconscious memories. Certainly, as Dower has recently argued, the attacks were experienced as a repeat of Pearl Harbor. George W. Bush wrote in his diary, "The Pearl Harbor of the Twenty-First Century took place today." Numerous newspapers bore such headlines as "New Day of Infamy," while a billboard on the Kennedy Expressway in Chicago emblazoned the legend "Never Forget!" between the two dates December 7, 1941 and September 11, 2001. Not only Pearl Harbor but World War II and the atomic bomb were also invoked. The famous photo of Marines raising the Stars and Stripes on Iwo Jima was recycled as a poster and postage stamp showing firemen raising the flag over the devastated World Trade Center site. The site, in turn, was renamed Ground Zero, until then a term reserved for the bombed out areas of Hiroshima and Nagasaki.

There were other parallels to be drawn between Pearl Harbor and 9/11. Both attacks had been foreseen for years, but the warnings were ignored not only because of an underestimation of the enemy's intelligence and will but also because a defensive psychological barrier had been erected by Americans to distance themselves from the possibility of enemy attacks. Before and during World War II, American understandings of Japan were blinded by racism. Likewise, before and after 9/11, Americans could not or were not willing to understand "Islamo-fascist" anger. In fact, beneath the barrier, there were many similarities between America and its attackers. During World War II, Japan was as racist as the United States. And in the era of 9/11 both the American leaders and the terrorists were caught up in quasi-religious modes of thought. Thus, the top-secret Pentagon reports to President Bush during the invasion of Iraq were headlined by biblical quotations, while Al Qaeda embraced the conviction that lethal shock tactics could undermine the spirit and will of the enemy, mirroring the rationale for the U.S. bombing of German and Japanese cities during World War II as well as for the U.S. invasion of Iraq.[37]

There were also important differences between Pearl Harbor and 9/11. Pearl Harbor fell upon a nation in which strong ties still existed among its people. These ties were considerably weakened by 2001. The disputed election the year before the attacks provided a kind of X-ray into the American body politic: nodes of disease, murrains of corruption. World War II was waged through universal military service, but the draft was abolished in 1973, after the war in Vietnam. After 9/11, while the code of sacrifice was still honored in principle, the only demand President Bush placed on the country was to "keep shopping." The country's historic predisposition to mobilize technological superiority in the service of *in*vulnerability, while present in 1941, had been heightened by 2001 by the new quasi-personalized digital and electronic technology. "The electro-shock of repeated doses of the unreal and the unbelievable," as Frederic Jameson wrote, prepared the way for a culture of paranoia and victimhood.[38] Finally the American sense of being "exceptional," a term that Tocqueville had coined to indicate that the U.S. was sui generis, had taken on the connotation of "superior" by 1941. By way of contrast, in 2001 the country had gone through several decades of worrying that it was losing its exceptionalness and entering into decline.

Even so, the U.S. response to the attacks was not predetermined. The hijackers chose the World Trade Center and the Pentagon as icons of U.S. power. Yet, many Americans responded by attempting to *dere-ify* those iconic objects into the individuals that comprised them. One could see such attempts in the pictures of the "missing" found on public walls in New York for many weeks afterward, the *New York Times* project of publishing capsule biographies sometimes with pictures of each and every victim, and the attempt to find every shard or bone fragment by which an individual could be identified, even though this prolonged the clean-up process and deferred the achievement of what was called "closure." In this process the ordinary and the everyday were infused with personal meaning. The shopping emporia and the office suites of the World Trade Center no longer appeared as sites of consumerism and shady high-finance dealing, but as life-worlds suffused with individual aspirations. Equally important was the face-to-face recognition that marked the normally impersonal streets of New York as strangers recognized, with a new level of depth, they inhabited a common world.

Nevertheless, very quickly the human response of sadness and the desire to connect to others was aborted. Ten days after the attack, Bush addressed Congress, saying, "Our grief has turned to anger and anger to resolution. Whether we bring our enemies to justice or bring justice to our enemies, justice will be done." The characteristic expressions of self-righteous victimhood appeared: the constant replaying of images of the towers in flames, the pilgrimages to the site, the wearing of the American flag. Jacques Derrida, in New York several weeks after the attack, remarked: "Not only is it impossible not to speak on this subject, but you feel or are made to feel that it is actually *forbidden,* that you do not have the right, to begin speaking of anything . . . without making an always somewhat blind reference to this date."[39]

In seeking to understand why the balance of forces led away from intersubjective sadness and deliberation and toward vengeful, blind reaction, Butler stressed the agonizing experience of violated vulnerability, the nakedness the attacks lay bare, the shame of being naked and exposed, and the inability to bear that shame; in other words, the same defensive denial of vulnerability that had animated analytic thought in the previous two wars. However, she also added something new. She saw that if the experience of being violated was not to generate a cycle of retribution and counterretribution, it had to be followed by communication between victim and aggressor. To this end she drew upon the teachings of the phenomenological tradition, and especially on philosopher Emmanuel Levinas's emphasis on face-to-face recognition. According to Levinas, "the approach to the face [is] the most basic mode of responsibility." Through the injunction to look at the face of the other, Levinas was trying to get at the primary, precognitive core in which human vulnerability shows itself: communication with a particular other. From psychoanalysis we are used to this vulnerability in considering the infant's relation to the mother, and even the patient's (nonvisual) relation to the analyst, but Levinas added the awareness of mortality. In his words, the gaze of the other ultimately "is the other before death, looking through and exposing death. . . . The face is the other who asks me not to let him die alone."

Butler drew on this most primal of fears, the fear of dying alone, to pierce through the chaos and violence of September 11 and reestablish the intersubjective world that the attack and the president's foolish and malevolent response to the attack had disrupted. To do this she not only had to look beyond the victim-enemy mind frame, but also to penetrate the large group/mass media or spectacle character of the event, which threatened loss of identity even as it created an imagined community or, rather, an imagined public. How, she asked, is it possible to sustain intersubjectivity with any concreteness in the age of the spectacle? For Butler, the thread leading to genuine intersubjectivity was the recognition of vulnerability. For Freud, this recognition lay behind the autonomy of the ego; for Klein, it was the key to the creation of whole objects, and now for Butler it became the key to democratic deliberation in the midst of the first major twenty-first-century war.

Since the recognition of vulnerability, for Butler, was an effort to rebuild the intersubjective ties that had been shattered, that recognition entailed the creation of an intersubjective narrative. According to Butler, everyone in the United States remembers where they were and what they were doing when they learned that the planes hit the towers. But everyone begins the story of that day by invoking a first-person narrative point of view. That narrative is part of a healing process, an attempt to rebuild a shattered world. As Butler writes, "a narrative form emerges to compensate for the enormous narcissistic wound opened up by the public display of our physical vulnerability." But, she continues, the first-person restoration of narcissism is not sufficient. Also necessary is a process of decentering and reintegration. The goal, Butler argues, is "the ability to narrate ourselves not from the first person alone, but from, say, the position of the third, or to receive an account delivered in the second." In other words, we need to be able to decenter ourselves from our own ego, and narrate our experience not only personally but also from the point of view of the wounding and wounded other.

In achieving the goal of intersubjectivity, *mourning* plays a critical part. Through mourning, as Freud argued, we retain our connection to an object that no longer exists, even though this causes us pain. Mourning, then, is intersubjective; it incorporates the dead into our present-day egos and in that way into an ongoing human community. Mourning also is linked to justice, as is suggested by the common Old French root of the words *grievance* and *grief, grever*, which means sadness.[40] To understand 2001, then, Butler's argument is that we must broaden the circle of mourning, beyond the universal obligations recognized by Freud and beyond the particularistic loyalties described by the object-relational schools. Counterintuitive as it may seem, we have to rethink the community's economy of grieving if we are to prevent future 9/11s and future wars in Iraq. This rethinking implies transcending the nation-state.

In Butler's view, "the differential allocation of grievability," in the sense of its restriction to the nation-state, operates to produce and maintain exclusionary conceptions of "what counts as a livable life and a grievable death." While American deaths are "consecrated in public obituaries that constitute so many acts of nation-building," the names, images, and narratives of those whom the U.S. kills are suppressed. Our capacity to mourn beyond the nation is foreclosed by our failure to conceive of Arab lives *as lives* worth mourning. Guantanamo becomes the purgatorial locus of "unlivable lives." The result, Butler suggests, is that many, excluded from the circle of grievability, die alone, while the homeland itself suffers "a national melancholia," the result of "disavowed mourning." In arguing this point, Butler was relying on the profound way that psychoanalysis was rooted in a global—archaeological and anthropological—perspective that had been lost in the era of the social-democratic nation-state, but she was also calling attention to the importance of mourning.

According to Butler, the unique place that mourning occupies in the building and preservation of intersubjective ties rests on the way it entails a loss of control or the acceptance of vulnerability. Grief, she writes, entails "moments in which one undergoes something outside one's control and finds that one is beside oneself, not at one with oneself." In mourning one *submits* to a transformation that "de-constitutes choice at some level." Thus mourning disrupts a bounded and protective sense of self as one "accepts that by the loss one undergoes one will be changed, possibly forever." "When we lose someone we do not always know what it is *in* that person that has been lost."[41] We lose not just the person but also our former sense of identity. Grief, therefore "contains the possibility of apprehending a mode of dispossession that is fundamental to who I am." It exposes "my unknowingness, the unconscious imprint of my primary sociality." Butler ends her reflection with a question: What form might "political reflection and deliberation take if we take injurability and aggression as [our] points of departure for political life," rather than independence and self-mastery. What form would our politics take, in other words, if we began from "an understanding of how easily human life is annulled?"

Butler's analysis of 9/11 helps clarify the nature of the political Freudian tradition that has sought to comprehend war. In the three case studies considered here, solidarity based on awareness of our common vulnerability lies at the center of that tradition. In the first episode, the encounter with World War I, we see men's defensive wish to avoid vulnerability. In the second, object relations during World War II, we see a corresponding responsibility to protect loved ones. In the third, the "War on Terror," we see defensive reactions among the population at large aimed at warding off vulnerability as well as the possibility of a counterproject aimed at achieving solidarity in mourning and beyond. All three moments reflect an expanding sense of human connection: from the self to immediate others, especially the family, and then to the nation, and finally, potentially, to the global community as a whole. In his letter to Einstein, Freud called this widening "civilization," meaning *eros* or binding, the work of the life instinct. In each case the awareness of human vulnerability connects individuals to one another while also broadening the circle of those who feel solidarity through shared feelings of vulnerability.

At the same time, Butler's insistence that we take "an understanding of how easily human life is annulled" as a point of departure for political life can lead in two different directions. In one scenario, the focus on vulnerability is normative; it moves to the core of ethics and politics. In the other, it is genetic; it explains where we come from, but not who we are. The difference leads to two different political positions. In the first, normative case, our deepening understanding of vulnerability *displaces* the liberal emphasis on individual rights in favor of a politics of recognition and mutual support. In the second, genetic case it *imbues* a liberal polity with an awareness of the inherent vulnerability of the subject, but does not displace the preexisting paradigm of individual rights. In my view, the psychoanalytic picture of the mind, which begins in prolonged dependence but culminates in the autonomous ego, tends toward the latter option. It revises the liberal social contract theory, which so often served as a cloak for destructiveness, as it did for Woodrow Wilson, and as it did for Bush, but it does not abandon the core ideal of the liberal tradition, which comes down to us from the Reformation and from the Enlightenment, that the keystone of all progress is the independent, free-thinking individual. In other words, the political Freudian tradition concerning war suggests that we will be in a better position to avert, limit, and ultimately end war if we consider our fellow human beings not only as vulnerable bodies but also as potentially rational coequal participants in creating the binding forces of civilization and resisting the destructive forces, both internal and societal.

In this regard, the words of Fred Weinstein and Gerald Platt are worth considering: "From the standpoint of psychic structure . . . the important development historically has been the strengthening of the ego." This strengthening has been the result of the radical "break with authority in religion, politics, economics and the family." This break— "not the productive facilities . . . established nor [the] commitment to rationality *as such*"—has been the signal contribution of modern progressive movements.[42] Freud's theory of the ego belongs in this tradition. It was formulated during what is often called the general crisis of the twentieth century, marked by the rise of mass propaganda, images, and charismatic father figures, and is centered on the difficulty, above all the internal difficulty, of attaining and preserving individual autonomy or freedom. As such works as Erich Fromm's *Escape from Freedom* (1940) suggested, the move from communal to individualistic societies was fraught, and humanity was always prone to relapse into infantile dependencies and paranoid fears. Psychoanalysis was important because it caught that transition. The point of its revelations of the depth of human vulnerability was to *deepen* rationality, independence, and self-mastery, in other words, to *strengthen* what political theorist Masao Maruyama, writing in Japan amid the crisis that followed World War II and the bombing of Hiroshima, called "the modern ego"—the ego that stands up to injustice or bullying—an effort that runs through the enormous Popular Front literature on family, education, culture, and politics.

The problem posed by 9/11 is the same. Anyone who lived through that event will remember the huge, passionate waves of fear, enforced loyalty, and sidelining of dissent that swept over the country and continue to this day. But if we are to understand what happened to America after 9/11, a liberal perspective is not enough. Butler explains the mass psychology of fear by the intensity of the blow to American narcissism, in other words, to American identity or the American "self," but she does not ask how American narcissism became so fragile as to produce such a twisted, warped, and self-destructive response. Missing from her account is the liberal drive to extend and render autonomous market relations, which had already atomized the public when it responded to 9/11 by enabling the invasion of Iraq. Seen by classic liberals as the locus of rationality, the disembedded market also eroded or decimated collective ties, whether in the form of communities, trade unions, cooperatives, or the welfare state, and thereby obscured the role that the recognition of dependency plays in binding the social world together, including in this respect the market itself. There is a difference, then, which Butler misses, between the narrow self-interested ego presumed by neoclassical (i.e., liberal) economics and rational choice political science, on the one hand, and the self-reflective ego with its deep connections to the unconscious, as described by Freud, on the other. The Marxist critique of the market is an indispensable supplement to Freud here. As a product of the cultural revolution of the 1970s and 1980s, and therefore lacking the anticapitalist perspective still alive in the earlier political Freudian tradition, Butler's approach fails to grasp that deepening the web of connections that enable collective action coheres with strengthening the ego, as Freud understood it. The true force of the tradition of political Freud lies in its refusal to counterpose dependence and independence as if they were antitheses. It demonstrates rather that the ego reaches down into its earliest, most primal, and essentially immortal dependencies precisely when it is strongest and most independent.

# 5

## From the Maturity Ethic to the Psychology of Power

*The New Left, Feminism, and the Return to "Social Reality"*

Psychoanalysis and the Long 1960s

When we talk about the role of psychoanalysis in repressive or authoritarian societies, we typically have in mind Nazi Germany and Vichy France, where forms of psychoanalysis were practiced, as well as the Soviet Union and Eastern Europe, where analysis was banned but continued to exert an underground influence. More recently, we have come to think about psychoanalysis in the Latin American dictatorships: its hermeticism, its complicity, and its counterintuitive flourishing. But what is the role of psychoanalysis in nominally democratic societies like the United States? Are questions of authority, authoritarianism, and repression relevant there?

In the 1960s New Leftists answered these questions with a resounding yes. According to them, an ostensibly apolitical or "neutral" psychoanalysis was in fact deeply political, serving the cold war elites. Ego psychology and the maturity ethic, as I will term the predominant psychoanalytic worldview of the time, were integral to what has been called the "administered society" of postwar America, infusing the work of school psychologists, guidance counselors, urban planners, medical doctors, therapists, juvenile court justices, and religious counselors. The maturity ethic stressed the strength and adaptability of the ego in the practical world, while also maintaining that the deeper experiences of life were to be found in the private realm. Its essence was its rejection of "utopian," i.e., left-wing, politics of the sort that had characterized the United States during the New Deal. In Philip Rieff's formulation, maturity implied "an attitude of ironic insight on the part of the self toward all that is not self." Maturity required withdrawing from "the painful tension of assent and dissent" in relation to society in order to relate more affirmatively to one's depths.[1]

In challenging the maturity ethic, New Leftists were effectively insisting that psychoanalysis supported a repressive system of authority in a putatively democratic society. To challenge that system, New Leftists expounded a range of theories, including critiques of objectivity and scientism, the idea of "repressive tolerance," meaning that dissent was accepted so long as it remained impotent, and the idea of "repressive desublimation," meaning instinctual release that sustained existing power rather than challenging it. In doing so, they often relied on *anti*authoritarian trends within the analytic tradition itself. Drawing especially on Herbert Marcuse's *Eros and Civilization* (1955) and Norman O. Brown's *Life Against Death* (1959), New Leftists rejected the goal of ego autonomy and embraced instead the idea of an "oceanic feeling," or primal unity, rooted in the infant's earliest relation to the mother. Associated historically with the mystic's dissolution of the self, the oceanic feeling resonated with the carnivalesque experiences of the 1960s, such as the fervor of the crowd, the blurring of sexual boundaries and "polymorphous perversity," the eroticization of the entire body. From the new if unstable ground of a dissolved or boundless self, New

Leftists challenged analytic complicity with the cold war, its idealization of the private sphere, and the maturity ethic.

Before long, however, in the 1970s, a new set of social movements, especially radical feminism and gay liberation, supplanted the New Left. Whereas the New Left had distinguished a repressive psychoanalysis from an emancipatory one, most radical feminists rejected Freud *in toto*. Characterizing Freud as the fount of twentieth-century sexism and homophobia, they attacked such ideas as penis envy, the vaginal orgasm, and the female castration complex as if they were the whole of analysis. After some debate, analysts themselves took on board a good portion of the critique. In the ensuing paradigm shift, the study of the unconscious gave way to a critique of power relations, sexuality gave way to gender, bisexuality gave way to androgyny, analytic restraint and neutrality gave way to relational psychotherapy. Yet it would be hard to claim that the problem of repressive authority, identified by the New Left, had been resolved. In fact, just as the maturity ethic complemented the military Keynesianism of the fifties, so the new feminist-inspired relational therapeutic paradigm complemented the market revolution of the seventies.

These three episodes—the rise of the maturity ethic, the New Left's antinomian overturning of that ethic, and radical feminism's fervent and wholesale rejection of Freud—had an intensity, even ferocity, to them, that reflected the centrality of psychoanalysis to U.S. culture at that time. In chapter 1 I sought to elucidate this centrality by arguing that psychoanalysis played a critical role in mediating between an older Protestant ethic, characterized by savings, compulsivity, and hypocrisy, and the post-Fordist ethic that emerged in the 1970s, characterized by hedonism (or narcissism), flexibility, and empowerment. In the present chapter I want to develop that idea by foregrounding the changes in the nature of traditional authority, and especially the family, that were intrinsic to the changes in the spirit of capitalism.

My argument runs roughly like this: the New Deal and World War II created the economic conditions—Keynesianism—for the shift from restraint to release that led to the new spirit of capitalism. But it simultaneously unleashed a revolution in the structure of familial and societal authority. The result was the demise of an older, status-bound, WASP-dominated America in which immigrants were not recognized as Americans, even after they gained citizenship, Black males were referred to as "boy," and women worked outside the home only when they were single, Black, or Irish. In place of an obsolescent status hierarchy, reforming elites sought to create a rationalized society based not on traditional authority but on internalized self-control. Psychoanalysis, in the form of ego psychology, was enlisted in this project. Rationalization weakened traditional authority but substituted the adjustment, labeling, and manipulation that the New Left criticized. At the same time, the import of psychoanalysis exceeded the project of social control. As a charismatic source of meaning, analysis embodied powerful sexual and other emancipatory currents that key socializing institutions, above all the family, could not contain. By the 1960s, antinomian upsurges linked to analysis overflowed the boundaries of the new socializing agencies, the heterosexual family, and the welfare state, inspiring both the New Left and the new social movements, especially feminism and gay liberation. The result was ironic and unintended: although these currents viewed themselves as critical of capitalism, they helped to bring about the revolution in family structure and authority relations that converged with the new post-Fordist spirit of capitalism.

To grasp the changes that occurred in the 1960s, along with the changes that did not, it will be helpful to recall the experience of the Puritans, who founded so much of American civilization. Puritanism was itself a cultural revolution aimed at the medieval worldview, in other words against traditional authority. In Freudian terms, the original Puritan moment was also a *Geistigkeit* moment, in the sense explained in chapter 3. Because of the momentous implications of predestination, the Puritans were forced into a new form of introspection, asking themselves: Am I really saved? Am I really good? However, just as Mosaic monotheism did not last, so the intense self-questioning of the Puritans did not survive the growth of capitalism and of new democratically inclined masses. Instead Puritan overattention to the demands of the superego produced two heresies: antinomianism, which claimed to know God through direct experience, and Arminianism, which claimed to reach salvation through good works. Arminianism, expressed in such ideologies as the self-made man, the can-do spirit, and America's self-definition as a "land of opportunity," predominated because it converged with the American preoccupation with economic life. Nevertheless, the country veered regularly into antinomian periods, "Great Awakenings," radical upsurges, and periods of communal aspiration that renewed and revised the Arminian tradition, feeding it, so to speak, from the well of primary narcissism. The 1960s were just such an antinomian period. Afterward, as in the case of the Puritans, the original tendency toward guilt and self-abasement did not disappear, but emerged, strengthened, in the form of political correctness.

In describing the upheavals of the years from the 1950s to the 1970s in a way that restores psychoanalysis to its important place, I hope also to explain why we need the tradition of political Freud today. There is a different way to tell the story of the long 1960s from mine: the liberal story of how a country based on ideals of freedom and equality unwittingly ignored slavery, patriarchy, and ethnic hatred at the time of its founding, but gradually improved itself, always perfecting its inner convictions, so that the civil rights movement, the women's movement, and the other protest movements of the sixties were essentially fulfillments of a foundational dream. There is an important truth to this story, but it is also partial and distorted. It ignores the deep, psychic structure of the individuals who comprise society and the deep structure of capitalist society itself.

As early as 1835, Alexis de Tocqueville warned that democracy was double-edged. On the one hand, it tended to erode "social" or "aristocratic" distinctions, such as those of race and sex; on the other hand, it created a new hierarchy based on "manufactures."[2] That is what happened in the 1960s and 70s, although finance, not manufacturing, was the agent of change. Tocqueville intuited, to use our terms, that as *cultural* inequality weakened, *structural* inequality would strengthen;

in other words, that an intrinsically capitalist society such as America could achieve meritocracy but would resist equality. By examining the long 1960s through the lens of structures of authority historically rooted in the family and today exerted through personal life we may approach the deeper understanding toward which Tocqueville's *aperçu* points. At root, the conflicts of the 1960s were conflicts over what psychoanalysts called the father imago, over the relations of men and women, and over the place of the unconscious in society, all of which pervade and buttress the class structure that gives America its truest and deepest character. What emerged from these conflicts was a profound mutation in both the structure of capitalism and in the psyche of the individuals comprising it. Tracing the role played by political Freudianism makes this clear.

## The Maturity Ethic

In August 1945, a few months after Franklin Roosevelt's death, the United States dropped atomic bombs on Hiroshima and Nagasaki. The dawning of the atomic age brought to a terrible end World War II's unprecedented pain and misery. Writing in the *Saturday Review*, Norman Cousins described "a primitive fear, the fear of the unknown [which] has burst out of the subconscious and into the conscious, filling the mind with primordial apprehensions."[3] At the same time, the tragic fate of the Russian Revolution was politicized through the still little understood outburst of McCarthyism, the largest wave of repression in American history. Ten thousand people suspected of having Communist sympathies lost their jobs with barely a peep of protest.[4] On the contrary, a new anticommunist ideology, exemplified by Whittaker Chambers's *Witness*, described the West as sick and helped spawn a paranoid mentality based on the themes of suspicion, victimhood, and witnessing. Fifty years later it was possible to recognize Chambers's influence when conservative spokesperson Ann Coulter wrote that the liberals "have the media, the universities, the textbooks. We have ourselves. We are the witnesses."[5]

American liberal elites responded to the traumatic explosion of McCarthyism in two successive waves. To begin with, they created the national security state, a unified pattern of attitudes, policies, and institutions designed to put the United States on a permanent war footing.[6] Although a postwar conflict between the Soviet Union and the United States was almost inevitable, given the vacuum created by the destruction of the Third Reich, the national security state turned that conflict into a highly ideological global crusade that persists even now, over two decades after the collapse of communism, in the form of the "war on terror." Eventually, however, liberals condemned McCarthyism as a form of irrational populism, a condemnation classically expressed in Richard Hofstadter's 1965 essay "The Paranoid Style in American History." Opposition to what liberal elites regarded as the paranoia and unbridled aggressivity of the right wing confirmed their turn toward a new, technocratic, "growth"-oriented liberalism that supplanted the New Deal and created the context in which the maturity ethic flourished.

The heart of the new, technocratic liberalism was a politics of economic growth centered on familial consumption. Economics, so the theory went, was "transpolitical." In other words, economic growth would allow the country to bypass the divisiveness and conflict that had characterized the New Deal era and provoked the McCarthyist outbreak.[7] Political scientists espoused pluralism as the political complement to economic growth. Rejecting the New Deal conception of capitalism as the deep structure of American society, they portrayed "business" as one interest group among others, such as unions, churches, or neighborhood associations. Drawing on the ideologies of both growth and pluralism, liberal thinkers such as Arthur Schlesinger Jr. advocated a post-New Deal politics cleansed of "ideology" and "class struggle." As Schlesinger explained, American reform divides between those "who regard liberalism as a practical program to be put into effect; and those . . . who use liberalism as an outlet for private grievances and frustrations."[8] Both left and right, Schlesinger held, were more concerned with the symbolic aspects of politics than they were with practical results.[9]

The idea that "extremists" translated "private grievances and frustrations" into politics was fertile ground for a debased reading of psychoanalysis. Freud had been a Zionist, and a Social Democrat, who referred in the twenties to the Bolshevik Revolution as a "great experiment." But, according to political scientist Harold Lasswell, Freud's work demonstrated that radical politics was driven by irrational needs originating in the private sphere.[10] Psychologizing the "true believer" or "revolutionary personality" stiffened the resolve of a liberal tradition that had lost credibility by enabling McCarthy. Whereas, during the Popular Front, Freud's emphasis on the difficulty of self-knowledge informed democratic reform, now it infused an antidemocratic technocratic liberalism with curdled fervor. The liberal co-opting of psychoanalysis—the repudiation of political Freud—compromised the maturity ethic from the first.

The cold war liberal turn toward Freud was accompanied by a rediscovery of the Puritans. Perry Miller's profound interpretations of the Augustinian moment in Puritanism in *The New England Mind*, published in two volumes in 1939 and 1953, became canonical. What struck readers especially was the high intellectual level of the Puritans, as well as their contempt for shallow "Pelagian" rejections of the ideas of predestination and original sin, their scorn for fatuous conceptions of free will, and their appreciation of the snares of narcissism, which Miller termed "self-hood." As intellectuals recast American history as American studies, freed from the "populist" bias of progressive historiography, they saw the Puritan moment as an anticipation of their version of Freudianism. Just as the Puritan, Max Weber wrote, "was forced to follow his path alone to meet a destiny which had been decreed for him from eternity," so the Freudian was condemned to be alone with his unconscious. How shallow the Popular Front seemed when one understood, in Philip Rieff's Freudian-inflected words, that social relations no longer defined man. Rooted in the Puritan revolution, remade by modernism, populated by Jewish Americans and ex-Communists, the New York intellectual culture that promoted psychoanalysis in the 1950s placed the highest value on irony, complexity, and ambiguity, while despising the "simple," "reductionist" materialism of the story-book Marxist.

Moreover, the United States had provided a nurturant soil for psychoanalysts, many of whom immigrated in the 1930s and 1940s. Thanks in part to its Puritan beginnings, in the nineteenth century the country had pioneered the ideas of psychological illness and psychotherapy, identifying the world's first psychologically defined illness, neurasthenia, in 1869. Freud's 1909 Clark Lectures, delivered in the original Puritan redoubt of New England, turned him into a world figure at a time when he was still largely ignored in Europe. While the Depression generated such headlines as "Farewell to Freud," analytic psychiatry actually exploded in the 1930s. But it was above all World War II, the greatest engine of mass rationalization and social control in history, that made psychoanalysis central to the U.S. Every doctor in the military was taught its basic principles and encouraged to use them not only for recruitment and training but to manage the interpersonal dimensions of medicine.[11] After the war, when doctors could not meet the demand for psychological treatment, the newly founded professions of clinical psychology and psychiatric social work stepped into the breach. The year 1947, which witnessed an intensification of the cold war, was "something of a gold rush" for analysts, who increasingly ran America's psychiatric profession, hospitals, and training programs.[12] Six years later, the president of the American Psychoanalytic Association celebrated the fact that his science had "finally become legitimate and respectable" in contrast to its checkered career in Europe.[13]

Just as Puritanism meant a break with medieval communal controls and a shift toward individual responsibility, so the postwar therapeutic revolution was based on the idea of internalized self-control. The traditional psychiatrist embodied what Michel Foucault has called "repressive power," in other words, paternal authority, the sort that a father imposes on a well-ordered family. By contrast, under the impact of ego psychology, as the émigré analysts termed their project, psychiatry became a "psychodynamic" discipline, aimed at strengthening what Michel Foucault called "productive power," power that works "not from the outside but from within . . . not by constraining individuals and their actions but by producing them."[14] Numerous depictions of psychiatry in films of the period, such as Anatol Litvak's *The Snake Pit* (1948), contrasted the old-style, ham-handed psychiatrist, still oriented to isolation, electroshock, and other forms of repressive power, to the newer "talking therapies." Typically, the turning point in these films occurs when analysts refused to retaliate against their patient's anger, thus working not from the outside of the patient, but from within, giving individuals the "space" in which they could generate the desired self-control or ego autonomy.

Freud's theory of the ego, formulated during World War I, was ideally situated for the project of internalized self-control. In classical psychoanalytic treatment (as with monotheism in Freud's interpretation), the powerful instinctual drives of the unconscious were not to be repressed but rather frustrated by the analyst's refusal to satisfy them. In theory the result would be that patients would learn to sublimate, turning their instinctual energies away from immediate sensual gratifications and toward insight, rational thought, or *Geistigkeit*. But sublimation was not inevitable. Thus Freud's approach could inform the new therapeutic modalities as well as the new liberal theories of management and political order. In 1942, for example, Talcott Parsons advised Franklin Roosevelt that in order to avoid the kind of antiwar hysteria that had plagued World War I, the government should decline to respond "to hostile interpretations of government policy—thus defeating them in the manner of a therapist whose non-responsive behavior" undermines the "patient's neurotic perceptions by withholding confirmation from them."[15] Five years later, George F. Kennan's containment policy was based on the same idea, namely that a calm, unintimidating presence on Soviet borders would force the Soviets to change internally, eventually generating rationality, whereas military interventions and "tests" of resolve would deepen Soviet paranoia. As these examples suggest, the maturity ethic was not, in reality, apolitical but rather aimed at a higher level of individual responsibility and autonomy than the imagined leftism against which it was directed. In the words of Erik Erikson, cited in chapter I, a mature person was "tolerant of differences, cautious and methodical in evaluation, just in judgment, circumspect in action, and capable of faith and indignation."[16]

While the maturity ethic linked analysis with liberal ideals of integrity and fairness, it also aimed at keeping emotionally charged or so-called moral issues out of politics. Psychoanalysts, and the many professionals influenced by them, were called upon to help damp down "excessive" outbreaks of public emotion, which was considered especially important in the nuclear age. The Korean War (1950–1953), which killed several million Koreans and tens of thousands of Americans, was accompanied by very few antiwar demonstrations of the sort that exploded with the war in Vietnam. Arthur Miller could "not help suspecting that psychoanalysis was . . . being used as a substitute not only for Marxism but for social activism of any kind."[17] Analysts policed "excesses" of conscience precipitated by the McCarthy investigations. When the actor Sterling Hayden reported that "the FBI isn't going to let me off the hook without my implicating people who never did anything wrong," his analyst advised, "the FBI would probably treat this information confidentially."[18]

The counterpart to the postwar cooling out of protest and rancor was the infusion of private life with intensity and purpose. Christopher Lasch, writing autobiographically, situated the analytically inflected turn toward private life historically. "My generation," Lasch wrote, "invested personal relations with an intensity they could hardly support, as it turned out; but our passionate interest in each other's lives cannot very well be described as a form of emotional retreat. We tried to re-create in the circle of our friends the intensity of a common purpose, which could no longer be found in politics or the workplace."[19] Lasch's words suggest the transformation of family life that the maturity ethic promoted. The maturity ethic meant the rejection not only of the traditional working-class family based on paternal authority but also of the New Deal era's male, homosocial, adolescent world of "mates" or "buddies." It meant reorienting men to the heterosexual dyad, to acceptance of the responsibilities of marriage, and to friendship networks that included both sexes. The maturity ethic also applied to women. As we saw in chapter 1, in the 1956 movie *The Man in the Grey Flannel Suit*, the wife (Jennifer Jones) learns of her husband's wartime affair with a Roman woman, overcomes her wounded narcissism, recommits to her marriage, and agrees to accept financial responsibility for her husband's war child, thus symbolizing America's financial responsibility for Italy in the mid-1950s.

Just as Puritanism was a post-traditional, individualizing ethic that placed high expectations on its followers, so too was psychoanalysis. This, however, was also its Achilles heel. A kind of internalized authoritarianism or identification with the aggressor, perpetuated through the training process itself, often led postwar analysts to despise what they saw as "weakness" in their patients. That, more than anything, explains their much noted "coldness"—sadism, really—toward women such as Annie Parsons who were rejected for analytic training for failure "to come to terms with their basic feminine instincts"; toward male homosexuals, such as Howard Brown, told by his analyst that he "was inherently impaired because of my sexual orientation"; toward victims of sexual discrimination, characterized by at least one analyst as "injustice collectors"; and toward "narcissistic patients," whose problems analysts blamed for their countless "failed" analyses. The ego psychologists, many of whom were émigré Jews seeking acceptance, identified with powerful male authority in the United States, which put them on the wrong side of the sixties as the decade unfolded.

Ironically, however, other currents of analysis, especially those focused on sexual love, were central to the revolt against the maturity ethic. Sexual love, as Max Weber wrote, was "as radical as possible in its opposition to all functionality, rationality and generality." "The lover realizes himself to be rooted in the kernel of the truly living . . . freed from the cold, skeleton hands of rational orders."[20] By the late fifties, the explosiveness of sexuality and the unconscious was coinciding with a youth rebellion. Jack Kerouac's *On the Road* (1957), with its "intense, out-of-focus hurtling across America, the absolute lack of social pretensions, the seeking of something somehow important, somewhere, the experimentation with life and the gobbling of books . . . showed an American youth different from any before."[21] Meanwhile, a work contemporaneous with Kerouac's, David Riesman's *The Lonely Crowd*, dated the growing demotic spirit of youth to the death of Henry Ford in 1947, which symbolically precipitated a shift from inner- to outer-directedness or, in psychoanalytic terms, from the ego to the self.[22] One of the great episodes of antinomian boundlessness in American history was about to begin.

## The New Left and Antinomianism

In the early 1960s a new spirit of hope entered Western societies. The context was the epochal transition from traditional or "repressive" authority to new forms of individualizing empowerment, which had begun in the 1950s. This shift was not easily contained. Global tendencies toward relaxation of the cold war as well as growing abundance provided the backdrop for an eruption of vibrancy and sex appeal, racial and sexual subcultures, and a mass consumer culture oriented to youth. Bob Dylan, the Beatles, the Grateful Dead, Pop Art, Jimi Hendrix, John F. Kennedy, Marshall McLuhan, Buckminster Fuller, Mary Quant, color TV, jet travel, transistors, and the pill set the stage for the democratic surge of the 1960s.

The essence of that surge was a general challenge to existing systems of authority, public and private. According to Samuel Huntington, who was by no means happy about the change, "people no longer felt the same compulsion to obey those whom they had previously considered superior to themselves in age, rank, status, expertise, character, or talents. Within most organizations, discipline eased and differences in status became blurred. . . . Authority based on hierarchy, expertise, and wealth all, obviously, ran counter to the democratic and egalitarian temper of the times." A New Left, then called "the movement," sought to politicize this surge. Previous revolutions, whether "bourgeois" or "socialist," had been state-building enterprises, but the New Left was critical of statism. As Sabine Von Dirke summarized, "the cultural revolution of late capitalism is more impatient, more generous and less easily satisfied than the economic-political revolution. It includes . . . a revolution of all relationships in which the human being becomes a commodity."[23]

Like cold war liberalism, the New Left was deeply influenced by the prevailing Freudianism. Reflecting this provenance, the New Left was critical of authority relations within the family. To be sure, a familial critique—the "world turned upside down," in Christopher Hill's phrase—had been a subcurrent in previous revolutions. During the French Revolution, for example, the Marquis de Sade insisted that incest provides better cement for a revolutionary society than fraternity, because it frees up libidinal energies for citizens to lavish on their country.[24] But such views had remained marginal and *provocateur*. In the sixties, however, the critique of familial relations moved to the center of leftist politics and was closely linked to the critique of other modes of authority, including those that promoted rationalized self-control or "productive power." This placed the New Left in confrontation with the maturity ethic and thereby with psychoanalysis in its ego psychology form.

As critics of the maturity ethic, New Leftists felt they had a choice in regard to psychoanalysis: to condemn it wholesale or to locate a critical strain within it. They responded by developing what might be called the theory of the two Freuds. One Freud was an apolitical, sexist medical doctor. The other was a theorist of suppressed longings, utopia and desire, surrealism and the Situationist International, in a word, of revolution. One Freud authorized American world hegemony, the sanctified middle-class family, and the classifying regimes of the welfare state. The other held that reason arose from madness and encouraged the libratory explosions of the 1960s. The fact that neither corresponded to the historical Freud was less important than the uses to which Freud's powerful imago could be put.

In drawing upon Freud as a warrant for revolution, the New Left rejected the earlier tradition of Freudo-Marxism. In prewar Austria and Germany Wilhelm Reich had traced the "mass psychology of fascism" to the German patriarchal family and called for the construction of sex clinics in working-class neighborhoods as a way of resisting the Nazis. Reich also traced the Stalinist counterrevolution to its reactionary sexual and familial practices. But Reich's work rested on what he took to be the suppressed genital longings of the industrial working class. Progenitors of the New Left such as Dwight MacDonald, C. Wright Mills, and Paul Goodman followed Reich in tracing the failures of the Popular Front to what Mills called "miscalculation of the psychology of the masses."[25] But they differed in orienting themselves to a youth-centered postindustrial society rather than a tradition- and family-centered working class. Goodman—homosexual, communitarian, anarchist, and a follower of John Dewey--was especially important in the genesis of the New Left. Ego psychology, Goodman complained, fostered a "rationalized sociolatry," "the smooth running of the social machine *as it exists*." Instead of the *ego*, Goodman urged therapists and educators "to think of the *self* as a process of structuring the organism-environment field."[26]

Goodman's contrast between the "ego" and the "self" exemplified the change that occurred in psychoanalysis in the 1960s. Like many changes in the history of psychoanalysis, this one can be understood through examining language. Freud's original term (*Ich*) had been ambiguous, but deliberately so. On the one hand, Freud's term referred to a psychic agency, the ego as opposed to the id and superego. On the other hand, it referred to the subject as opposed to the object. Freud's usage exploited this duality. On the one hand, he described the mind as made up of different agencies (id, ego, superego), each pursuing its own ends. On the other hand, the ego had to have a sense of the interests of the subject as a whole in order to fulfill its task of mediating between the different parts of the mind. The ego began to develop this sense at the stage of narcissism, the initial taking of one's self as a love object. The ego also derived much of its energies from narcissism but was not reducible to the self. What happened in the sixties was that the idea of the ego became increasingly associated with repression, authoritarianism, or productive power, in Foucault's sense. The idea of the self replaced it, eventually generating a new, affirmative approach to narcissism.

The substitution of the self for the ego was also an *antinomian* response to the Puritanism of the maturity ethic. To see how, recall that Perry Miller's Puritans followed Augustine in identifying self-love with original sin. "Piety," reverence for the moral law through which God reveals "His" will, was the opposite of self-love. Antinomianism, by contrast, affirmed the self by claiming that the self can know God directly, without the mediation of God's law. Indeed, antinomianism means opposition to the law. In line with its reverence for the moral law, furthermore, Puritan authority was patriarchal; authority passed from father to son. By contrast, antinomianism was imbued with the spirit of women and other outsiders. The antinomian heresy of Anne Hutchinson, which began almost immediately (1636–1638) after the establishment of Massachusetts Bay Colony in 1620, was a rebellion against conservative Puritan elders. Nor was the antinomian rejection of conventional morality and conviction in the truth of direct experience restricted to religion. Since original sin was the classic justification for all forms of injustice, including slavery, an affirmative approach to the self became linked to antislavery, feminism, transcendentalism, and romantic reform long before it influenced the culture of the sixties.

The antinomian tradition had also shaped American psychotherapy, taking the shape of "mind cure" or suggestion. Mind cure rested on relaxation techniques such as meditation, which allowed for the dissolution and ultimate reconstruction of the self. Mind cure's conversion-based idea of dying and being reborn lies behind the powerful self-help traditions of American psychology, from Christian Science and mesmerism to Alcoholics Anonymous, EST, Lifespring, and theories of "positive thinking" and "codependency." As the antinomian version of psychotherapy, mind cure was also the favored therapy among American women. Mary Baker Eddy (the founder of Christian Science), Clara Barton (a founder of the U.S. nursing profession), Dorothea Dix (a reformer of psychiatric asylums), and Jane Addams (a founder of the U.S. social work profession) all practiced mind cure as positive thinking.

All had been sick when young but then discovered their vocations and went on to rich, healthy, and productive lives. Far from constituting a shallow, "affirmative" alternative to psychoanalysis, mind cure was recognized internationally. When William James gave the Gifford Lectures in Scotland in 1902, he rejected the sick-minded morbidity of the Puritans for what he called an "anti-moralistic method." "Healthy mindedness"—as James called mind cure—which held that you already are saved if you only knew it, prepared the way for the American reception of psychoanalysis, even as psychoanalysts condemned mind cure as the terrain of uncredentialed female amateurs.

In the sixties, antinomian and mind cure currents, often taking the form of new age psychologies, provided strong if unacknowledged backing for the shift away from the maturity ethic and to the affirmation of the self. We can trace the unfolding theory behind this shift along two terrains: professional psychoanalysts and psychotherapists, on the one hand, and the New Left, on the other. Among analysts, one witnessed an increasingly affirmative therapeutic approach; analysis became kinder and gentler, but also began to lose its distinctive project, the analysis of the resistance. As early as 1946 Heinz Hartmann, Ernst Kris, and Rudolph Loewenstein had urged analysts to replace the word *ego* in Freud's 1914 text on narcissism with the word *self.* Narcissism, they argued, was not the libidinal investment of the *ego* as opposed to the id, but of the *self* as opposed to the world.[27] In doing this they lost the depth of Freud's conception. By the 1960s, analysts like Heinz Kohut were arguing for an *affirmative* attitude toward narcissism. The ego psychologists who espoused the maturity ethic, Kohut insisted, wielded a brutal "courageously facing the truth morality," a "health-and maturity-morality" in the service of building up the ego. According to Kohut, the need was not to encourage the strengthening of the ego by practicing analytic restraint or "abstinence" (Freud's favored term), but rather to reassure injured selves.

New Left Freudianism, exemplified by Marcuse's *Eros and Civilization* and Brown's *Life Against Death*, also rejected the maturity ethic's focus on the ego, but explicitly made this part of an ongoing transformation of authority relations. In other words, they politicized Freud. By distinguishing *surplus* repression (caused by capitalism, the work ethic, racism, or sexism) from *necessary* repression (built into our lives as mortal, vulnerable animals), Marcuse diagnosed the maturity ethic as an artifact of postwar American capitalism and not as a logical outcome of Freud's thought. Brown, too, argued that the "neutrality" and confinement of the maturity ethic were not necessitated by Freud's theory and that a new way of life was implicit in Freud's vision of infantile sexuality, which Brown called "polymorphous perversity." Both thinkers argued that Freud's writings contained a revolutionary conception of a nonrepressive society rooted in the explosive possibilities of the instinctual life.

What distinguished the New Left approach to narcissism from the therapeutic approach was that therapists and analysts wanted to affirm the self, as they had earlier sought to strengthen the ego, while Marcuse, Brown, and the New Left wished rather to dissolve it. Instead of considering narcissism in the sense of self-esteem, or *secondary* narcissism, they called attention to *primary* narcissism, the infantile well of self-love and merger with the mother's body. Freud had proposed the latter concept to explain what he called the "oceanic feeling" in *Civilization and Its Discontents,* writing, "originally the ego includes everything, later it detaches from itself the external world. The ego-feeling we are aware of now is thus only a shrunken vestige of a far more extensive feeling—a feeling which embraced the universe and expressed an inseparable connection of the ego with the external world."[28] With the oceanic feeling in mind, Marcuse argued that primary narcissism existed *prior* to the emergence of the "I" or self. Far from producing a psychic investment in the self, primary narcissism characterized intrauterine life and sleep. Because primary narcissism reflected the ego's original, "inseparable connection with the external world," Marcuse contrasted it to the ego that underpinned the maturity ethic, which he described as "an essentially aggressive, offensive subject, whose thoughts and actions were designed for mastering objects. It was a subject against an object. . . . Nature (its own as well as the external world) was 'given' to the ego as something that had to be fought, conquered, and even violated." The maturity ethic ego, Marcuse concluded, was "antagonistic to those faculties and attitudes which are receptive rather than productive, which tend toward gratification rather than transcendence [and] which remain strongly committed to the pleasure principle."[29]

Whereas Marcuse wrote in the traditions of critical theory and radical politics, Brown drew on the mystical loss of self to challenge the maturity ethic. Brown's heroes were Lao-tse, Jakob Boehme, and William Blake and their latter-day descendants like Alan Ginsberg. In his preface, Brown explained that "the superannuation of the political categories, which informed liberal thought and action in the 1930s," meaning Marxism, as well as his profound antipathy to "the politics of sin, cynicism and despair," meaning cold war liberalism, compelled him "to re-examine the classic assumptions about the nature of politics and about the political character of human nature." Brown joined Marcuse in rejecting the genitally based, 1950s-style "ego of mastery" and in equating boundlessness with "feminine" motifs, such as receptivity and gratification. Rejecting the "pseudo-individuation" of ego psychology as "based on hostile trends directed against the mother," Brown sought to rescue Johann Bachofen's discovery of the role that matriarchy played in human history from "the Jungian *Schwärmerei.*"[30]

Such readings of Freud, which were widespread in the New Left, flourished against a background of "altered states of consciousness" (drugs), be-ins, the blurring of identity, huge crowd formations, and the demotic world of newborn mass consumption, pulsating with the color, vitality, and primal rhythms of the unconscious id. Communes, attacks on monogamy, rock music, the onstage performance of backstage behaviors such as nudity, informal dress, and self-disclosure, an activist culture whose only regulative ideal was "participation": these constituted a social basis for a new postmaturity ethic based on release of the self. Primary narcissism pointed the way, Marcuse held, "from sexuality constrained under genital supremacy" to eroticization of the entire body, from instrumental rationality to art, play, and narcissistic display. Articulating the utopian element in narcissism, Marcuse identified artists and homosexuals as the vanguard of the forces breaking down the maturity ethic. Both found expression in the poet/musician Orpheus, who now replaced Prometheus, Marx's hero from the ancient world who had stolen the secret of fire from the gods and thereby become the hero of a productivist culture. Orpheus, by contrast, was a figure of postscarcity society. Like Narcissus, Orpheus rejected "the normal Eros, not for an ascetic ideal, but for a fuller Eros." He was not only able to charm all living things with his music; he also introduced homosexuality into human history.

The sixties' regression to primary narcissism reflected what Lou Andreas-Salomé, in 1921, called narcissism's potentiality for "conjugation and fusion."[31] This was the moment when societal and gender distinctions dissolved, an antinomian moment that abstracts individuals from their social context and brings them face-to-face with God. In psychoanalysis the antinomian moment was preserved in the form of free association, which depended on the suspension of action, but prepared the way for interpretation. By contrast, the New Left lifted individuals out of their social and cultural situations in an effort to spur new forms of action. Kristin Ross has called this New Left capacity "dis-identification," writing, "May '68 had little to do with the social group—students or 'youth'—who were its instigators. It had much more to do with the flight from social determinants, with displacements that took people out of their location in society, with a disjunction that is, between political subjectivity and the social group." Ross also calls this "a shattering of social identity that allowed politics to take place."[32] Disidentification constituted a form of political antinomianism during which established forms of authority or social distinction dissolved.

The maturity ethic had already begun to erode traditional authority by encouraging a distanced and ironic attitude toward society. The New Left, however, went much further by challenging the antipolitical connotations of the maturity ethic and securing a place for radical or left-wing politics. To grasp the importance of this, it is helpful to recall that the liberal portrayal of Freud as a conservative opponent of utopian and progressive thought was deeply rooted in two centuries of mainstream American antipolitical thinking, which had originated in the effort to keep the slavery issue out of politics. Hence the revolutionary impact of the civil rights movement—for example, the sit-ins over segregation—that exploded the codes of propriety governing and delimiting protest. The antiwar movement built on the civil rights precedent. During its demonstrations, sit-ins, and marches, cold war liberals, university presidents, and social scientists regularly complained that the students would not honor the pluralist expectations, mechanisms, and procedures, such as the formulation of "clear demands," compromise, and bargaining, that, according to liberals and pluralists, kept society together. In fact, the students recognized that only a continuous, activist challenge to hierarchy, including hierarchy within the radical movement, could lead toward genuine equality.[33] The line that regulated what could be challenged politically and what needed to remain private was the same line that operated within individuals, cutting off the genteel from the crude, the loud from the soft, the manly from the feminine, the acceptable from the truly challenging. Suppression of the instincts, New Left activism in effect demonstrated, was tied to the survival of the older status hierarchies in America, as well as to capitalism itself.

By its nature, an antinomian upheaval such as the sixties cannot last. In fact, much of the antinomian spirit of the sixties was consumed in the flames of Vietnam. Memorialized in quasi-surreal works such as Michael Herr's *Dispatches* and Tim O'Brien's *The Things They Carried*, the fiery war reached a turning point with the January 1968 Tet offensive. April brought an uprising in Prague, and May a worker/student general strike in Paris. In Mexico City left-wing students were massacred at the university. In Chile, Paraguay, Brazil, Argentina, and Uruguay, New Left activists were "disappeared," in some cases thrown alive from military airplanes. Against such a background, and under the saturated light of TV and film cameras ("the whole world is watching"), elements of the New Left began to disintegrate into assorted grouplets and crowd crystals, of which radical feminism was the most enduring. At the same time, any number of new journals, preparty organizations, university reform manifestos, conferences, and other intellectual and political efforts were underway, attempting to turn the largely inchoate upsurge of the New Left into a permanent radical presence.

Meanwhile, too, the neoliberal revolution was germinating. A new form of consumerism, symbolized by the *Whole Earth Catalog,* and a new model of work, symbolized by Silicon Valley, bridged the utopianism of the sixties with the entrepreneurialism of the seventies. Although the dominant ideology associated with the market was one of rational choice, neoliberalism was also able to capture much of the creativity previously associated with the unconscious and with private life. A new affirmative approach to narcissism was integral to this. As the seventies dawned, journalists labeled the new generation the "me generation," supposedly marked by widespread fear "of not belonging to the company of the great, rich and powerful, and of belonging instead to the 'mediocre.'"[34] A pivotal work, Christopher Lasch's *The Culture of Narcissism* (1978), argued that the New Left had degenerated into "a struggle not for social change but for self-realization." Lasch quoted Susan Stern, later a Weatherman, describing her state of mind at the demonstrations at the Democratic National Convention in Chicago in 1968: "I felt good. I could feel my body supple and strong and slim, and ready to run miles, and my legs moving sure and swift under me . . . I felt real . . . I felt I was part of a vast network of intense, exciting and brilliant people."[35] Even as Lasch belittled the phenomenon of narcissism, he unconsciously cited a passage focused on a woman's experience of her body.

## Women's Liberation and the Consolidation of Consumer Capitalism

In spite of widespread interest in Marcuse and other Freudo-Marxian thinkers during the sixties, opposition to Freud remained second nature to most leftists. To them Freud was a Victorian thinker who accepted the backward ideologies of his day, such as innate aggression, the patriarchal family, and women's inferiority, while ignoring the palpable social realities of capitalism, racism, and sexism. In the early seventies, however, radical feminists and advocates of women's liberation argued that Freud's work was central to addressing the kinds of problems that had emerged in the evolution of the New Left: authority, domination, sexuality, the socialization of temperament and "sex roles," the relation of the private and the public, the difference between the sexes, and, above all, women's oppression. Still, they maintained that his influence had been essentially, even intensely, negative. Indeed, because psychoanalysis supplied the ideological core of the maturity ethic, radical feminism largely defined itself through its attacks on Freud, at least in its early, formative years. At the same time, radical feminism was also the heir of political Freudianism in that it too assumed that the psychosexual dynamics of the family were crucial to understanding politics, culture, and society. As a result of this proximity to Freudian thought, the feminist break with Freud was highly ambivalent, passing through three conflicting but overlapping phases.

In the first phase, psychoanalysis was rejected *tout court* as an enemy, or even *the* enemy. In the second, it was redescribed as "feminist theory *manqué*," meaning a flawed theory of patriarchy that had to be reconstructed by feminists. In the third phase, which persists today, Freudianism was revised again in a relational or "self-object" form that converged with the neoliberal turn and, especially, with the consolidation of the new spirit of capitalism. All told, the feminist focus on Freud was short-lived but intense and historically consequential. The concepts and ethical ideals formulated in the early seventies proved remarkably enduring, in good part because they became symbiotically entangled with the emerging spirit of capitalism.

In the first, rejectionist phase, radical feminists argued that "the discoveries of a great pioneer" had been "invoked to sponsor a point of view essentially conservative." By 1970, when Kate Millet published these words, they had become a New Left commonplace, but radical feminism gave them new meaning. The theory of penis envy,

Millett adumbrated, had been a "superbly timed accusation" against "any woman unwilling to 'stay in her place.'" In Millet's reading of Freud, "a female's discovery of her sex is, in and of itself, a catastrophe of such vast proportions that it haunts a woman all through life."[36]

The key to the first phase was a credo: "the personal is political." This notion challenged the very idea of a relatively autonomous intra-psychic life in favor of what would later be called social construction. A direct attack on the maturity ethic, the credo had deep roots in the culture of the period. The cold war ideology of totalitarianism, reflected in the imagery of "brainwashing," had encouraged the idea that society could be all-powerful, while New Leftists held that even madness was a social construction. Drawing on such precedents, the first wave of radical feminists insisted that anything that affected women negatively must come from outside the female psyche. Naturally, psychoanalysis fell to the axe. Feminists discouraged "individual explanations" in favor of "consciousness-raising" groups. Commenting on this development, the pro-Freudian feminist Juliet Mitchell protested that feminists had gotten "rid of mental life." For second-wave feminism, Mitchell insisted, "It all actually happens. . . . There is no other sort of reality than social reality."[37]

As Mitchell's remark suggests, the first feminist attacks were too simple to dispel so complex and imposing a figure as Freud. More promising was a second, reconstructionist phase in which feminists adapted proto-Freudian figures of thought to penetrate more deeply into the personal or familial terrain. Here, however, feminists experienced a fateful ambivalence. On the one hand, the family was the locus of traditional authority, and therefore of women's subordination, but it was also the main site of love between men and women, of their struggle to establish sexual and parental bonds, and of personal life, beyond the determinations of a rationalized capitalist order. In general, feminists resolved this ambivalence negatively by defining the family as a site of oppression or power simpliciter. Harkening back to Wilhelm Reich, this approach was reinforced in the early seventies by the neo-Marxist-cum-feminist discovery that the family was part of what Marx called the "economic structure" of society—a site of socially necessary but unrecognized because nonmonetized labor. While that discovery might have nudged America in a very different direction than the one it adopted, namely toward social democracy, its chief effect was rather to further the deidealization of sexual and romantic love, which was the key achievement of the second phase of the feminist encounter with Freud.[38]

Coitus "*appears* a biological and physical activity," Millet elucidated, but in fact it is "a charged microcosm" of "power-structured relationships . . . whereby one group of persons is controlled by another."[39] Shulamith Firestone's *The Dialectic of Sex* (1970) was the *locus classicus* for this approach. According to Firestone, "the ultimate cause and the great moving power of all historic events" lay in the "biological family," which gave rise to a father-dominated "power psychology," a "psychological pattern of dominance-submission." Penis envy was power envy. "From the beginning," she wrote, intending to improve on Freud, the infant is "sensitive to the hierarchy of power."[40] Firestone offered this as a general approach to history, one that would supplant Marxism. In fact, its main area of application was the family.

Understanding the family as the site of labor and power transformed the meaning of heterosexuality, sometimes to near the point of caricature. Even self-proclaimed socialist feminists like Ellen DuBois and Linda Gordon wrote that women's heterosexual experience involved "ecstasy on the battlefield," implying that whatever instants of sexual pleasure a woman might glean during intercourse had to be stolen from her unremitting struggle against predation.[41] Radical feminist Catharine MacKinnon was more blunt: "sexuality is to feminism what work is to Marxism: that which is most one's own, yet most taken away." Heterosexual sex, MacKinnon explained, is "something men *do* to women." "Domination, penile penetration, possession, constitute the *male* definition of sex."[42] "A woman is a being who identifies and is identified as one whose sexuality exists for someone else who is socially male."[43] The logical implication was that there is at least a touch of rape in all heterosexuality; even when they appear voluntary, sexual relations between men and women are eroticized forms of dominance and submission.[44] Not all women agreed with these formulations, but very few failed to be affected by them.

Highlighting sexual ambivalence touched a nerve among women. Juliet Mitchell's *Psychoanalysis and Feminism* (1974) drew on the same painful strain of feeling, but this time to *rescue* psychoanalysis for the feminist project. Rejecting the idea that Freud's work was a sexist account, Mitchell characterized it as a theory of how a psychology of female inferiority is created in early childhood. "In setting out to analyze the operations of ideology and the laws of the human order," she wrote, "Freud had to realize that that order and ideology are patriarchal."[45] Hence psychoanalysis was a *description of* a patriarchal society, not a *prescription for* one.

To make this case, Mitchell returned to the debates over the infantile "prehistory" of womanhood that had consumed psychoanalysis in the thirties. Freud's core preoccupation, she explained, was to explain how a child with an innately bisexual constitution turns into a heterosexual woman. For Freud, the girl faced a problem in changing her sexual object from her mother to her father and, in the process, modifying her drives so that they became less active, more passive. Thus, in Freud's view, boys and girls had different oedipal experiences. The boy's Oedipus complex (his early love for his mother) was "smashed," whereas the girl entered into a difficult and circuitous path, turning herself into an object of desire first for her father and then for men in general. What Freud called "the difficult development toward femininity" in infancy could exhaust a young girl psychologically. For his early feminist critics, such as Karen Horney, this was a nonproblem, since girls developed into women by identifying with their mothers. For Mitchell, however, such critics missed the point, which was the created, precarious, and almost artificial character of what is called femininity.

Although Mitchell was trying to defend Freud, she shared the underlying radical feminist assumption that the family was the site of patriarchal power. She also agreed with her feminist critics that the passive, receptive, "feminine" side of women's sexuality reflected the structure of domination in the traditional family. Mitchell went beyond radical feminism, however, by situating the patriarchal or traditional family anthropologically, thereby further supplanting the Marxist focus on economic structure with a new focus on kinship, which placed sexual difference at the origin and foundation of society. The existence of the incest taboo, she argued, following Claude Lévi-Strauss, presupposed the distinction between the sexes. That distinction gives us "that smallest of differences" which forces men to leave their biological families and find other men's sisters and daughters to marry, thus generating the patriarchal kinship ties that underlie all prior social organization.[46] Mitchell's interest in the cultural as opposed to biological character of sexual difference converged with Lévi-Strauss's interest in distinguishing culture from nature. What the girl "learns" in infancy, Mitchell explained, is not the superiority of the penis over the clitoris, but the superiority of culture over biology. As a result of her infantile experience, the girl feels "*originally* deprived . . . not, like other deprivations, a culturally demanded necessity."[47]

In this second phase in their encounter with Freudianism, feminists were trying to remake psychoanalysis so that it could contribute to a feminist theory. However, reciprocal blind spots in feminism and psychoanalysis scuttled this project. Psychoanalysis implied a patriarchal law that stands over both sexes, but did not fully appreciate the way that law subordinated women to men. Feminists saw the rule of men over women, but neither the weight of "the law" in the Kafkaesque sense of command or tradition nor in the sense of the superego, as Freud envisioned the rule of the father. Freud believed that the proper conflict for understanding the logic of domination was "not between masculine and feminine but between libido and repression," implying that men and women would advance in tandem.[48] Feminists held that the conflict between men and women was at least as important as sexual repression, and arguably prior, implying that sexual progress presupposed the earlier overthrow of male domination. For Freud, the "repudiation of femininity" explained both misogyny and penis envy. For feminists, the idea of penis envy was already an expression of misogyny. Gayle Rubin called psychoanalysis "feminist theory *manqué*," but radical feminism could equally be termed psychoanalysis *manqué*. In any case, Mitchell's effort to rescue Freud for feminism failed, as the emotional mistrust and bitterness dividing the two outlooks proved insuperable.

Behind the impasse lay two different conceptions of the family and, ultimately of human evolution. The feminist conception stressed the role of power, as expressed in the idea of patriarchy, understood as male control over women's sexuality and labor. According to Gerda Lerner, feminists had to explain thirty-five hundred years of "women's historical 'complicity' in upholding the patriarchal system that subordinated them and . . . in transmitting that system, generation after generation, to their children of both sexes."[49] Freud, by contrast, saw both sexes suffering, albeit differently, from the aftereffects of the father complex, which left a legacy of guilt and repression. Whereas feminists like Lerner tended to go back to an originary "world historic defeat of the female sex," situated, for example, in ancient Mesopotamia, Freud drew on an evolutionary (Lamarckian) conception of the sexes that emphasized the importance of pair-bonding, the prolongation of infancy, and kinship in the long Paleolithic era, especially in its later prehistoric phase. Undoubtedly the two strands of thinking—male power, on the one hand, the father complex, sexuality, and guilt, on the other—were ultimately reconcilable, but the feminists of this period rejected the Freudian strand. The result was a one-sided emphasis on power that facilitated the third phase in the encounter between feminism and Freudianism, ultimately weakening feminism's critical dimension and facilitating its convergence with the ongoing neoliberal ascendancy.

Two aspects of the feminist concept of patriarchy proved consequential. First, that model focused on one-to-one relations of domination, analogous to those of slavery. Thus it lent itself to the classic liberal solution of the "rights revolution," i.e., protection of the individual against discrimination as opposed to structural reform. Insofar as feminists moved from immediate domination to social structures, they remained within the liberal paradigm in emphasizing meritocracy

(discrimination against women) as opposed to a more robust conception of equality that would require the transformation of the society as a whole. That liberal paradigm lay behind the radical feminist
assumption that men as a group sought to maximize their power vis-
à-vis women as a group. Examples of this assumption include Mitchell
and Rubin's idea that kinship was a matter of men exchanging women,
Heidi Hartmann's idea that the family wage should be understood as
the outcome of men's struggle against women, and Joan Kelly's idea
that women did not have a Renaissance.[50] In all these formulations
there were elements of truth, but too much was obscured or denied:
men and women cooperate in kinship, the family wage was supported
by most working-class women as part of the struggle of labor against
capital, and women did have a Renaissance, albeit a different one than
men. Grasping these complications required a more anthropologically
and historically grounded approach to gender relations as rooted in
social production and reproduction and especially in the changing role
of the family as a unit of production and consumption.

In addition, the patriarchal model misconstrued the problem of
authority, which by its nature involves an intrapsychic and unconscious dimension. In fact, the sharp division between paternal authority and maternal nurturance so central to the radical feminist vision
was recent, largely originating in the Victorian era, which had spawned
the ideology of the "haven in a heartless world" in response to the
growing divide between capitalism and personal life. For Freud, who
supplied the first overall theory of modern personal life, obedience to
the laws of civilization was based on love for the primal figures of childhood, not just on command and fear. Thus the patriarchal father was as
much protector as castrator, tucking his children in at night even while
threatening them with the loss of their genitals. Hence, to analyze gender inequality, feminists needed a theory encompassing not only domination but also respect, love, and sexual desire.

Most important, the one-sided interpretation of the family as
the site of patriarchal power severely circumscribed feminist self-
reflection. It encouraged questions that affirmed the paradigm of

patriarchal subjection, such as the self-critique of women's racism or homophobia, but discouraged reflection on feminism's psychological content itself. Crucial to understanding the cultural revolution consuming America at that time, the unconscious content of the feminist revolution was and was to remain largely unanalyzed. Central here was the new centrality of the maternal imago, or preoedipal mother, precipitated by the eruption of feminism.[51] Potentially revolutionary in its implications, the explosive moment of the early seventies drew on the intensely primitive forms of dependence that underlie all group psychology, the tendency toward splitting and paranoia that periodically animate groups, and the cathexis of narcissism, idealization, and identity, all of which were critical for understanding the neoliberal society then emerging.

Loosening the ties that bound women to men, feminists strengthened the ties that bound women to one another. New Left antinomianism, with its fantasies of primitive merger, its blurring of identity and huge crowd formations, had prepared the way for the explosively growing women's community, which was based on the idea of the "woman-identified woman," whether overtly as in lesbianism or in the sublimated form of women's loyalty to women. The result was a joyful reunion among mothers and daughters, or sisters and sisters, the intense feelings of pleasure released indicating the lifting of a repression. Kathy Amatniek, wrote, "when those meetings began. . . . suddenly everyone had a story about the negative response of the man she lived with." For Nancy Hawley, "The flood broke loose gradually and then more swiftly. We talked about our families, our mothers, our fathers, our siblings; we talked about our men; we talked about school; we talked about 'the movement' (which meant New Left men). For hours we talked and unburdened our souls and left feeling high." Joanne Cook, a feminist economist, wrote, "not one woman apologized for complaints about her lot. . . . Every woman was a sister."[52] It is true that in the immediate aftermath of the radical feminist explosion, the euphoria of sisterhood generated struggles over maternal power—so-called trashing—directed against women who "slept with the enemy" or women who were "male-identified" or "unsisterly" in their ambitions. But in the long run the idea of sisterhood became an enduring point of reference in historical writing, social theory, and politics.

Here, then, was the triumph of narcissism in its group-psychological form. Whereas New Left antinomianism promoted a politics of "disidentification," a "shattering of social identity," the emotional drive behind seventies' feminism lay in *identification,* the earliest tie with another person, the basis for the building up of the self, and the mechanism of group formation. What appeared from one perspective as solidarity across women's difference was, from another, self-assertion for the members of the group. Cathy Cade, a lesbian documentary photographer, explained, "in the black movement I had been fighting for someone else's [freedom from] oppression and now there was a way that I could fight for my own freedom." For Mimi Feingold, "women couldn't burn draft cards and couldn't go to jail so all they could do was to relate through their men and that seemed to me the most really demeaning kind of thing."[53] As these statements suggest, the woman-identified woman meant a wrenching break with the New Left, a break that proved crucial in precipitating the convergence of feminism with neoliberalism. But the key to understanding the break is that the "mixed" left was premised less on a *general* assumption of sacrifice to advance collective goals and more on the assumption that *women* would sacrifice, an assumption that rested on women's self-sacrificing role within the family. Women's liberation was a way of saying that was no longer acceptable, neither on the left nor in the society as a whole.

The break with the left precipitated the third phase in the feminist encounter with psychoanalysis—the feminist revision of psychoanalysis in a relational form that helped consolidate the neoliberal extension of the market. The most important expression of the new relational ideology was Nancy Chodorow's *The Reproduction of Mothering* (1978), which replaced Mitchell's and Firestone's works as the leading feminist/psychoanalytic text. The core of Chodorow's book lay in what Julia Kristeva called "the homosexual facet" of motherhood—the mother-daughter relationship, which feminist psychoanalysts of the

1930s, such as Karen Horney, had counterposed to Freud to explain female development. Like her 1930s predecessors, Chodorow substituted the theme of identification for the theme of sexual object choice that characterized classical psychoanalysis. According to Chodorow, the preoedipal mother *identifies* with her daughter, but treats her son as *different.* The important axis of infantile development, then, is the formation of gender identity, not the choice of a sexual object. Through identification with their mothers, girls achieve "an unambiguous and unquestioned gender identity and realistically sexed body-ego," whereas boys' gender identity and "relational potential" is less secure. Thus, women value merger and closeness, whereas men insist on separation. From a theory that stressed the difficulty that girls had in finding their way to heterosexual desire, psychoanalysis became a theory that described the difficulty boys had in achieving intimacy. Even as public expressions of sexuality exploded in mass culture, advertising, and pornography, the emerging focus on identification and identity suggested desexualization.[54]

Largely through its transformation of the maturity ethic into a relational ethic, women's liberation was able to replace Freudianism as the final form of the spirit of capitalism for the era of mass consumption. Like the original Protestant ethic described by Weber, the feminist version of the spirit of capitalism reflected an ongoing transformation of the family. That transformation had begun with the maturity ethic, which drew men and women from their traditional, homosocial worlds into the sexual dyad. It continued with the New Left's struggles against *in loco parentis*, chivalry, and the idealization of female virginity. And it culminated in the feminist critique of nepotism and the "old boy's network." The effect was to buttress support for the two-earner family, fictive kinship, and gay marriage. In the context of this transformation of the family, the third stage in the feminist encounter with psychoanalysis complemented and enriched American society's turn toward the market, rational choice, and neuroscience. Like those Americans who, in the 1730s, turned away from the difficult, ascetic doctrine of predestination and toward the common sense of free will, the feminists of the 1970s moved away from Freudian analysis and toward secondary narcissism or self-assertion, thus providing an Arminian resolution to the cultural conflicts of the era.

The first and most important of the changes in the spirit of capitalism occurred when narcissism, as the libidinal face of egoism, replaced asceticism, the first component of the spirit of capitalism as described by Weber. For Weber, capitalism required instinctual renunciation, or asceticism, because of the imperatives of saving. As we saw, when the mantra shifted from saving to spending, the Protestant ethic faded. By the seventies, the new spirit of capitalism assumed the naturalness of egoism or, as it came to be called, rational choice. The legitimation of egoism had a profound effect on psychotherapy. Society, to the neoliberal imagination, should be a "timeless, placeless, self-equilibrating register of individual preferences."[55] To achieve this register, neoliberals unleashed a totalizing project meant to remake society by valorizing distancing, objectification, behavioral criteria, quantification, and scientism. Considerations of "the bottom line" were applied to every institution, at the cost of any self-reflection over goals. But a special effort was made to subdue those professions that relied on immeasurable human qualities: medicine, teaching, the arts, and psychotherapy. Here the tendentious and inaccurate feminist labeling of Freud as "sexist" was a gift of inestimable value. Managed care, cost-benefit accounting, the "diagnosis-based" medical model, "effectiveness" measures, and Big Pharma's well-documented "cooking" of research results, as well as the wave of "Freud-bashing," followed in its wake. Psychoanalysis did not disappear, but it was increasingly adapted to America's prevailing psychological culture: mind cure.

As this suggests, the redefinition of the subject in egoistic terms was only the surface of the neoliberal turn. The embrace of egoism rested on the validation of narcissism. Here, again, the radical feminist revolt against the oedipal theory, the redefinition of psychoanalysis as a theory of the self, and the triumph of group narcissism or identity would all prove crucial. Foucault's theory of productive power, instantiated in the maturity ethic, received a libidinal basis not only in the secondary narcissism of self-assertion but even more deeply in the primary narcissism of identity politics. Once again, there was an element of repetition. In the 1730s Jonathan Edwards had called Arminianism "a lust for selfhood" whose chief doctrine was "I am my own cause."[56] Now, nearly three hundred years later, a recognition of the importance of narcissism to capitalist social organization informs Kazuo Ishiguro's novella *Never Let Me Go* (2005), in which educators cultivate an artistic sense in children being raised as clones, their organs to be eventually harvested for the benefit of neoliberal, technocratic elites.

The second component of the new spirit of capitalism was the ideology of flexibility, which supplanted the compulsivity of the Protestant ethic in what was sometimes termed the network society, typically linked to globalization, enhanced immigration, and the two-earner family. Here, too, the New Left and feminist rejections of depth psychology set the stage for the new dispensation. On the one hand, intrapsychic life was redescribed in terms of information, cybernetics, and neuroscience. "Gender" was cut off from its roots in sexuality or biology and redefined as a sign or token. On the other hand, the "relational" psychoanalyst, based on the imago of the pre-oedipal Mother, *complemented* the neoliberal, cybernetic world of neurobiology, her techniques of holding, mirroring, and the so-called real relationship with the patient replacing the "cold," "withholding," oedipally oriented Freudian. Drive theory, according to which individuals sought objects primarily to realize their own aims, such as orality (through talking) or genitality (through sexual intercourse), gave way to the idea that individuals sought objects for the intrinsic satisfaction of the relationship. Pragmatic thinkers like George Herbert Mead, who had created a desexualized, infant-based social psychology, were rediscovered. Subjectivity was subordinated to *inter*subjectivity, especially in the therapeutic context of a "holding," quasi-maternal relationship. Together these trends supposedly decentered authority and encouraged pluralism, contextualism, and sensitivity to difference. In fact, however, they distracted attention from the unconscious structure of authority, which is rooted in the appeal to *amour propre* in liberal societies. Just as the emerging language of "networks" and "flat-worldism" obscured economic and political structure, which generates class domination, so the language of "difference" and "recognition" obscured authority, which sustains that domination.

Complementing narcissism and sensitivity to difference, the third component of the new spirit of capitalism was the ideology of empowerment, successor to puritanical hypocrisy. Here, too, there were good reasons to question classical psychoanalysis. Could it be that Freud was so focused on the backward-moving tendencies in the mind that he failed to see the positive, optimistic, outward-directed side of human character? Perhaps he devised an analytic method premised on analyzing the resistance while underestimating the narcissistic and self-interested forces that make men and women want to learn more about themselves? William James, for one, thought so. The "sick soul," he wrote, goes "grubbing in rat-holes," manufactures fears, and is preoccupied "with every unwholesome kind of misery." With the appearance of the healthy-minded, James rejoiced, "the deliberate adoption of an optimistic turn of mind [makes] its entrance into philosophy."[57]

Certainly empowerment converged with the application of the symptom-oriented medical model to psychotherapy. But it also drew the narcissistic energies released from the traditional family into a new form of political life, "identity politics," the counterpart to the spread of the market. Although presaged by the Black Power movement, radical feminism, with its valorization of the woman-identified woman, gave the identity paradigm its general character. Sociologists and historians, such as Carol Smith-Rosenberg, evoked the nineteenth-century "female world of love and ritual," lifelong sisterly friendships, allegedly more important to women than their relations with their husbands, and ultimately based on mother-daughter ties.[58] The poet Adrienne Rich captured the powerful regressive forces that infused the new politics: "women are talking to each other, recovering an oral culture, telling our life-stories, reading aloud to one another the books that have moved and healed us, analyzing the language that has lied about us, reading our own words aloud and to each other."[59] By the 1980s such

philosophers as Charles Taylor were insisting that the future of progressive politics rested on the politics of identity,[60] while Axel Honneth extended identity into a more general politics of recognition,
which arose out of, and in turn reinforced, the relational turn.[61]

No group embodied the new focus on identity better than homosexuals, meaning both gays and lesbians. In the 1890s, when psychoanalysis was born, homosexuals exemplified the then new idea of personal
life, that is, a sexual life not defined by one's place in the family. At that
time, Freudians could understand a homosexual object choice psychologically, but there was no such entity as a "homosexual."[62] In the course
of the 1970s, however, efforts to understand the psychology of homosexuality began to seem bigoted, like efforts to understand the psychology of races. The last thing homosexuals needed, spokespeople for the
community argued, was psychoanalysis; rather, they needed services,
community institutions, and political organizations. In time, homosexuals began to understand themselves as persons with a distinct way
of life who belonged to a historically specific community. At that point
homosexuality became an *identity* based on membership in a community. Lesbians, explained one theorist, are "women who love women,
who choose women to nurture and to create a living environment in
which to work creatively and independently. . . . Lesbians cannot be
defined simply as women who practice certain physical rites together."[63]

Radical feminism, then, was the culmination of a great historical transformation, on whose achievements it rested, and which it
brought to an end. In its blazing intensity, enormous gains were made
but two great resources necessary to understand and advance those
gains were lost. The first is the psychoanalytic exploration of what
Freud called the "long period of time during which the young of the
human species is in a condition of helplessness and dependence," an
epoch that enhances "the value of the object which can alone protect"
the infant, creating "the need to be loved which will accompany the
child through the rest of its life."[64] A whole world is implicit in this
insight. The second, which is closely related, is the socialist vision
of a just society, which assumes that human beings can rise above

egoism and narcissism to form cooperative relations that are in everyone's interest. Neither Freudianism nor socialism are rooted in an ahistorical patriarchy but rather in a view of evolution that has a place for the recognition of paternity and for the cooperation between the sexes that made the prolonging of infancy (the growth of the human brain) possible. Both visions underlie an understanding of personal life as a *historical* development. Not just Freud, but political Freud is crucial to its comprehension.

The loss of the two great critical paradigms generated during the preceding two centuries paved the way for the rise of neoliberalism, the governing philosophy since the seventies. In liberating not only egoism but also narcissism, neoliberals found a new and more effective way to achieve a core objective of the maturity ethic: to contain and restrict the political sphere. The channeling of narcissism into powerful demands for meritocracy, minority cultural rights, and recognition served effectively to transform personal life from a critical to an affirmative development and to blunt any overall opposition to the assault on collective values such as public goods and social solidarity. The understanding of the past in terms of power has left men and women powerless. Here again we see the ambiguous character of political Freudianism. Mounted in the sixties as a banner of revolution, it ended by reflecting the mirror of the self.

# Afterword—Freud in the Twenty-First Century

Is Freud's thought solely of historical interest, or is it relevant to our lives today? Is Freud, in any meaningful sense, still our contemporary, and if he is not, can he and should he become one again? Let me attempt to answer this question by recalling why psychoanalysis once commanded such extraordinary attention and why that changed.

To understand why psychoanalysis was once so compelling, it helps to think of it as an uneasy synthesis of three different projects: a therapy or medical practice, a paradigm for interpreting culture, and an ethical current in everyday life. All three projects ultimately stemmed from the interrelated political crises of twentieth-century Europe and the rise of consumer society, centered on such new media as advertising and film. Together, the three projects marked a profound change in Western thinking about subjectivity and the individual, a change reflected in Freud's imposing synthesis. Nevertheless, each project also had a discrete character and followed a distinct trajectory.

The therapeutic project began as a solution to the riddle of the neurosis, a force that Freud described as "inexpedient, and running counter to the flow of life." To explain this riddle Freud brought together British empiricism, which gave him the concept of the association of ideas; French medicine, which gave him the theory of transference; and German idealist philosophy, which gave him the idea of the unconscious. He rethought these currents through the Darwinian lens of the human being as an organism driven by internal needs that it sought to satisfy in specific environmental niches. His solution to the riddle of the neurosis also drew on the Hebrew Bible and the Greek tragedies, archaeology and sculpture, and everyday or "folk" understandings of psychology. Ultimately, Freud fused all these currents into a powerful synthesis, neither wholly scientific nor wholly humanistic. In the microcosm of the consulting room, this synthesis illuminated the ethical struggles of the human being, which arose in relation to the parents and ended in the confrontation with death.

While history records many other treatments for maladies of the soul, psychoanalysis was based on an innovative psychological theory that viewed the human being as an arena of internal conflict. Individuals, in Freud's conception, did not come to therapy primarily to solve their problems. They largely came to satisfy infantile wishes, wishes they simultaneously struggled to suppress. According to analytic theory, the drive to satisfy these wishes, along with the drive to suppress them, was displaced onto a struggle with the doctor or analyst. Only when that struggle subsided could the real gain of the treatment reveal itself, namely access to one's inner life, including its points of conflict or disharmony. When viewed as a therapy, then, psychoanalysis was an ambitious project that far transcended conventional medical aims. Even at the highpoint of its influence, it was clear that other treatments could relieve many symptoms better. But analysis promised something different: an open-ended, noninstrumental, and "free" orientation aimed at promoting individual autonomy and self-understanding.

The therapeutic project was joined to the second great project of psychoanalysis, its contribution to the modern understanding of culture. As with the therapeutic project, the starting point of the Freudian approach to cultural hermeneutics was the observation of neurosis, understood as a clue to the general situation of human beings vis-à-vis the social and cultural systems into which they were born. In Freud's view, culture—or civilization (he refused to distinguish them)—was a kind of collective project imposed by considerations both of love and economic necessity, but also internally resisted and experienced as somewhat alien. As he put it in *Civilization and Its Discontents*, the difficulty human beings have in regulating their relations to one another leads to the suspicion that "a bit of unconquerable nature lurks" inside the individual. This approach to culture—it was barely more than that—was situated in the context of comparative religion and mythology, archaeology and anthropology, ritual and totemism, non-Western family forms, and mother goddesses. Moreover, all Freudian theories of culture stressed the unique role of the family, which, as Freud wrote, "carries on its task of binding men and women to one another, and . . . with greater intensity than can be achieved through the interest of work in common."[1]

In addition, Freud was a pioneer of the contemporary tendency to rethink culture as *memory*, meaning collective processes of group self-knowledge and self-interpretation, which are to be distinguished from *history*, the project of professional historians and social theorists. The heart of the Freudian approach to culture was the idea that culture had a kind of unconscious, in other words, a memory. Like the individual unconscious, cultural memory was the product of conflict. Just as analysts viewed individual consciousness as symptomatic rather than transparent, so they viewed architecture, religious rituals, novels, films, clothing, advertisements, philosophical texts, even works of mathematics as screens, performances, expressions of defensive conflicts, efforts to impose order where none exists, which did not mean that cultural products could not also be valued in their own right. This analytic approach worked its way into anthropology, literary criticism, and artistic practice—think of the surrealists, the stream-of-consciousness novel, but also photography, film, and contemporary music. However, the bedrock of Freudian cultural interpretation, as of Freudian psychotherapy, was the interpretation of dreams. Freudians understood cultural practices as they understood dreams, as palimpsests or archaeological sites, collections of traces, having a complex structure, laid down in strata, almost geological in character. Like dreams, cultural expressions evince slippages, fractures, inconsistencies, and distortions that require interpretation or decoding. Cultural practices respond to these slippages in the same way that individuals respond to their dreams: they work over unconscious contents to make them acceptable to the ego or, in the case of culture, to the collective ego or memory of the social group. Culture, then, is secondary revision: "only a dream." In its second guise, therefore, Freudianism heralded a new way of reading cultural artifacts, directing attention to what was not openly said. In an age of exploding new media, this enhanced Freudianism's contribution to a critical perspective.

The third strand comprising analysis was an ethical project of self-reflection, a project of special importance to young people and to the new middle classes. Seeking honesty and directness in personal life, as well as clarity and simplicity in such areas as architecture, design, and philosophical thought, young people gravitated to the idea that a meaningful life necessitated self-reflection in depth. Sometimes the ethic of self-reflection was imbued with the passion of a calling, as when Floyd Dell called himself a "missionary" on the subject of psychoanalysis or when Max Eastman said that he had become a kind of "amateur specialist" on analytic theory. Underlying this ethic too was the new Freudian conception of the human subject. Neither situated through universal reason, morality, and self-control, as the Victorians maintained, nor defined through collective labor, as the socialists claimed, the twentieth-century subject was individual, unique, idiosyncratic. Alienated from large-scale bureaucratic structures, he or she was intensely involved with a few love objects or rivals that populated a rich, meaning-saturated, morally inflected inner life. Analysis supplied the ethic for this life, an ethic based more on personal honesty than on morality or aesthetics. In this regard, too, psychoanalysis marked an epochal advance. Although sometimes attacked as amoral, analysis extended the pre-Freudian sense of individual morality beyond deliberate, conscious decisions and acts to unconscious wishes. Encouraging the capacity to look at oneself objectively—"analytically"—and to enter empathically into other person's inner worlds, analysis promoted the expansion of the moral capacity while delimiting and contextualizing its scope.

This third project—the psychoanalytic ethic of everyday personal life—was never directly political, but neither could it be described as apolitical. Tellingly, Freud was widely read and discussed in the new milieus of artistic modernism, bohemia, and cultural revolution, which mixed politics with new thinking concerning the self. Recall from chapter 1 Lincoln Steffens's account of the first time—1911—he was introduced to the idea that "the minds of men were distorted by unconscious suppressions": "There were no warmer, quieter, more intensely thoughtful conversations at Mabel Dodge's [her Greenwich Village salon], than those on Freud and his implications." Throughout Europe, especially central Europe, but also England and even Russia, analysis was linked to socialist and Zionist politics; witness the polyclinics, sex education, and low-cost or free analysis described in Elizabeth Danto's *Freud's Free Clinics*. In Weimar Germany, Kurt Tucholsky, the editor of the left-wing *Die Weltbühne*, identified Freud with the position that reforms "are of no use if a basic honesty [*Redlichkeit*] does not permeate the country."[2] Even—perhaps especially—in periods of alienation, analysis was never separated from political awareness. In Latin America, where the dictatorships promoted psychoanalysis because it seemed to encourage quietism, and where many analysts collaborated, other analysts insisted on keeping the memory of counterrevolutionary violence alive. Likewise in communist-era Czechoslovakia, secret networks, while no doubt compromised, kept analysis going amid tanks and Stasi-like intrusions. In the United States, too, as Christopher Lasch remarked, the passionate interest that he and his friends took in each other's lives could not "be described as a form of emotional retreat."

The striking fact about these three projects—the therapeutic, the hermeneutic, and the ethical—is that they were connected at all. Operating on different terrains, pursuing different aims, and facing different obstacles, this labyrinth of diverging impulses nonetheless cohered. What held them together was the innovative Freudian conception of the human mind, which reflected the historically new phenomenon of personal life: an intrapsychic life that could not be reduced to one's social relations, but in which one's early family retained an unwonted power. This conception converged with the progressive currents of the time, so long as older currents for instinctual restraint contradicted newer possibilities for release. But in the 1970s, when release became a form of social control itself, the three projects began to part ways. Since then the therapeutic project has given way to neuroscience, brain research, and psychopharmacology. The cultural hermeneutic has been absorbed into popular culture in such forms as entertainment and "cynical reason," cybernetics, information and data collection, as well as into academic enclaves, such as cultural studies, feminist theory, and queer theory. And the ethic of self-reflection has lost its privileged place in postmodern milieus, if it has not fallen away entirely.

Consider first the fate of analysis as a therapy. Today, many—perhaps most—psychiatrists believe that the Freudian turn away from the study of the brain to the study of the unconscious mind was a wasteful detour, and they have returned to the nineteenth-century neurology in which Freud was originally trained. But this rests on a grave misunderstanding. As a neurologist, Freud spent twenty years (1876–1896) studying memory and neural action in the laboratory using roughly the same impersonal, empirical methods, and even much of the same language (although not the same technology) as such twenty-first-century neuroscientists as Eric Kandel and Gerald Edelman. Furthermore, Freud never repudiated this way of thinking. On the contrary, psychoanalysis presupposed the idea, still current today, that mental life is essentially unconscious in the sense of automatic, neurological, or reflex driven. As we have seen, however, the object of psychoanalytic research was not the *neurological unconscious* but the *repressed* or *dynamic unconscious*, which becomes available through regression, as in dreams, and can only be inferred from its effects on conscious psychic life. While scientists like Kandel argue that brain research will eventually be synthesized with cognitive psychology to produce a genuine science of the mind, their claim is questionable at best. The many centuries of effort that have gone into explaining the mind in terms of the brain or nervous system have produced nothing like a psychology that describes the mental life of living creatures, their experience of sexuality and family life, their capacities for empathy and abstract thought, and indeed their memories. Philosophers of science tell us that neuroscience represents an advance, and it does, but it is an advance over the brain science that preceded it—the science of Wilder Penfield or Charles Sherrington—and not over psychoanalysis. In reality, there is no reason to expect that the biology of the brain can replace psychoanalysis, nor to expect any reliable synthesis between the two disciplines in the foreseeable future.[3]

No wonder, then, that the principal advances in treatment since the 1970s pertain to highly delimited conditions such as autism, drug addiction, and bipolar disorder, where the biological factor may be uppermost, and which Freud did not pretend to treat.[4] American ego psychologists sowed the seeds for the shift from psychoanalysis to psychopharmacology when they re-described analysis to conform to the protocols of the medical model, such as behavioral diagnoses and testable hypotheses. In theory the medical model diagnoses illness on the basis of symptoms or tests and specifies treatment accordingly. Some psychological symptoms, such as compulsions, do conform to the medical model, but most do not. Most have to do, rather, with the kind of inner division or conflict that I foregrounded earlier. For that reason it is hopelessly restrictive to understand the human mind only in terms of outwardly observable behaviors, as psychiatrists claim they do. Once analysis was redefined to conform to the medical model, moreover, it could not resist the claims of quantitative, comparative outcome studies and legal tests of its scientific standing, as in the landmark case of Rafael Osheroff, the internist who was treated by analysts without success, but who claimed to have been cured by drugs.[5] There is no denying that some mental conditions can be treated successfully by drugs, but, overall, American analysts, therapists, and psychiatric social workers have ceded far too much to the medical model and neglected the distinctively subjective quality of the human mind.

If psychoanalysis has not fared well as a scientifically grounded medical practice, what can we say about its role as a cultural hermeneutic? In fact, the story is much the same. Since the "obsolescence" of psychoanalysis set in during the 1970s, the study of culture, too, has largely discounted subjectivity and privileged behavior instead. Two apparently opposed paradigms, the cybernetic or cognitive, on the one hand, and that of identity politics and cultural studies, on the other, share this penchant for excluding subjectivity.

The emergence of a cybernetic, networked, or digital worldview has deep intellectual roots in the projects of Anglo-American analytic philosophy and the Vienna Circle, which sought to model philosophy on the natural sciences. The most immediate source of the shift away from psychoanalysis and toward a digital conception of mental life lay in the cybernetics movement of the 1940s–1950s, which bracketed questions of subjectivity and interiority to generate instead what we today call data: behavioral probabilities subject to prediction and control. While the cybernetics movement did not survive, the data, informational, or network-based view of the world gained increasing ground. Turning points include the discovery of the double helix structure of DNA in 1953, which made it possible to think of biology in terms of informational algorithms; the growth of neuroscience and cognitive psychology in the 1970s, which replaced psychoanalysis in the universities; and the development of the microprocessor in the 1980s, which made small portable computers, screens, and interfaces ubiquitous. Within the polycentric, market-oriented, media-permeated world that developed, ideas of depth and interiority gave way to ideas of network, image, and feedback and of signs, folds, and nets. Gilles Deleuze is probably the most influential single exponent of this shift.

The radical political movements of the 1960s generated a second, complementary strand that replaced the Freudian approach to culture:

the idea that objective social conditions directly cause internal mental states such as madness. After the sixties, this idea led to the creation of such academic fields as cultural studies, women's studies, and queer studies and influenced other fields such as film studies and media studies. Although their point of departure was often psychoanalysis, cultural studies theorists wrote not of sexuality and neurosis but of power and resistance, often basing their thought on strong misreadings of psychoanalysis by such figures as Michel Foucault, Jacques Lacan, and Jacques Derrida. As a result of the "poststructuralist" distortions of psychoanalysis, those who practice cultural studies today have little sense of what a complex, multifaceted paradigm studying human subjectivity looks like. Consequently, they tend to fall back on moral-political formulations— in other words, on political correctness. Putting the focus on behaviors, including speech, they fail to attend to intrapsychic life, which is invariably multivalent and ambiguous and needs to be understood on its own terms. Significantly, political correctness converges with cybernetics through the idea that identities, such as race, gender, or sexuality, are points of relay, exchange, and intersection, which can be shifted as easily as computer codes, an idea that belies the psychoanalytic view of the subject as having a unique, relatively enduring, inner life.

Just as the shift toward neuroscience in therapeutics began within psychoanalysis, so did the shift from depth psychology to behavior. In the 1950s ego psychologists such as Ernst Kris and Lawrence Kubie encouraged a subtle turn away from the overemphasis on interiority or depth and toward surface, image, and self-presentation. Freud had already been aware of the corporeality of language, image, and "writing" in the Derridean sense, as Derrida himself showed in 1964.[6] This aspect of psychoanalysis converged with the vast growth in such new media as film, photography, and TV, which led to the question of how an individual subject was represented, framed, or contextualized. In principle, there is certainly no contradiction between the study of the surface and the study of depth. However, with the scientistic and totalizing approach that became hegemonic in the 1970s, there was a shift from subjectivity to behavior, evident in the language of psychotheraphy itself. Whereas classical psychoanalysis understood bisexuality as ambivalence over sexual object choice, today's meaning has shifted to sleeping with individuals of both sexes. Whereas homosexuality meant a sexual current common to both men and women, today it refers to an identity, meaning a way of life. Gender, a sociological concept based on power differential, displaced the analytic focus on the unconscious recognition of sexual difference. For now we have lost the sense of an idiosyncratic unconscious intrapsychic life, which was the real gain of psychoanalysis. Thus, as one great slope of the psychoanalytic edifice disappeared into psychopharmacology and brain science, the other slid into identity politics and the Internet.

Where did this leave the third great project associated with psychoanalysis, namely the ethical project of honesty, directness, and self-knowledge? Simply put, a great deal of the energy once devoted to practices fostering self-knowledge and reflection on one's group life has been given over to those enhancing empowerment, sociability, and participation. In this regard, as in so many others, the fate of psychoanalysis was tied to a momentous historical shift. In formulating and promoting such ideas as the instincts or the unconscious, Freud—as Wittgenstein pointed out—always called attention to the powerful social forces that operated to repress or marginalize his discoveries while neglecting the powerful attraction they exerted. In fact, the appeal of psychoanalysis came—as we have seen repeatedly in this book—because it rode the wave of an epochal historical movement away from the awesome power of the patriarchal imago and toward release, toward the abandonment of renunciation in favor of gratification, and toward a massive reduction in, or sidelining of, guilt. Freud's emphasis on sublimation or "instinctual renunciation," intended as an alternative to restraint or suppression, was already obsolescent by the 1960s, partly as a result of the successes of psychoanalysis itself. Accordingly, the revolts of that epoch found it necessary to refashion Freud as a liberator of the instincts and thereby put the final nail in the coffin of the repressions and renunciations that Freudians had confronted in the past. But was the result truly the success it claimed to be? Can we honestly say that a society that is based on release of the instincts, on gratification, and on a turning away from guilt, at least at the conscious level, is a freer, more just, and more civilized society than the repressive one it replaced?

This question leads us back to our initial query. Is Freud, in any sense, still our contemporary? And if he is not, can he and should he become one again? Certainly he is no longer a living force in most people's lives, but does that matter? After all, change is normal, and every thinker becomes part of history, at least when they are lucky. As to the scientific standing of psychoanalysis, any empirically minded researcher expects, and even hopes, to become outmoded. Why should we worry if the very complicated psychoanalytic picture of the mind, essentially the creation of one highly imaginative, dangerously charismatic, extremely enthusiastic individual, has given way to a slow, steady collective effort to locate the mechanisms of memory, thought, and emotion in the genes, amino acids, proteins, and neurons of the brain? As for the project of cultural hermeneutics, our current understanding of the role that race, gender, sexual orientation, and ethnicity play in human life certainly corrects a political blind spot, or deliberate obfuscation, to which psychoanalysis sometimes lent itself.

Finally, what is there to say about the high value placed on self-exploration during the long Freudian century? The long, pointless analyses, the hopeless pursuit of ever receding insights, the turning of individuals into lifelong patients, never quite submissive enough, never quite ready to leave their doctor: all this suggests that analytic self-knowledge was at the very least oversold. Why shouldn't empowerment, sociability, and group identity replace self-knowledge, at least in part? In fact, the inward, self-reflective turn represented by psychoanalysis typically occurs only intermittently in life, for example, in adolescence, during traumatic interruptions such as death, illness, or divorce, and perhaps in old age. The normal direction of the mind is outward, toward desired objects, with the aim of thwarting rivals and outmaneuvering obstacles. Whereas introspection did once define an epoch of social and cultural history—the Freudian epoch—there were historical reasons for this, and it was bound to pass.

These are powerful arguments. I could believe them myself if it were not for a single reservation. The analytic project had a critical dimension, as this book has amply demonstrated. If psychoanalysis was able to help Black radicals think through the long-term effects of slavery and racism, if it was able to characterize World War II in a way that illuminated the special role played by anti-Semitism, if it was able to show that femininity could be torturous for women, can we really do without it today? What characterizes the modern radical tradition and distinguishes it from Anglo-American liberalism is the idea that individual subjectivity and a critical approach to society requires a depth psychology. The fact that the three analytic projects—therapy, cultural studies, and self-examination— were fused into a unity suggests that different aspects of society—science, culture psychology—are interwoven in the individual mind. Simply looking at a single individual, as Robert Musil noted in describing his character Moosbrugger, a carpenter on trial for cutting up a young girl in fin de siècle Vienna, was like looking at "a loose end of a thread hanging out, and if one pulls at it, the whole tightly knit fabric of society begins to come undone." The dispersion of the analytic synthesis, its transformation into a series of three separate, unrelated projects, portended the weakening of its critical dimension, as is painfully evident today.

To answer the question of whether Freud is still a relevant figure, we might finally consider how he became a part of history. Freud's image—his imago, to use an analytic term—did not succumb to the slow processes of deidealization and mourning that normally characterizes the passing on of a major figure. Rather, much of Freud's true identity, and much of the actual contribution of Freudianism, was suppressed through explosive, demagogic, and profoundly misleading attacks by such figures as Frederick Crews and Jeffrey Masson, who themselves relied on the tendentious but at least comprehensible caricatures produced by radical feminists. Paradoxically, Freud became a historical figure to those who respected and even revered him, while to his enemies he remained a vital contemporary, invested with powerful emotions and zeal. This point alone should make us doubt that "the Freudian conception of man" is obsolete.

# NOTES

Introduction—Political Freud

1. I can give an example of this. In January 2012 I received a phone call from a *New York Times* reporter, Paul Vitello, who told me that at the suggestion of Frederick Crews he was contemplating an obituary for the philosopher Frank Cioffi based on Cioffi's role in bringing about the decline in Freud's reputation. I told Vitello that Crews had a deep personal animus toward Freud and that Cioffi, though certainly worth an obituary for his philosophical work, had little role in Freud's declining reputation. I further explained that the main factors for that decline were the criticisms that came from the feminist movement, the neoliberal "reforms" of the world of mental health, followed distantly by the work of revisionist historians like Henri Ellenberger and Frank Sulloway. When the obituary appeared on February 1, 2012, it parroted the view, carefully constructed by Crews and his associates, that Cioffi had demonstrated that psychoanalysis was a pseudoscience. The picture of Cioffi as a giant slayer was far more "newsworthy" than an obituary for a highly technical philosopher of science or a nonsimplistic discussion of the changing fortunes of psychoanalysis.
2. The citations for these statements are found in the chapter itself.
3. Sigmund Freud, "The Interpretation of Dreams," in *The Standard Edition of the Complete Psychological Works of Sigmund Freud,* ed. and trans. James Strachey, in collaboration with Anna Freud, assisted by Alix Strachey and Alan Tyson (New York: Norton, 1976), 5:541.
4. Yosef Hayim Yerushalmi, *Freud's Moses: Judaism Terminable and Interminable* (New Haven: Yale University Press, 1993); Jacques Derrida, *Archive Fever: A Freudian Impression* (Chicago: University of Chicago Press, 1998).

## 1. Psychoanalysis and the Spirit of Capitalism

1.  Carl Schorske, *Fin-de-Siècle Vienna: Politics and Culture* (New York: Vintage, 1980).

2.  It may be more precise to say that the English political economists believed in *external* incentives. That they *tended* to take the culture of capitalism for granted is suggested by the following passage: "The principal [*sic*] which prompts to save is the desire of bettering our condition, a desire which, though generally calm and dispassionate, comes with us from the womb and never leaves us till we go into the grave. . . . There is scarce perhaps a single instant in which any man is so perfectly and completely satisfied with his situation, as to be without any wish of altera-tion or improvement of any kind." Adam Smith, *The Wealth of Nations,* quoted in Gordon Marshall, *In Search of the Spirit of Capitalism: An Essay on Max Weber's Protestant Ethic Thesis* (New York: Columbia University Press, 1982), 24.

3.  For a description of Weber's theory of capitalism, as opposed to his concept of the spirit of capitalism, see Randall Collins, "Weber's Last Theory of Capitalism," in Mark Granovetter and Richard Swedberg, *The Sociology of Economic Life* (Boulder: Westview, 1992).

4.  Max Weber, *The Protestant Ethic and the Spirit of Capitalism* (New York: Rout-ledge 1992). Weber's essay was originally published as a two-part article in 1904–5 in the *Archiv für Sozialwissenschaft und Sozialpolitik,* of which Weber was an edi-tor. A revised version appeared as the opening study in Weber's *Gessamelte Aufsätze zur Religionssoziologie* (Collected Essays on the Sociology of Religion) published in 1920–21, just after Weber's death. In 1930 Talcott Parsons translated the latter version, along with the introduction to the *Gessamelte Aufsätze,* and this remains the authoritative English version. A second essay of Weber's, "The Protestant Sects and the Spirit of Capitalism," largely devoted to the relations of Protestantism and capitalism in the United States, is often included in discussions of Weber's thesis. It can be found in Hans Gerth and C. Wright Mills, *From Max Weber: Essays in Sociology* (New York: Oxford University Press, 1946). The page numbers in the text and all other references are to the Routledge 1992 republication of Parsons's trans-lation. It is also worth noting that Weber's thesis is among the most commented upon, and the most controversial, in the history of social science. Social theorists who have engaged importantly with it include Robert Bellah, Clifford Geertz, Michael Walzer, Robert Merton, Daniel Bell, Jürgen Habermas, and Erich Fromm. Historians include Henri Sée, Richard Tawney, Christopher Hill, Henri Pirenne, Perry Miller, E. P. Thompson, Eric Hobsbawm, and Le Roi Ladurie. I will not enter into the many controversies surrounding it here.

5.  Shmuel N. Eisenstadt, ed., *Max Weber on Charisma and Institution Building* (Chi-cago: University of Chicago Press, 1968).

6.  Weber's definition of charisma is worth noting: "a certain quality of an individ-ual personality by virtue of which he is set apart from ordinary men and treated as endowed with supernatural, superhuman, or at least specifically exceptional

qualities." Recognition of charisma is "a matter of complete personal devotion aris-ing out of enthusiasm, or of despair and hope." Max Weber, *Theory of Social and Economic Organization* (New York: Bedminster, 1968), 329.

7. The best discussion of the term *elective affinity* is to be found in Michael Löwy, *Redemption and Utopia. Jewish Libertarian Thought in Central Europe: A Study in Elective Affinity* (London: Athlone, 1992). The term came to Weber from alchemy via Goethe. The key idea is that, instead of Newtonian causation, the universe is understood in terms of similarities and difference, attractions and repulsions. Although elective affinity by no means offers a wholly adequate theory of social or cultural causation, neither do the positivist methodologies that derive from Isaac Newton and John Locke.

8. The relevance of Weber's argument to Anglo-American as opposed to continen-tal capitalism is one of the most contested questions inspired by Weber's work. For a good introduction see Philip Benedict, "The Historiography of Continen-tal Calvinism," in Hartmut Lehmann and Guenther Roth, *Weber's Protestant Ethic: Origins, Evidence, Contexts* (New York: Cambridge University Press,1993), 305–25.

9. The term *second industrial revolution* is sometimes ascribed to Patrick Geddes's 1915 *Cities in Evolution*. Important discussions can be found in David Landes, *The Unbound Prometheus* (New York: Cambridge University Press, 1969), which emphasizes technological change and financial innovation, and Eric Hobsbawm, *Industry and Empire* (London: Weidenfield and Nicholson, 1968), 144–49, which points to the new role of science, the assembly line, and consumerism. Other useful discussions include N. Rosenberg, "The Growing Role of Science in the Innovation Process," in Carl Gustaf Bernhard et al., eds. *Science, Technology and Society in the Time of Alfred Nobel* (New York: Oxford University Press, 1982), 231–46; P. Temin, "The Future of the New Economic History," *Journal of Interdisciplinary History* 12, no. 2 (Autumn 1981); and James P. Hull, "From Rostow to Chandler to You: How Revolutionary Was the Second Industrial Revolution?" *Journal of European Economic History* 25 (Spring 1996): 191–208.

10. Let me address one objection. How can I call psychoanalysis the "Calvinism" of the second industrial revolution when it had relatively little to say about economic life? The main exception was its analysis of the anal basis of the bourgeois character structure. See, for example, Otto Fenichel, "The Drive to Amass Wealth," *Psychoan-alytic Quarterly* (1938); as well as Norman O. Brown's *Life Against Death* (Middle-town: Wesleyan University Press, 1959). Perhaps I should follow the lead of Robert Skidelsky, who agrees that twentieth-century capitalism was based on a new, post-Calvinist spirit, but argues that Keynes, with his radical demotion of savings and his appreciation of spending, should be considered the twentieth-century "Calvin." Robert Skidelsky, *The End of the Keynesian Era* (New York: Palgrave Macmillan, 1977), 2. I emphasize the role of psychoanalysis because it spoke to the individual's self-relation and relation to the family, relations that are at the core of the spirit of capitalism.

11. Luc Boltanski and Eve Chiapello, *The New Spirit of Capitalism* (London: Verso, 2006). See also Colin Campbell, *The Romantic Ethic and the Spirit of Modern Consumerism* (New York: Oxford University Press, 1989).

12. Boltanski and Chiapello, *The New Spirit of Capitalism*, 57.

13. Eli Zaretsky, *Secrets of the Soul: A Social and Cultural History of Psychoanalysis* (New York: Knopf, 2004).

14. Philip Rieff, *Freud: The Mind of the Moralist* (New York: Viking, 1959).

15. For the relations of sexual and familial life, see such standard histories of the family as Louise A. Tilly and Joan Scott, *Women, Work, and the Family* (New York: Routledge, 1988).

16. Elizabeth Cady Stanton, "Solitude of the Self," address before the U.S. Senate Committee on Woman Suffrage, February 20, 1892, reprinted in Mari Jo Buhle and Paul Buhle, eds., *The Concise History of Women's Suffrage* (Urbana: University of Illinois Press, 1978), 325–26.

17. Sigmund Freud, "The Dynamics of Transference," in *The Standard Edition of the Complete Psychological Works of Sigmund Freud*, ed. and trans. James Strachey, in collaboration with Anna Freud, assisted by Alix Strachey and Alan Tyson (New York: Norton, 1976), 12:99. I have followed the translation in Philip Rieff, ed., *Sigmund Freud: Collected Papers* (New York: Collier, 1963).

18. To be sure, women generally read more than men. See, for example, Alastair Jamieson, "Women More Avid Readers Than Men," *Telegraph*, March 23, 2009.

19. Freud, "A Difficulty in the Path of Psychoanalysis," in *The Standard Edition*, 17:144.

20. Stephen P. Waring, *Taylorism Transformed: Scientific Management Theory Since 1945* (Chapel Hill, NC: University of North Carolina Press, 1991) shows that the roots of the transformation of Taylorism antedate the Second World War.

21. Luxury goods were produced for elites and for an expanding middle class earlier, but not for the mass of the working class. See Neil McKendrick, *The Birth of a Consumer Society: The Commercialization of Eighteenth Century England* (Bloomington: Indiana University Press, 1982).

22. For the thesis of the general crisis, see Arno Mayer, *Why Did the Heavens Not Darken?* (New York: Pantheon, 1988).

23. Antonio Gramsci, "Americanism and Fordism," in Quintin Hoare and Geoffrey Nowell Smith, eds., *Selections from the Prison Notebooks of Antonio Gramsci* (New York: International, 1971), 277–321.

24. Ann Douglas, *Terrible Honesty: Mongrel Manhattan in the 1920s* (New York: Farrar, Straus and Giroux, 1996), 123.

25. For example, Jonathan Ned Katz, *The Invention of Heterosexuality* (Chicago: University of Chicago Press, 2007).

26. John G. Howells, ed., *World History of Psychiatry* (New York: Brunner/Mazel, 1975), 464; William Claire Menninger, *Psychiatry in a Troubled World: Yesterday's War and Today's Challenge* (New York: Macmillan, 1948), 452.

27. E. Fuller Torrey, *Freudian Fraud: The Malignant Effect of Freud's Theory on American Thought and Culture* (New York: Harper Perennial, 1992), 165; Nathan Hale,

The Rise and *Crisis of Psychoanalysis in the United States:* (New York: Oxford University Press, 1995), 211–12; Thomas Stephen Szasz, *Law, Liberty, and Psychiatry; an Inquiry into the Social Uses of Mental Health Practices* (New York: Macmillan, 1963).

28. Samuel Klausner, *Psychiatry and Religion* (New York: Free Press of Glencoe, 1964).

29. Morris Janowitz, *Last Half Century* (Chicago: University of Chicago Press, 1978), 417–29.

30. Quoted in Christopher Lasch, *Haven in a Heartless World* (New York: Basic Books, 1977), 108. Lasch's brilliant work, as well as the antagonism it stirred in the post-1960s feminist movement, rests in good part on his continued loyalty to the maturity ethic of the 1950s.

31. On the funding of analytic research, see Ellen Herman, *The Romance of American Psychology: Political Culture in the Age of Experts, 1940–1970* (Berkeley: University of California Press, 1995); and Alton Chase, *Harvard and the Unabomber: The Education of an American Terrorist* (New York: Norton, 2003).

32. Masao Maruyama, *Thought and Behavior in Modern Japanese Politics* (London: Oxford University Press, 1963); Alexander and Margarete Mitschlich, *The Inability to Mourn* (New York: Grove, 1975 [1967]); Richard Hofstadter, "The Paranoid Style in American Politics," *Harpers,* November 1964.

33. It is sometimes said that the 1950s were a conservative period and that American psychoanalysts simply reflected the conservatism of the times. In fact, they were at one extreme.

34. Lewis A. Coser, *Refugee Scholars in America: Their Impact and Their Experiences* (New Haven: Yale University Press, 1984), 20; Hans Gerth and C. Wright Mills, *From Max Weber: Essays in Sociology* (New York: Oxford University Press, 1946), 345.

35. Max Runciman, ed, *Max Weber: Selections in Translation* (New York: Cambridge University Press, 1978), 383ff. See also Marianne Weber, *Max Weber: A Biography* (New York: Wiley, 1975), 375ff.

36. Harry Stack Sullivan, "The Illusion of Personal Individuality," *Psychiatry* 13 (1950): 317–32. The shift toward relational theories needs to be distinguished from classical object-relational theories such as Melanie Klein's. Klein's theory was concerned with the *inner* object world; the new intersubjective theories were concerned with interpersonal relations. Klein's roots were in Freud; the new intersubjective theories looked toward American social psychology, especially George Herbert Mead.

37. Karl Abraham, "Psychoanalytic Notes on Coué's System of Self-Mastery," *International Journal of Psychoanalysis* 7 (1926).

38. Lynn Z. Bloom, *Doctor Spock* (Indianapolis: Bobbs-Merrill, 1972), 72, 83–84.

39. Betty Friedan, *The Feminine Mystique* (New York: Norton, 1963), 112.

40. Shulamith Firestone, *The Dialectic of Sex* (New York: Morrow, 1970), 49, 51. For other examples, see Charles Bernheimer and Claire Kahane, *In Dora's Case* (New York: Columbia University Press, 1985), 5–6; Maria Ramas, "Freud's Dora, Dora's Hysteria," *Feminist Studies* 6 (1980): 472–510.

41. For Hélène Cixous, Dora was "the one who resists the system, the one who cannot stand that the family and society are founded on the body of women, bodies despised, rejected, bodies that are humiliated once they have been used." Hélène Cixous and Cathérine Clement, *The Newly Born Woman* (Minneapolis: University of Minnesota Pres, 1986), 153–54.

42. Gayle Rubin, "The Traffic in Women," in Rayna R, Reiter, ed., *Toward an Anthropology of Women* (New York: Monthly Review, 1975), 185.

43. Erica Jong, *Fear of Flying: A Novel* (New York: Holt, Rinehart and Winston, 1973), 20–22.

## 2. Beyond the Blues

1. My reading of Hegel is based on Alexandre Kojève's famous account, which draws on Marxist and existentialist themes as well.

2. Ralph Ellison, "Richard Wright's Blues," *Antioch Review* 50, nos. 1–2 (Winter-Spring 1992): 61–74.

3. This imperative to work through resistance might also be called deconstructive by analogy to Jacques Derrida's view that the meaning of a text can never be understood directly but only through working through the text's defensive operations.

4. James Weldon Johnson, "Preface," in *Book of American Negro Poetry* (New York: Harcourt Brace, 1922).

5. William E. B. Du Bois, *The Souls of Black Folk* (New York: Dover, 1994), 10–11.

6. Badia Sahar Ahad, *Freud Upside Down: African American Literature and Psychoanalytic Culture* (Urbana: University of Illinois Press, 2010).

7. Robert E. Hemenway, *Zora Neale Hurston: A Literary Biography* (Urbana: University of Illinois Press, 1977), 8.

8. Ibid., 114.

9. Henry Louis Gates Jr., *The Signifying Monkey: A Theory of Afro-American Literary Criticism* (New York: Oxford University Press, 1988), 170–216.

10. Jean Toomer, "Negro Psychology in *The Emperor Jones*," in *Jean Toomer: Selected Essays and Literary Criticism*, ed. Robert B. Jones (Knoxville: University of Tennessee Press, 1996), 6.

11. Werner Sollors, "Jean Toomer's *Cane*: Modernism and Race in Interwar America," in Geneviève Fabre and Michael Feith, *Jean Toomer and the Harlem Renaissance* (New Brunswick, NJ: Rutgers University Press, 2001), 20.

12. Zora Neale Hurston, *Moses, Man of the Mountain* (New York: Lippincott, 1939).

13. W. E. B. DuBois, "My Evolving Program," quoted in Claudia Tate, *Psychoanalysis and Black Novels: Desire and the Protocols of Race* (New York: Oxford University Press, 1998), 51.

14. Orlando Patterson, *Slavery and Social Death: A Comparative Study* (Cambridge: Harvard University Press, 1985).

15. Abdul R. Janmohamed, "The Economy of Manichean Allegory: The Function of

Racial Difference in Colonialist Literature," in *"Race," Writing and Difference*, ed. Henry Louis Gates Jr. and Kwame Anthony Appiah (Chicago: University of Chicago Press, 1986).

16. Richard Wright, *Black Boy: A Record of Childhood and Youth* (New York: Harper and Row, 1945), 284.

17. Janmohamed, "The Economy of Manichean Allegory."

18. Wright, *Black Boy*, 271–72; Margaret Walker, *Richard Wright. Demonic Genius: A Portrait of the Man, a Critical Look at His Work* (New York: Warner, 1988), 41. Elsewhere he speaks of Mencken as "slashing with his pen."

19. St Clair Drake and Horace Cayton, *Black Metropolis* (Chicago: University of Chicago Press), 1970.

20. Quoted in Donald Gibson, *Five Black Writers: Essays on Wright, Ellison, Baldwin, Hughes, and Le Roi Jones* (New York: New York University Press, 1970), 24–25.

21. On Ellison's early leftism see Barbara Foley, *Wrestling with the Left: The Making of Ralph Edison's Invisible Man* (Durham, NC: Duke University Press, 2010).

22. Wright, *Black Boy*, 135; Richard Crossman, ed., *The God That Failed* (New York: Columbia University Press, 2001 [1949]), 131.

23. Richard Wright, "Blueprint for Negro Writing," *New Challenge* 2 (1937).

24. "We are not attempting to restage the 'revolt' and 'renaissance,' which grew unsteadily and upon false foundations ten years ago," Wright added. Hazel Rowley, *Richard Wright: The Life and Times* (New York: Henry Holt, 2001), 136–37.

25. Henry Louis Gates and Anthony Appiah, *Richard Wright: Critical Perspectives, Past and Present* (New York: Amistad, 1993); Russell C. Brignano, *Richard Wright: An Introduction to the Man and His Works* (Pittsburgh: University of Pittsburgh Press, 1970), 35.

26. Rowley, *Richard Wright*, 33.

27. Ralph Ellison, "Richard Wright's Blues" quoted in Margaret Walker, *Richard Wright*, 190.

28. Richard Wright journal, January 6, 1945, box 117, folder 1860, Wright Papers, quoted in Gabriel N. Mendes, "A Deeper Science: Richard Wright, Frederick Wertham, and the Fight for Mental Health Care in Harlem, N.Y., 1940–1960." Ph.D. diss., Brown University, 2010.

29. Karpman, in turn, edited a series of psychoanalytic articles on such matters as the Negro church, Negro suicide, and the Negro poet, Paul Laurence Dunbar (1872–1906). Jay Garcia, *Psychology Comes to Harlem: Rethinking the Race Question in Twentieth-century America* (Baltimore: Johns Hopkins University Press, 2012), 133. Charles V. Charles, "Optimism and Frustration in the American Negro," *Psychoanalytic Review* 29 (1942): 270–99. Also see Benjamin Karpman, *The Sexual Offender and His Offenses: Etiology, Pathology, Psychodynamics, and Treatment* (New York: Julian, 1954).

30. After publishing *Native Son*, Wright received many letters from black prisoners and in 1940 responded to one from Clinton Brewer, a murderer who had become a composer in prison. Wright visited Brewer and wrote the governor of New Jersey

on his behalf. Three months after being released, Brewer murdered again. Wertham helped prevent the execution of Brewer as well as treating Wright analytically, in part to help him stay out of World War II. Brewer, in turn, served as the model for one of Wright's last novels, *Savage Holiday*, a novel that takes the form of the psychoanalytic case study.

31. Horace Cayton, "A Psychological Approach to Race Relations," *Presence Africaine*, no. 5 (1948).

32. Horace R. Cayton, *Long Old Road* (New York: Trident, 1965), 260. See also Horace R. Cayton, "Personal Experience of Race Relations" (1967), box 3, Cayton Collection, Chicago Public Library.

33. Horace Cayton, "The Search for Richard Wright" (1969), box 4, Cayton Collection, Chicago Public Library.

34. "Psychiatry in Harlem," in *Time*, December 1, 1947; "Clinic for Sick Minds," *Life*, February 23, 1948.

35. Throughout his life, Sullivan remained "curious as to how one could put Freud and Marx together."

36. Richard Kluger, *Simple Justice: The History of Brown v. Board of Education and Black America's Struggle for Equality* (New York: Knopf, 1976), 443–44.

37. LeRoi Jones, *Blues People: Negro Music in White America* (New York: Harper, 1999), 67.

38. C. L. R. James, *Black Jacobins* (New York: Penguin, 1980 [1938]), 232–34.

39. Aimé Césaire, *Discours sur le Colonialisme* (Paris: Présence Africaine, 1955).

40. Jean Paul Sartre, *Being and Nothingness: An Essay on Phenomenological Ontology* (New York: Taylor and Francis, 1956), 364.

41. W. R. Bion, "Attacks on Linking," *International Journal of Psychoanalysis* 40 (1959): 308–15.

42. Frantz Fanon, *Wretched of the Earth* (New York: Grove, 1999), 232. Fanon also wrote of Algeria, where the French had introduced concentration camps, that "for the colonized . . . to live simply means not to die."

43. Ortigues quoted in Frederic Jameson, "Imaginary and Symbolic in Lacan," *Yale French Studies* 55–56 (1977): 348.

44. Chester Himes, too, described the embodied experience of being the target of racism as seeping "down my spine, into my arms . . . through my groin." Chester Himes, *If He Hollers Let Him Go* (Cambridge: Da Capo, 2002 [1947]), 2.

45. Frantz Fanon, *Black Skin, White Masks* (New York: Grove, 2008), 143.

46. Later Jacques Lacan would emphasize the visual and discursive aspects of Freud's conception of trauma, and Lacan's Freud is the basis of Homi Bhaba's well-known reading of Fanon. However, at the time, Fanon was under the spell of Freud, not Lacan. Bhaba's introduction can be found in his edition of *Black Skin, White Masks*.

47. Albert Memmi, "The Impossible Life of Frantz Fanon," *Massachusetts Review* 14, no. 1(Winter 1973): 9–39.

48. Fanon, *Black Skin, White Masks*, 119, 116.

49. Françoise Vergès, "Creole Skin, Black Mask: Fanon and Disavowal," *Critical Inquiry* 23, no. 3 (Spring 1997): 593.
50. I suggest some of the reasons for this in discussing paternalization in chapters 3 and 5.
51. Fanon, *Black Skin, White Masks,* 57.
52. Ibid., 63.
53. Baldwin is quoted in David W. Blight, *American Oracle: The Civil War in the Civil Rights Era* (Cambridge: Harvard University Press, 2011), 208.
54. Lou Turner, "Fanon Reading (W)right, the (W)right Reading of Fanon: Race, Modernity and the Fate of Humanism," in Robert Bernasconi with Sybol Cook, eds., *Race and Racism in Continental Philosophy* (Bloomington: University of Indiana Press, 2003), p. 152; Michel Fabre, *From Harlem to Paris: Black American Writers in France, 1840–1980* (Urbana: University of Illinois Press, 1991), 191; see also Michel Fabre, "Frantz Fanon et Richard Wright," in Elo Dacy, ed., *L'Actualité de Frantz Fanon* (Paris: Karthala, 1986), 169–80.
55. The first statement is quoted in Garcia, *Psychology Comes to Harlem,* 162; Richard Wright quoted in Cedric J. Robinson, "The Emergent Marxism of Richard Wright's Ideology," in *Race and Class,* January 1, 1978, p. 227.
56. Richard Wright, *The Outsider* (New York: Library of America, 1991 [1953]). Excerpt from book 2: "Dream," 499–501.
57. Richard Wright, *White Man, Listen* (New York: Harper, 1995), 36; John M. Reilly, "Richard Wright and the Art of Non-Fiction: Stepping Out on the Stage of the World," *Callaloo* 29 (1986): 507–20.
58. Richard Wright, *The Color Curtain* (Jackson, MS: Banner, 1995) 200. Wright, *White Man, Listen,* 59. Also see Wright's review of Mannoni in the *Nation,* October 20, 1956, pp. 330–33.
59. Memmi, "The Impossible Life of Frantz Fanon."
60. Wright was also fascinated by the black soldiers in the Abraham Lincoln brigade, writing "The fate of Spain had hurt me, had haunted me, I had never been able to stifle a hunger to understand what happened there and why."
61. Richard Wright, *Pagan Spain* (New York: Harper and Row, 1957), 1, 97–98.
62. Richard Wright, "Forward" to Paul Oliver, *Blues Fell This Morning: The Meaning of the Blues* (New York: Horizon, 1960), ix.
63. Fanon, *Wretched of the Earth,* 242–43.
64. W. E. B. Du Bois, *The Suppression of the African Slave Trade* (New York: Russell and Russell, 1965), 327–29.
65. Claude Bowers's *The Tragic Era: The Revolution After Lincoln* was published in 1929.
66. Toni Morrison quoted in Lawrence Buell, *The Dream of the Great American Novel* (Cambridge: Harvard University Press, 2014), 324.
67. Stanley Sadie and John Tyrell, *The New Grove Dictionary of Music and Musicians* (London: Macmillan, 2001), 3:730.

## 3. In the Shadow of the Holocaust

1. Freud to Arnold Zweig, September 1934, in Edith Kurzweil, *The Freudians: A Comparative Perspective* (New Haven: Yale University Press, 1989), 293.

2. This achievement, to be sure, was related to the problem of Jewish identity. For Freud, there was a *mystery* at the center of Judaism. In saying, as he often did, that he *did not know* what it means to be Jewish, Freud was also saying that not knowing was internal to Judaism. Eli Zaretsky, "The Place of Psychoanalysis in the History of the Jews," *Psychoanalysis and History* 8, no. 2 (2006): 235–54.

3. Sigmund Freud, *The Standard Edition of the Complete Psychological Works of Sigmund Freud,* ed. and trans. James Strachey, in collaboration with Anna Freud, assisted by Alix Strachey and Alan Tyson (New York: Norton, 1976), 14:22, 4:xivff.

4. Freud, "The Unconscious," in *The Standard Edition,* 14:171.

5. Rudolph Bultmann, *Primitive Christianity in Its Contemporary Setting* (Philadelphia: Fortress, 1980 [1956]), 25.

6. In his Third Critique Kant wrote, "There is perhaps no passage in the Jewish law code more sublime than the commandment "Thou shalt make thyself no graven image nor any likeness neither of what is in heaven not beneath the earth."

7. John Boyer, "Freud, Marriage, and Late Viennese Liberalism: A Commentary from 1905," *Journal of Modern History* 50 (1978): 91–99.

8. Carl E. Schorske, *Fin-de-Siècle Vienna: Politics and Culture* (New York: Vintage, 1981), 186. Freud was a member of B'nai Brith from 1897 to 1902.

9. W. H. Auden, "In Memory of Sigmund Freud," in *Another Time* (New York: Random House, 1940).

10. Sigmund Freud, *Moses and Monotheism* (New York: Knopf, 1939), 115, 118.

11. Freud, *Moses and Monotheism,* in *The Standard Edition,* 23:113.

12. Sándor Ferenczi to Sigmund Freud, October 25, 1912, in *The Correspondence of Sigmund Freud and Sándor Ferenczi,* vol. 1: *1908–1914,* 417.

13. Sándor Ferenczi to Sigmund Freud, December 26, 1912, ibid., 450.

14. Phillip Rieff, "The Meaning of History and Religion in Freud's Thought," *Journal of Religion* 31, no. 2 (April 1951): 121.

15. Sigmund Freud and Karl Abraham, *A Psychoanalytic Dialogue: The Letters of Sigmund Freud and Karl Abraham, 1907–1926,* ed. Hilda C. Abraham and Ernst L. Freud (New York: Basic Books, 1965), 46–47.

16. Alfred Adler, "On the Psychology of Marxism," March 10, 1909, in *Minutes of the Vienna Psychoanalytic Society,* vol. 2: *1908–1910,* 172–78. See also the minutes of June 2, 1909.

17. Adler's main presentation before the Vienna Society was on February 23, 1910. Ibid., 425–27. Alfred Adler, "Masculine Protest and a Critique of Freud," in Alfred Adler, *Cooperation Between the Sexes,* ed. Heinz C. Anbacher and Rowena R. Anbacher (New York: Anchor, 1978).

18. Letter from Sigmund Freud to Sándor Ferenczi, June 17, 1913, in *The Correspondence of Freud and Ferenczi,* 499; Freud to Jung, December 3, 1910, in Sigmund

Freud and C. G. Jung, *The Freud/Jung Letters,* ed. William McGuire and Ralph Manheim (Princeton: Princeton University Press, 1994), 376.

19. Freud, "On the History of the Psychoanalytic Movement," in *The Standard Edition*, 14:57.

20. Richard Noll, *The Jung Cult* (Princeton: Princeton University Press, 1994).

21. *The Freud/Jung Letters*, 223; *New York Times*, September 29, 1912.

22. Ferenczi to Freud, July 9, 1910, in *Correspondence*, 186.

23. Rieff, "The Meaning of History and Religion," 121.

24. Freud, *Moses and Monotheism*, in *The Standard Edition*, 23:134.

25. Alon Confino, *A World Without Jews* (New Haven: Yale University Press, 2013).

26. Wilhelm Reich, *The Sexual Revolution* (New York: Farrar, Straus and Giroux, 1963 [1936]), 123–25, 142–43, 238; Wilhelm Reich, *The Sexual Struggle of Youth* (London: Socialist Reproduction, 1972 [1932]).

27. Paul A. Robinson, *The Freudian Left: Wilhelm Reich, Geza Roheim, Herbert Marcuse* (New York: Harper and Row, 1969), 53.

28. Sandor Ferenczi and John Rickman, *Further Contributions to the Theory and Technique of Psycho-analysis* (London: Hogarth, 1950), 193; Freud, *The Standard Edition* 11:145.

29. Sandor Ferenczi and Otto Rank, *The Development of Psychoanalysis* (New York: Nervous and Mental Disease, 1925), 20.

30. Freud, "The Future of an Illusion," in *The Standard Edition*, 21:8.

31. Freud, "Analysis Terminable and Interminable," in *The Standard Edition*, 23:215.

32. Ibid., 23:242.

33. Freud, "The Ego and the Id," in *The Standard Edition*, 19:12–59.

34. Freud, *Moses and Monotheism*, in *The Standard Edition*, 23:122.

35. Richard Sterba, *Reminiscences of a Viennese Psychoanalyst* (Detroit: Wayne State University Press, 1982), 116.

36. Michael Molnar, "Introduction," in *The Diary of Sigmund Freud, 1929–1939: A Record of the Final Decade* (New York: Scribner's, 1992), xxiv; Sander L. Gilman, *Freud, Race, and Gender* (Princeton: Princeton University Press, 1993), 35.

37. Freud, *Moses and Monotheism*, in *The Standard Edition*, 23:88.

38. Jung to Freud, April 27, 1912 in *The Freud/Jung Letters*, 228.

39. Jung to Freud, February 11, 1910, ibid., 18, 294; Carl Jung, *Analytical Psychology: Notes of the Seminar Given in 1925 by C. G. Jung* (Princeton: Princeton University Press, 1985).

40. Robert Graves, *The White Goddess* (New York: Farrar, Straus and Giroux, 2013 [1948]) continued this line of thought.

41. Marshall Stalley, in *Spokesman for Man and the Environment: A Selection,* ed. Patrick Geddes (New Brunswick, NJ: Rutgers University Press, 1972), 289–380; Frank G. Novak Jr., in Lewis Mumford and Patrick Geddes, *Lewis Mumford and Patrick Geddes: The Correspondence,* ed. Frank G. Novak (New York: Routledge, 1995).

42. Bernard Chapais, *Primeval Kinship: How Pair-Bonding Gave Birth to Human Society* (Cambridge: Harvard University Press, 2010), 196.

43. I should make clear that in situating psychoanalysis in relation to these three inter-twined aspects of our species—the pair-bond, prolonged infancy, and kinship—I am not entering into current debates as to those aspects of evolution that are genetically transmitted and those that are properly cultural, but rather relying on what is sometimes called "deep history," history that includes our evolutionary past.

44. David Bakan, *And They Took Themselves Wives: The Emergence of Patriarchy in Western Civilization* (New York: Harper and Row, 1979), 13, 30. Bakan also notes, the Torah "is the product of a multitude of hands, and each hand that wrote was informed by many hands that spoke."

45. Freud, "Female Sexuality," in *The Standard Edition,* 21:226.

46. Freud, "Outline of Psychoanalysis," in *The Standard Edition,* 24:187.

47. Friedrich Engels, *The Origin of the Family, Private Property and the State* (New York: Penguin, 2010 [1884]).

48. Alex Ross, "The Case for Wagner in Israel," *New Yorker,* September 25, 2012. I have been unable to find the original source for this remark.

49. Chandak Sengoopta, "The Unknown Weininger: Science, Philosophy, and Cultural Politics in Fin-de-Siècle Vienna," *Central European History* 29, no. 4 (December 1996): 490.

50. In recent years several thinkers such as Sander Gilman, Eric Santner, Jay Geller, and Daniel Boyarin have claimed to discover a link between women and Jews, generally along the lines of a supposed "femininity." No doubt there are many further complexities here.

51. Ann Douglas, *Terrible Honesty: Mongrel Manhattan in the 1920s* (New York: Farrar, Straus, and Giroux, 1995), 134–35, 139.

52. "It is proof of a special psychical fitness in the mass which became the Jewish people that it could bring forth so many persons who were ready to take upon themselves the burden of the Mosaic religion." Freud, *Moses and Monotheism,* in *The Standard Edition,* 23:176.

53. Gershom Scholem to Walter Benjamin, August 1, 1931, quoted in Rivka Horwitz, "Kafka and the Crisis in Jewish Religious Thought," *Modern Judaism* 15, no. 1 (February 1995): 23.

54. Freud, *Moses and Monotheism,* in *The Standard Edition,* 23:43.

55. Timothy Snyder, *Bloodlands: Europe Between Hitler and Stalin* (New York: Basic Books, 2010).

56. Freud, "The Interpretation of Dreams," in *The Standard Edition,* 5:421–22, 426–28, 441–22.

57. Carl E. Schorske, "Freud's Egyptian Dig," *New York Review of Books* 40, no. 10 (May 27, 1993).

58. Edward Said, *Freud and the Non-European* (London: Verso, 2003), 54.

59. For example, Peter Gay, *Freud: A Life for Our Time* (New York: Norton, 2006).

60. Mark Mazower, *Dark Continent* (New York: Knopf, 1999).

61. Richard J. Evans, "Who Remembers the Poles?" Review of *Bloodlands: Europe Between Hitler and Stalin,* by Timothy Snyder, *London Review of Books* 32, no. 21 (2010): 21–22.
62. Hannah Arendt, *Men in Dark Times* (New York: Harcourt Brace, 1968), 84; Julien Benda, *L'Espirit Européen* (Neuchatel: Baconniere, 1947), 294.
63. Yuri Slezkine, *The Jewish Century* (Princeton: Princeton University Press, 2004), 211.

## 4. The Ego at War

1. Elaine Scarry, *The Body in Pain: The Making and Unmaking of the World* (New York: Oxford University Press, 1987).
2. Ernst Simmel, *Kriegs-Neuroses und 'Psychisches Trauma'* (Munich: Otto Nemnich, 1918), 5–6, 82–84.
3. W. M. Maxwell, *A Psychological Retrospect of the Great War* (London: Macmillan, 1923).
4. Eric J. Leed, *No Man's Land: Combat and Identity in World War One* (Cambridge: Cambridge University Press, 1981), 181–83.
5. Sigmund Freud, "Beyond the Pleasure Principle," in *The Standard Edition of the Complete Psychological Works of Sigmund Freud,* ed. and trans. James Strachey, in collaboration with Anna Freud, assisted by Alix Strachey and Alan Tyson (New York: Norton, 1976), 18:16.
6. See the discussion in Freud, "The Ego and the Id," in *The Standard Edition,* 19:18.
7. Quoted in Modris Eksteins, *Rites of Spring: The Great War and the Birth of the Modern Age* (Boston: Houghton Mifflin, 1989), 173.
8. Pat Barker, *Regeneration* (London: Dutton, 1992).
9. Quoted Paul Fussell, *The Great War and Modern Memory* (New York: Oxford University Press, 2013), 102.
10. Vera Brittain, *Testament of Youth: An Autobiographical Study of the Years 1900–1925* (New York: Macmillan, 1933), 165–67.
11. Alex Zwerdling, *Virginia Woolf and the Real World* (Berkeley: University of California Press, 1987), 294–96.
12. *New York Times,* July 16, 1922, quoted in Ann Douglas, *Terrible Honesty: Mongrel Manhattan in the 1920s* (New York: Farrar, Straus and Giroux, 1995), 246–47.
13. Thomas Mann, entry of May 24, 1921, in Thomas Mann, *Diaries: 1918–1939* (London: Robin Clark, 1984).
14. The phrase is Walter Benjamin's.
15. Oliver Wendell Holmes Jr., "The Soldier's Faith," address delivered in 1895, in Oliver Wendell Holmes Jr. and Richard Posner, eds., *The Essential Holmes* (Chicago: University of Chicago Press, 1987), 87. See also Freud to Jones, February 18, 1919, in *The Complete Correspondence of Sigmund Freud and Ernest Jones* (Cambridge: Belknap, 1995), 334f.

16. Hemingway's 1929 *The Farewell to Arms*, quoted in Fussell, *The Great War and Modern Memory*, 21.

17. Freud, "Lines of Advance in Psycho-Analytic Therapy" (1919), in *The Standard Edition*, 17:167

18. Elizabeth Danto, *Freud's Free Clinics: Psychoanalysis and Social Justice, 1918–1938* (New York: Columbia University Press, 2005).

19. John Gittings, *The Glorious Art of Peace* (New York: Oxford University Press, 2012), 169.

20. Freud, "Why War?" in *The Standard Edition*, 22:214.

21. Freud, "Inhibitions, Symptoms and Anxiety," in *The Standard Edition*, 20:15.

22. Freud, "Analysis Terminable and Interminable," in *The Standard Edition*, 23:242–43.

23. Peter Stansky and William Abrahams, *London's Burning: Life, Death, and Art in the Second World War* (London: Constable, 1994), 101.

24. John Dower, *Cultures of War* (New York: Norton, 2010), 21.

25. Freud, "The Uncanny," in *The Standard Edition*, 17:245.

26. Robert Westbrook, *Why We Fought: Forging American Obligations in World War II* (Washington, DC: Smithsonian, 2004).

27. John G. Howells, ed., *World History of Psychiatry* (New York: Brunner/Mazel, 1975), 464; William Claire Menninger, *Psychiatry in a Troubled World: Yesterday's War and Today's Challenge* (New York: Macmillan, 1948), 452.

28. Marshall Stalley, ed., *Patrick Geddes: Spokesman for Man and the Environment* (New Brunswick, NJ: Rutgers University Press, 1972), 289–380; Frank G. Novak Jr., ed., *Lewis Mumford and Patrick Geddes: The Correspondence* (New York: Routledge, 1995); Sandra J. Peacock, *Jane Ellen Harrison: The Mask and the Self* (New Haven: Yale University Press, 1988), 237 and 179–223; Elizabeth Abel, *Virginia Woolf and the Fictions of Psychoanalysis* (Chicago: University of Chicago Press, 1989), 27–28.

29. Joan Riviere to Melanie Klein, June 3, 1940, PP/KLE/C95, British Psychoanalytic Society Archives.

30. Harold James Perkin, *The Rise of Professional Society: England Since 1880* (New York: Routledge, 1989).

31. Ibid., 411.

32. Stansky and Abrahams, *London's Burning*, 65.

33. Ibid.

34. Peter Hennessy, *Never Again* (New York: Pantheon, 1993), 37.

35. According to Rudolph Klein: "At the time of its creation it was a unique example of the collectivist provision of health care in a market society." Ibid., 132.

36. Peter Homans, *The Ability to Mourn* (Chicago: University of Chicago Press, 1989), 114, 226f; Ian Suttie, *The Origins of Love and Hate* (London: Paul, 1945).

37. Dower, *Cultures of War*, 19, 85, 299.

38. Jameson quoted in Perry Anderson, "From Progress to Catastrophe," *London Review of Books* 33, no. 15 (July 28, 2911). See also, on narcissism, Otto Kernberg,

*Love Relations: Normality and Pathology* (New Haven: Yale University Press, 1998).

39. Giovanna Borradori, *Philosophy in a Time of Terror: Dialogues with Jurgen Habermas and Jacques Derrida* (Chicago: University of Chicago Press, 2003), 87.

40. Paul Hoggett, "Politics and the Relative Autonomy of Affect," unpublished MS.

41. Judith Butler, *Precarious Life* (London: Verso, 2006), 21.

42. Fred Weinstein and Gerald Platt, *The Wish to Be Free: Society, Psyche, and Value Change* (Berkeley: University of California Press, 1969), 214, 221 (my emphasis).

## 5. From the Maturity Ethic to the Psychology of Power

1. Philip Rieff, *Freud: The Mind of the Moralist* (Chicago: University of Chicago Press, 1971 [1959]), 330.

2. Alexis de Tocqueville, *Democracy in America* (New York: Vintage, 1945), 2:169–71.

3. William Graebner, *The Age of Doubt: American Thought and Culture in the 1940s* (Boston: Twayne, 1991), 20.

4. Ellen Schrecker, *Many Are the Crimes* (Princeton: Princeton University Press, 1999).

5. Michael Kimmage, *The Conservative Turn: Lionel Trilling, Whittaker Chambers, and the Lessons of Anti-Communism* (Cambridge: Harvard University Press, 2009), 11.

6. Daniel Yergin, *Shattered Peace* (New York: Penguin, 1990).

7. Alan Wolfe, *America's Impasse: The Rise and Fall of the Politics of Growth* (New York: Pantheon, 1981); Charles S. Maier, "The Politics of Productivity: Foundations of American International Economic Policy After WWII," *International Organization* 31 (Autumn 1977): 607–33.

8. Arthur Schlesinger Jr., *The Vital Center: The Politics of Freedom* (London: Deutsch, 1970), 159, 233.

9. Michael Paul Rogin, *The Intellectuals and McCarthy: The Radical Specter* (Cambridge: MIT Press, 1967), 6; Richard Hofstadter, "The Pseudo-Conservative Revolt" (1955), in Daniel Bell, ed., *The Radical Right* (New York: Doubleday, 1963), 39.

10. Harold Lasswell, *Propaganda Technique in World War I* (Cambridge: MIT Press, 1971 [1927]), 4–5.

11. William Claire Menninger, *Psychiatry in a Troubled World: Yesterday's War and Today's Challenge* (New York: Macmillan, 1948), 452.

12. Nathan G. Hale, *The Rise and Crisis of Psychoanalysis in the United States: Freud and the Americans, 1917–1985* (New York: Oxford University Press, 1995), 211–12.

13. Lewis A. Coser, *Refugee Scholars in America: Their Impact and Their Experiences* (New Haven: Yale University Press, 1984); Edith Kurzweil, *The Freudians: A Comparative Perspective* (New Haven: Yale University Press, 1989), 54, 208.

14. Michel Foucault, *Discipline and Punish* (New York: Vintage, 1979), 203.

15. Talcott Parsons, "Propaganda and Social Control" (1942). In *Essays in Sociological Theory, Pure and Applied* (Glencoe, IL: Free Press, 1954 [1949]), 89–103.

16. Christopher Lasch, *Haven in a Heartless World* (New York: Basic Books, 1977), 108.

17. Arthur Miller, *Timebends: A Life* (New York: Grove, 1987), 320–21.

18. Sterling Hayden, *Wanderer* (New York: Knopf, 1964), 371, 377, 387.

19. Christopher Lasch, *The True and Only Heaven* (New York: Norton, 2013 [1991]), 32.

20. Hans Gerth and C. Wright Mills, *From Max Weber: Essays in Sociology* (New York: Oxford University Press, 1946), 345.

21. John Knowles, "Outstanding Books 1931–1961," *American Scholar* 30, no. 4 (Autumn 1961): 612.

22. David Riesman, *The Lonely Crowd* (New Haven: Yale University Press, 2001 [1950]), 139.

23. Sabine Von Dirke, *All Power to the Imagination! The West German Counterculture from the Student Movement to the Greens* (Lincoln: University of Nebraska Press, 1997), 44.

24. Fred Weinstein and Gerald Platt, *The Wish to Be Free: Society, Psyche, and Value Change* (Berkeley: University of California Press, 1969), 59.

25. Daniel Geary, *Radical Ambition: C. Wright Mills, the Left, and American Social Thought* (Berkeley: University of California Press, 2009), 114.

26. Frederick S. Perls, Ralph Hefferline, and Paul Goodman, *Excitement and Growth in the Human Personality* (New York: Julian, 1951), 235. The words are Goodman's (my emphasis).

27. Heinz Hartmann, Ernst Kris, and Rudolph M. Loewenstein, "Comments on the Formation of Psychic Structure," *Psychoanalytic Study of the Child* 2 (1946): 16.

28. Sigmund Freud, *Civilization and Its Discontents,* in *The Standard Edition of the Complete Psychological Works of Sigmund Freud,* ed. and trans. James Strachey, in collaboration with Anna Freud, assisted by Alix Strachey and Alan Tyson (New York: Norton, 1976), 21:67.

29. Herbert Marcuse, *Eros and Civilization: A Philosophical Inquiry Into Freud* (Boston: Beacon, 1974).

30. Norman Oliver Brown, *Life Against Death* (Middletown, CT: Wesleyan University Press, 1959), 118, 123, 128–29, 132, 142.

31. Lou Andreas-Salomé, "The Dual Orientation of Narcissism." *Psychoanalytic Quarterly* 31 (1962): 1–30.

32. Kristin Ross, *May '68 and Its After-Lives* (Chicago: University of Chicago Press, 2002), 2–3.

33. Wini Breines, *Community and Organization in the New Left, 1962–1968: The Great Refusal* (New York: Praeger, 1982), xiv.

34. Otto F. Kernberg, *Borderline Conditions and Pathological Narcissism* (New York: Jason Aronson, 1995), 234.

35. Christopher Lasch, *The Culture of Narcissism: American Life in an Age of Diminishing Expectations* (New York: Warner, 1978), 34.

36. Kate Millett, *Sexual Politics* (New York: Doubleday, 1969), 180.

37. Juliet Mitchell, *Psychoanalysis and Feminism* (New York: Pantheon, 1974).

38. As it was, the recognition that women's labor was integral to the functioning of capitalism produced such movements as wages for housework, flextime, and maternity leave.

39. Millett, *Sexual Politics*, 23 (my emphasis).

40. Shulamith Firestone, *The Dialectic of Sex* (New York: Morrow, 1970), 45, 48.

41. Ellen DuBois and Linda Gordon, "Seeking Ecstasy on the Battlefield: Danger and Pleasure in Nineteenth-Century Feminist Thought," *Feminist Studies* 9, no. 1 (Spring 1983): 7–25.

42. Jennifer Ring, "Saving Objectivity for Feminism: MacKinnon, Marx, and Other Possibilities," *Review of Politics* 49, no. 4 (Autumn 1987): 471.

43. Catharine A. MacKinnon, "Feminism, Marxism, Method, and the State: An Agenda for Theory," *Signs* 7, no. 3 (Spring 1982): 532.

44. Catharine A. MacKinnon, "Sexuality, Pornography, and Method: 'Pleasure Under Patriarchy,'" *Ethics* 99, no. 2 (January 1989): 318.

45. Mitchell, *Psychoanalysis and Feminism*, 375.

46. Mitchell's anthropological starting point could have led her to situate patriarchal law in a Marxist context: the enormous mass of precapitalist history, its inertia, its antediluvian choices, its animism, magical thinking, and omnipotence of thought, and its enduring structures of unfreedom, beginning with the sexual division of labor. Eli Zaretsky, "Male Supremacy and the Unconscious," *Socialist Revolution* 21, no. 2 (January 1975), criticizes Mitchell from this point of view.

47. Mitchell, *Psychoanalysis and Feminism*, 87 (my emphasis).

48. *Minutes of the Vienna Psychoanalytic Society*, vol. 2: *1908–1910*, ed. Hermann Nunberg and Ernst Federn (New York: International Universities Press, 1962–75), 541.

49. Gerda Lerner, *The Creation of Patriarchy* (New York: Oxford University Press, 1986), 6.

50. Heidi Hartmann, "The Unhappy Marriage of Feminism and Socialism," in Linda Nicholson, ed., *The Second Wave: A Reader in Feminist Theory* (New York: Routledge, 1997), 97–122. Joan Kelly, *Women, History and Theory* (Chicago: University of Chicago Press, 1984), 19–50.

51. In his last work, Freud wrote, "A child's first erotic object is the mother's breast that nourishes it. . . . This first object is later completed into the person of the child's mother, who not only nourishes it but also looks after it. . . . In these two relations lies the root of a mother's importance, unique, without parallel, established unalterably for a whole lifetime as the first and strongest love-object and as the prototype of all later love-relations—for both sexes." Freud, "An Outline of Psychoanalysis," in *The Standard Edition*, 24:187.

52. Karen V. Hansen and Ilene J. Philipson, eds., *Women, Class and the Feminist Imagination: A Socialist-Feminist Reader* (Philadelphia: Temple University Press, 1990),

7. See also Ruth Rosen, *The World Split Open: How the Modern Women's Movement Changed America* (New York: Penguin, 2006).

53. Sara Evans, *Personal Politics: The Roots of Women's Liberation in the Civil Rights Movement and the New Left* (New York: Vintage, 1980), 205, 182.

54. Nancy Chodorow, *The Reproduction of Mothering: Psychoanalysis and the Sociology of Gender* (Berkeley: University of California Press, 1978).

55. Daniel Rodgers, *The Age of Fracture* (Cambridge: Harvard University Press, 2012), 47.

56. Perry Miller, *Jonathan Edwards* (New York: World, 1949), 106, 124. Jean-Jacques Rousseau also caught the ambiguity of selfhood. Conceding that something less general, more personal than equal respect was needed in a republic, Rousseau also argued that, with the development of commerce, *amour propre* would become the basis for invidious forms of comparison, performance, and theatricality.

57. William James, *Varieties of Religious Experience* (Cambridge: Harvard University Press, 1985), 6, 108–9. From the point of view of psychotherapy, the idea that individuals actually do seek solutions to their problems by going to therapists and doctors comes very close to ego psychology, which emphasized the relative autonomy of the ego from unconscious wishes, its desire for control and mastery, and its ability to use the therapeutic situation to realize its aims.

58. Carol Smith-Rosenberg, "The Female World of Love and Ritual," *Signs* 1, no. 1 (Autumn 1975): 1–29.

59. Adrienne Rich, *On Lies, Secrets, and Silence: Selected Prose, 1966–1978* (New York: Norton, 1979), 13.

60. To be sure, more conventional forms of identity regarding nationality or language were exploding everywhere as well—in Quebec, Yugoslavia, Poland, and Belgium, for example. But, while the older concept of national self-determination presupposed strengthening the male-headed family, the new feminist-inspired identity politics sought to weaken it.

61. Axel Honneth, *The Struggle for Recognition: The Moral Grammar of Social Conflicts* (Cambridge: MIT Press, 1996); Charles Taylor, *Multiculturalism: Examining the Politics of Recognition* (Princeton: Princeton University Press, 1994). Jessica Benjamin, for example, described *The Story of O* as the story of a woman's quest for recognition, rather than of a woman's desire to submit, a desire one sees regularly in religion as well as in sexual life, but one that is apparently incomprehensible to the recognition-centered mind.

62. Before Freud wrote, lesbianism was largely ignored, while the male homosexual was understood as the passive sexual partner of an active male. In other words, the "pansy," "fairy," or whatever derogatory term one chooses, was the passive penetrated object; the penetrator was the "man." This usage reflected the overwhelming power of gender in such fields as psychology, sexology, and criminology. The assumption was that men were active, females passive, and this assumption was simply applied to homosexuality. Freud rejected this assumption when he formulated his conception of bisexuality. His concept is distinct from the concept of androgyny

that preceded him as well as from today's meaning of taking sexual partners from both sexes. Bisexuality for Freud rested on the distinction between aim and object and meant ambivalence in the choice of an object. Thus the pre-Freudian assumption that gender shaped all psychology gave way to Freud's idea that gender became relevant to psychology in the choice of a sexual object alone. Only after Freud enunciated that shift could one say that a (male) homosexual was a man who chose a male object, regardless of whether he used that object to satisfy active or passive aims. Thus the 1970s idea that homosexuals constitute an identity is not only a post-Freudian idea; it is also pre-Freudian.

63. Shane Phelan, *Identity Politics: Lesbian Feminism and the Limits of Community* (Philadelphia: Temple University Press, 1989), 73–74.

64. Freud, "Inhibitions, Symptoms and Anxiety," in *The Standard Edition*, 20:154–55.

## Afterword—Freud in the Twenty-First Century

1. Sigmund Freud, "Civilization and Its Discontents," in *The Standard Edition of the Complete Psychological Works of Sigmund Freud,* ed. and trans. James Strachey, in collaboration with Anna Freud, assisted by Alix Strachey and Alan Tyson (New York: Norton, 1976), 21:85, 101.

2. Harold L. Poor, *Kurt Tucholsky and the Ordeal of Germany, 1914–1935* (New York: Scribner's, 1968), 67.

3. Perhaps—it is an open question—we will eventually be able to bring together psychoanalysis, neuroscience, cognitive psychology, linguistics, epigenetics, artificial intelligence, and other branches of knowledge to create a new paradigm for studying the mind, but one thing is certain, that paradigm will not be reducible to biology any more than biology is reducible to physics.

4. Another area of advance is depression *insofar* as it is biological.

5. Tanya M. Luhrmann, *Of Two Minds: The Growing Disorder in American Psychiatry* (New York: Knopf, 2000).

6. Jacques Derrida, "Freud and the Scene of Writing" (1964), in *Writing and Difference* (London: Routledge, 1978), 246–91.

# INDEX